To Thomas,
It was a pleasure
to speak and I
look forward to
our continued discussion

With very best
wishes,

David

Governance Reimagined

"In the context of thinking that 'the organization' is the most important innovation of mankind, writing a book titled *Governance Reimagined* is quite ambitious. But David Koenig has delivered! I will recommend this book to friends and people I meet on my way."

— Knut Kjaer, Chairman, FSN Capital; former President, RiskMetrics Group; and former Chief Executive Officer of Norges Bank Investment Management, the Norwegian Sovereign Wealth Fund

"David Koenig has always been on the vanguard of innovative ways to think and practice risk management. I have known David for over a decade and saw him make the link between environmental sustainability and corporate governance way ahead of his peers. Readers will greatly benefit from his 'out-of-the box' and multi-disciplinary approach to how reimagined governance can help create value in these turbulent but exciting times."

— Richard Sandor, Chairman and CEO of the American Financial Exchange (AFX); CEO of Environmental Financial Products; "Father of Financial Futures," "Father of Carbon Trading," *Time* Magazine "Hero of the Planet"

"*Governance Reimagined* presents material about which I have thought long and reawakens memories of intellectual voyages in the past like Complexity Theory at the Santa Fe Institute. This is a well organized, presented, and written book. The writing is exceptionally jargon free and user friendly. It should be a great success."

— Robert A. G. Monks, Lens Governance Advisors; and author of *Corporate Governance, Corporate Valuation for Portfolio Investment, The New Global Investors, Corpocracy, Capitalism Without Owners Will Fail, Power and Accountability,* and *The Emperor's Nightingale*

"David Koenig is equally at home explaining what subtle factors drive you to buy an apple, for example, as why complex organizations can break without warning. What's amazing, however, is how he weaves common sense with thorough academic knowledge to create a rich fabric that will enable readers to use governance for what it was intended: creating value."

— Jon Lukomnik, Managing Partner, Sinclair Capital; Executive Director, IRRC Institute; past Deputy Comptroller, City of New York; and Co-author, *The New Capitalists*

"David Koenig has the rare gift of distilling complicated topics into logical components and then thoughtfully synthesizing them to make insightful points with such clarity that others can readily understand and grasp them. One reason for this is that David is an exceptional networker with real people who have 'been there, done that' credentials in the arena of hard knocks and know what works and what doesn't. For that reason, you won't find half-baked theories that will bore you in *Governance Reimagined*. David takes on the essential aspects of strong corporate governance in today's dynamic world and uses that foundation to contextually contrast and integrate the interrelated disciplines of value creation and risk management. I greatly enjoyed David's work in this book and have referenced it often in my own writings and discussions with other practitioners."

— Jim DeLoach, Protiviti Managing Director; Author, *Enterprise-wide Risk Management: Strategies for linking risk and opportunity*; named to NACD Directorship 100 (2012–18) as one of the most influential people in the boardroom community

"*Governance Reimagined* is an insightful exploration into the design, practice, and underpinnings of how organizations best use and manage risk in this post-financial crisis period. The book begins, and maintains a focus throughout, just where it should: on the motivations and drivers of people, and groups of people, making risk/reward decisions big and small. It is a book that will benefit anyone involved with designing or managing an organization, no matter the focus of that enterprise."

— Michael A.M. Keehner, Columbia Business School adjunct professor; Board Member, Oppenheimer Holdings

"A fast-paced, informative, witty and eminently readable guide. *Governance Reimagined* provides an excellent road map for creating organizations that use larger, freer collaborations to transform how we think about our work and about the value we give and get from each other — a way to better fulfill your mission and unlock the full value of your organization. Anyone building or managing a for-profit, charitable, political or even social organization will benefit from David's perspective on governance."

— Jean Hinrichs, former Chief Risk Officer, Barclays Global Investors; and Lecturer, Haas School of Business, UC Berkeley

"If there's anything that's long overdue for a little reimagination, it's governance. Not only does this book contain new ideas, it is a delightful read, full of analogies, metaphors, and linkages to common everyday situations. I know I will refer to this book again and again."

— Don M. Chance, Ph.D., CFA, James C. Flores Endowed Chair of MBA Studies and Professor of Finance, Louisiana State University

"David Koenig provides a fresh call to action in this comprehensive and stimulating discussion of organizational design and risk governance. His enthusiasm and straightforward style makes the wide-ranging illustrations drawn from economics, complexity science, behavioural finance, systems and network theory both easily accessible and stimulating as a different way to think about governance. A thoughtful work for those involved in leading and managing organizations in today's world."

— Ruth M. Whaley, Member, Board of Directors, Nuclear Electric
Insurance Limited; Principal, Barset Consulting LLC

"There are two sides to this book that make it extremely valuable. First, the book presents enlightening examples that illustrate the nature of risk which are unmatched by technical texts. Second, it addresses the major issue of governance in its relation to risk — unlike many of the classic texts that debate governance without a focus on this critical relationship — most notably in financial firms. The variety of approaches taken by David makes the book immediately relevant — once you start reading, you cannot stop until reading the end. Professionals will immediately absorb the substance. Academics will find the variety of approaches and the examples unique. Students will gain a new perspective on governance and risk. This is a bright text that readers will highly appreciate."

— Joel Bessis, Professor of Finance, HEC Paris;
and author, *Risk Management in Banking*

"This is an excellent book — David Koenig has presented some very important and complex ideas in a simple manner and is a must-read for board members and managements. The ideas of networked and distributed governance, along with the management of risk capital as commons are very powerful. These ideas are important for corporations, governments, and nonprofits that must be accountable for profits, people, and the planet, and be more sustainable. The current crisis has exposed weaknesses in governance that need to be fixed, so this book comes at a very important time, not in a negative sense but in a positive, forward looking manner."

— Saurabh Narain, Chief Executive, National Community Investment Fund

"David Koenig has masterfully broken down the complex components of governance and risk and challenges us to rethink our governance framework. This excellent book dares to break old governance models and re-govern with flexibility, and inclusivity, while bringing empowerment to all stakeholders."

— Jennifer R. Sawyer, Principal, Rebound Enterprises; and
Sustainer President, Junior League of Minneapolis

"*Governance Reimagined* is brilliantly simple to understand. The relevance to today's corporate boards and C-suite executives who have gone through the worst period of economic turmoil in nearly a century jumps out at the reader in every chapter. The author's risk management background, combined with a philosopher/psychologist's eye for understanding how human's operating in clusters and individually make decisions sets this book apart from all other economic, finance, and risk management books. Every board member and CEO who worried over unfathomable explanations of what can or did go wrong in an organization needs to read this book."

> — Allan M. Grody, President, Financial InterGroup Holdings Ltd; founder and retired Partner-in-charge of Coopers & Lybrand's Financial Services Consulting Practice; adjunct professor, New York University Stern Graduate Business School; Editorial Board Member, Journal of Risk Management in Financial Institutions

"This should be a business book bestseller. David has always impressed me as an intelligent and likeable guy. However, he surprised me with this book. I wasn't expecting a book so deep with such simple explanation — something abstract yet thoroughly grounded. It is a mixture and digestion of disparate sources like Systems Theory, Network Analysis, and Risk Management. The book simply and clearly explains the process of value creation. I highly recommend it."

> — Patrick Burns, Owner, Burns Statistics

"David Koenig lives and breathes governance and in this book he presents valuable perspectives along with contemporary examples that illuminate his innovations. The book is full of great citations and current situations spice up every chapter. He connects the entire governance social network, including potentially conflicting groups, and demonstrates how establishing appropriate missions and values complemented by diversity, a collaborative open culture and transparent governance process will improve chances for healthy long term success and increased enterprise value. *Governance Reimagined* is a great read that does not disappoint. It should be required reading for senior corporate management and boards."

> — Mark C. Abbott, PRM, Managing Director, Head of Quantitative Risk Management, Guardian Life; President, Buy Side Risk Managers Forum

"In my view there is a clear link between corporate governance and the success of corporations — it is the missing link in many corporate finance and strategy courses and texts. This book provides guidance to the amenable reader and brings the area to life. Highly recommended reading."

> — Steven Bishop, PhD, MCom(Hons) BEc FCPA; Visiting Fellow, Macquarie University Applied Finance Centre; Executive Director, Education & Management Consulting Services Pty Ltd

"Koenig envisions a fundamental redesign of capitalism based on a networked/ distributive model centered around risk capital viewed as a "commons." He weaves together ideas from a wide variety of sources, exploding many myths along the way. Central to Koenig's emerging model is the role of trust in networks and the connections between agents. Koenig's risk governance infrastructure could bring much more business intelligence to bear by more fully engaging employees and stakeholders. The habitability of Earth for future generations may depend on extending the concept of the commons to capitalism itself. Unless our businesses adopt a sustainable model, how can we expect to address our larger commons? Businesses are in the driver's seat. Adoption of Koenig's ideas could keep us from going off a cliff."

— James McRitchie, Publisher, CorpGov.net and Shareholder Advocate

"When noted jurist Richard Posner describes some of our imminent risks as having the potential for the extinction of the human race, it is time to address such complex concerns as global warming and cyberterrorism with new and as David Koenig likes to say 'fit for purpose' forms of governance. The innovative and imaginative work that he presents in *Governance Reimagined* includes recommendations for organizational design that should be applied to the governance of states, countries, and global institutions equally as well as corporations, providing perhaps a viable mechanism for responding to complex global concerns."

— Laurie Brooks, Board Member, Provident Financial Services; Former Director, NACD New Jersey, Former Chief Risk Officer, PG&E and PSEG; Co-author, *Teaching Controversial Issues*

"In *Governance Reimagined*, David R. Koenig goes to the heart of the role of the organization: creating value. He shows how risk-taking is fundamental to value creation, explores the role of behavioral economics in understanding risk, and provides insights about complex systems as they relate to good governance. With a fresh and thoughtful perspective of boards, this book should be on the reading list of everyone who's invested in effective governance."

— Alice Korngold, CEO, Korngold Consulting; Author, *A Better World, Inc.* and *Leveraging Good Will*

"*Governance Reimagined* is insightful, engaging, and simply a great read. It is now on my 'must-read' list for every board that I deal with. Excellent job, David!"

— Mark Briggs, CSP, Vice President, Safety Management Resources Corp., Former Chief Risk Officer, The Ohio State University

Governance Reimagined

Organizational Design, Risk, and Value Creation

David R. Koenig

(b)right governance

PUBLICATIONS

Second edition, published by (b)right governance publications, Northfield, Minnesota.
First edition published by John Wiley & Sons, Inc., Hoboken, New Jersey.

For more information about this title or the author, please visit *brightgovernance.com*.

Cover and book design by Holmes Design, Inc., Northfield, Minnesota.

Publisher's Cataloging-in-Publication Data:

Names: Koenig, David R., author
Title: Governance reimagined: organizational design, risk, and value creation / David R. Koenig
Description: Second edition. | Northfield, MN: (b)right governance publications, 2018 |
    Includes bibliographical references.
Identifiers: 978-0-692-19602-1 (hardcover); 9781723845413 (paperback)
Subjects: Economics — Economic theory. | Economics — Value. | Risk management. |
    Organizational effectiveness.
BISAC:
    BUS104000 BUSINESS & ECONOMICS / Corporate Governance
    BUS071000 BUSINESS & ECONOMICS / Leadership
    BUS042000 BUSINESS & ECONOMICS / Management Science
Classification: LCC HD2741.K56 2012 | DDC 338.5-dc23

Printed in the United States of America

10 9 8 7 6 5 4 3 2 1

Three weeks before the scheduled publication of the first edition of this book, my wife was diagnosed with a glioblastoma — an aggressive brain tumor that leaves few, if any, survivors. I still have the advance copy of the book that I gave to her just before we learned of her illness. Inside the cover, I wrote *"To my soul mate and love for life! This book is dedicated to you and our life together."* I was unaware how short that time together would be.

Three months after my wife passed away, I was diagnosed with a Stage IV cancer, leaving our children, aged 11 and 13 at the time, wondering if they would have any living parents to be with them. It's hard to imagine how difficult that uncertainty must have been. But they are doing well, and I continue to receive encouraging reports from my doctors. That would not be the case without the wonderful help we have received throughout our journey.

The first edition of this book contained the following dedication:

> *To my family, whose love, support, and*
> *encouragement know no bounds.*

This edition of the book is dedicated as follows:

> *To the many neighbors, friends, doctors, nurses, medical*
> *staff, and all who have helped us over these past six and*
> *one-half years of life. Our thanks to you knows no bounds.*

> *And to my children, who have done an amazing job of*
> *living life through tough times. I love you so very much!*

CONTENTS

ACKNOWLEDGMENTS

Each of us is shaped by people in our lives — our families, friends, colleagues, and even those who we are only able to observe from afar. I am fortunate to have been taught by individuals who are open to new ideas; to have been guided by those who continually challenge conventional wisdom; and to have discovered or been directed to the writings of scholars who seek to make us all better in our personal and professional interactions. This work is a product of all these relationships and their impact on my own beliefs.

We live in an incredibly exciting world, especially when considered from the perspective of intellectual challenge. We cannot understand it completely, but we can be amazed by it, confounded, and sometimes hurt by it. At the same time, we are able to use our knowledge and experience to transform it into something better. The continuous opportunity for improvement is one of the most alluring aspects of our world. It is a gift that we cannot do such work alone.

My most sincere thanks go to those who have given their time to reading drafts of this book, including Jean Hinrichs, Joel Bessis, Ruth Whaley, Bruce Benson, and Betsy Spethman. Their diverse perspectives helped improve the book immensely, although none of them should be held accountable for my views.

In addition, Helena Bachmann and Meg Freeborn have provided excellent editorial guidance on structure, syntax, context, coherence, and flow — to, as Helena says, "put the book on its best behavior!"

Don Bratland of Holmes Design is to be thanked for his cover work and the design and flow of the whole book. He and his wife, Beth, are incredibly good at all that they do.

Mentors like Ron Eaton, Jim Kamphoefner, Charlie Calomiris, and Lew Rhinehart have been tremendously positive influences on my development, both professional and intellectual. I am indebted to them and to others who have modeled excellence in leadership and innovation for me over the years. Marc Groz, Alexander and Olga Shipilov, and Beaumont Vance have each introduced me to new ideas that have significantly changed my way of thinking about the intersection of risk and value.

Leaders in service and life such as Paul and Lois Christenson, Robert and Donna Koenig, John I. Anderson, Bruce and Carol Benson, and family members too numerous to name here are also rare and greatly appreciated. We should all aspire to be like them.

I want to express my thanks to the people whose work is cited in this text and all those who influenced them. While writing this book, I attempted to bring together a highly diverse set of ideas, which may not have been assembled in such a way before. None of these authors is responsible for how I have integrated their work with that of others. And I hope that every reader of this book will be inspired to further explore the ideas of each cited author in much greater detail. Doing so will surely improve your use of their ideas as I envisioned herein.

Finally, I want to acknowledge the significant impact that my late wife had on my life and the lives of others. She lived a life of joyful service, especially seeking to help those with little power or in difficult situations. And she continually reminded us, even before her diagnosis, that life is fundamentally a gift. When one takes on that perspective, it brings a deep appreciation for every day.

INTRODUCTION

This is a story about creating things that never existed before. It's a story about people and how they best come together to build and do valuable things. Whether in for-profit companies or at nonprofit organizations, in virtual worlds, political economies, or informal associations, this story is about successfully governing the interactions of those who take risks in the pursuit of value.

My own journey towards a better understanding of how value is created began when I was 10 years old. At that time, my father purchased 50 shares of a company called Texaco. Every week we'd look up its price in the *Wall Street Journal* and, sure enough, this stock's worth grew over time. I noticed that it went up and down in price — sometimes for what seemed like extended durations. But mostly the value increased. This father–son activity of tracking the fluctuations of stock market prices, his explanations about why they happened, and the fact that the holding seemed to magically make money through no work on my part, intrigued me.

But stock markets are not the only place where value is created in our lives. And, even in this realm, there is far more to creating value that has to happen before we can watch a stock price go up. People have to imagine new ideas and take risks to bring them to life. Others must then see those ideas as worthy enough to invest in them or to acquire, experience, and enjoy them. And, since many people embrace diverse ideas of what is valuable, the interactions of people and technologies make the whole process of value creation quite "complex."

We begin our reimagination of governance by looking at how humans move from where they are today to a better place. We're not talking just about physical movement, although that is sometimes part of the process. Rather, we're referring to how we go about achieving an improved life through our innovations and collaborations. To understand how this can work, we need to re-examine some of our long-held beliefs about economics and take a closer look at the power that people have to self-organize in pursuit of safety, wealth, pleasure, and sometimes destruction.

Next, we move to an improved view of risk-taking. In order to create things of value, we must be willing to take risks. But the interaction of people and technology around risk is also not simple. Our organizations operate in a kind of social network, with rules and expectations. Hence, how others perceive us matters for our organization's success. In fact, the impact of perception and emotions on value is far more important than many of us realize.

For example, until a risk is realized, it is something we feel — it's an emotion. One important measure of success states that value can only be created when the gain from risk-taking is greater than the cost of the risk being taken. The emotion of fear affects our behavior and raises the cost of risk, making it more difficult for any organization that generates this feeling in us to create value.

Risk also has positive potential, as an understanding of it makes us smarter risk-takers and better creators of value.

This book brings together ideas from a variety of disciplines, from practitioners, advisers, and academics, including the ideas of multiple winners of the Nobel Prize in economics. Much of what you read here will be new to you, as it has never been assembled in such a manner before. And, once you finish the book, I promise that you won't be able to look at your work, your social life, or your day-to-day interactions with people and businesses in the same way again.

I've been flattered by the response to this book since it was first published in 2012. Some people whose work I greatly admire have provided their endorsements to encourage you to read the book as well. Others have reached out to me to learn how they can implement these ideas in their own work.

Our past and current governance of risk-taking in pursuit of value has left much to be desired — in politics, business, and even at charitable organizations. There is an opportunity here to understand and to take risk better. We need to understand how our organizations can best be structured both to innovate and to avoid disappointing those who will decide if they want to engage us and our ideas now and into the future. It's time for us to re-govern how we pursue our ambitions — to make our governance processes ones that help us realize our potential.

In the following pages, you'll be guided to reimagine a form of governance that begets the freedom to make decisions, fosters innovation, and improves the effective use of scarce resources. We're looking to re-govern what we've been doing, so that we can do it far more effectively — creating more value, in its many diverse measures, and at the same time, more ably fulfilling our highly diverse values.

Achieving that success is what this story is all about.

PART ONE

Creation and Evolution: The Source(s) of Wealth

"Authentic values are those by which a life can be lived, which can form a people that produces great deeds and thoughts."
— Allan Bloom, American Philosopher

"Over 97 percent of humanity's wealth was created in just the last 0.01 percent of our history."
— Eric Beinhocker, *The Origin of Wealth*

CHAPTER 1

Value, Values, and Value Creation

The reason that any organization exists is to create value. Whether serving the needs of the clients of a non-profit charity or generating market or intrinsic value for the owners of a company, the creation of value is the primary objective that all volunteer groups, management committees, and supervisory bodies necessarily pursue. Most organizations, however, don't fully understand the connections between value, their values, and the elements that drive value creation.

HOW MUCH IS THAT DUCK IN THE WINDOW?

One of the most difficult steps in developing this appreciation is to define the meaning of *value* to an organization. Most typically, we measure value in financial or economic terms. Hence, most businesses understand the notion that their products and services, marketed and sold or utilized successfully, will generate value. However, the story only begins there.

Whether you realize it or not, all of us encounter simple situations in our daily lives that demonstrate where value has been created. For example, I'm hungry, so my brain decides that I should walk two blocks to the local co-op for some food. As I enter the store, I'm greeted by a beautiful display of various fruits, including kiwis, nectarines, oranges, and apples. But how should I choose?

I've decided, or someone has convinced me, that I should prefer something healthy to eat. After all, it's better for my body and carries the promise of lower health costs and longer life (so I have been told). Therefore, my brain decides to opt for fruit. Since the fruit on display is organic, my brain tells me it's even better. For some reason, I'm drawn to the apples. Red Delicious, Braeburn, Gala, and Honeycrisp are all on offer. What colorful names! My brain jumps into action.

I check the prices and see that Honeycrisp are on sale, but still cost about 10 cents more per pound than my old standard, Red Delicious. I remember just how good Honeycrisp apples are and that they normally cost almost one dollar per pound more. I am thinking that this could be the right time to buy, but then wonder what is the cost of the same apple at the grocery store down the road? Another person enters the store, politely excuses himself, reaches past me, and confidently grabs a Honeycrisp. I buy one too. Delicious! Hunger satisfied, I march on in my day.

At this very moment and in this very situation, I found the value of the Honeycrisp to be high enough to justify whatever price the store charged. At that moment, the Honeycrisp apple I chose had a certain value to me, which was at least as much as the amount of money I paid for it. The same is true for the person who selected Honeycrisp before me and for any others who purchased Honeycrisp that day. But what determined that value? Why didn't my brain tell me that it was too expensive? Why wouldn't everyone agree to buy Honeycrisp in the same situation? Some purchase Gala apples, while others go past all of the apples and choose kiwis or oranges instead. Why?

The answers to these questions are not simple; actually, they are very complicated and even *complex*. The decision I made, and decisions we all make every day, are a result of our current desires, the influence that others have on us, as well as our *values* and the intersection of opportunity with all of these factors.

Think through your most recent purchases. What made them valuable enough to you that you were willing to part with your money?

This question is also considered by the other side in the transaction. What is it that makes a product sell? What drives the perception of value and what is the value of a good or service that a company offers to end-users or consumers of that product or service?

To begin to understand how value is determined, we have to start with some basics. If you have something I want and I have something you want, we can possibly agree on an exchange — some amount of what I have for some amount of what you have. If we are successful in our negotiation, this barter of physical goods or services determines their value to each of us at that very specific point in time.

When more than two people participate in the discussion and more than two goods or services are involved, the determination of value has a changed dynamic. Another person may also have something that we want. There will be a barter rate of exchange at which you decide you want what he has more than what I offer. That point of substitution is usually determined by the respective values the third person ascribes to what item(s) we individually offer to him.

You can imagine that as the number of people involved in the discussion grows, the determination of the value of what we have can become very complicated. This type of bartering, or haggling between two parties who only have goods to exchange with each other, was an early form of trading and helped the growth of small economies.

But trading of physical goods can be difficult. For one, suppose someone offers you three live ducks for four of your shoes. If you only own four shoes, you may be willing to part with just two of them, because you don't want to walk around barefoot. But how can you exchange one and a half live ducks for two shoes? It's messy, needless to say, and the indivisibility of a live duck may actually cause the transaction to fail.

Enter a common medium of exchange: money. For the moment, let's ignore why money has value overall, but just look at its help in facilitating an exchange. If you are only willing to sell two of your shoes and the other party is willing to give you one live duck and five dollars for those two shoes, you may find a way to transact your desired exchange without the sacrifice of an indivisible live duck.

Money has given us a way to determine in a fairly precise manner the value of shoes and ducks, at this particular time, in this particular quantity, and between these two people.

Now, let's look at another way to determine the value of money. We're going to leave out some critical elements in this next examination of value, so just consider it a mental exercise for the time being. We'll get back to the details later in the book.

Suppose your cousin Louie wants to borrow $1,000 from you. Being a good cousin, he offers to pay you back in one year. Remove your long-held feelings about Cousin Louie's poor grooming habits from the equation and simply look at what choices you have to consider in determining if a loan to sloppy Louie is a good value to you.

First, if you lend the money to Louie, you will not have that money for one year (in this example, we're going to guarantee that Louie will pay you back). That money is not available for Red Delicious, Honeycrisp, Gala, or any other kind of apples for that whole year, and you will not be able to use it to buy shoes, live ducks, or any other items, for that matter. Because of this loss of use, you're potentially going to miss out on something of value to you in the future.

Let's assume that you neutralize this part of the equation by concluding it's worth the trade off to help a member of the family. Still, you realize that you are investing in Louie and while in the story it's guaranteed that he'll repay you, you might also choose to invest your $1,000 in a savings account, insured Certificate of Deposit, Treasury Bill or even the stock market. In this case, you will (except if you invest in stocks) be almost certain to have more than $1,000 given back to you at the end of one year. So it only seems fair that Louie should give you more back than he borrows and maybe more than the bank or U.S. government would. But how much is the right amount?

Louie has a sense of what the $1,000 is worth to him. He has some need and some appreciation for the value of satisfying that need. You, by looking at your alternative investments, have a sense for what Louie should pay you in additional interest in one year to make you feel like he was a good investment. If the value of the loan is high enough to both of you, you'll lend him the money and he'll agree to borrow it.

We can begin to see that goods, services, and even money can have a determined value when two or more people discuss what they would be willing to give in exchange for their use. Ultimately, we can substitute any of the items in the discussion to describe the value of the other item. It might be worth one and one-half ducks, two shoes, or 15 dollars.

To make things a little more interesting, now consider that someone offers a service, like cleaning your house, once every week for one year. But they want to be paid in advance. Cousin Louie might even offer to clean your house in exchange for the $1,000 loan, but since he's a slob, we'll leave him out of this part of the story. In any case, in order to determine how much you are willing to pay for the cleaning services, you have to take several factors into account.

First, what is the value of having someone clean your house for you? Second, will the person really provide the services every week for one year? Third, what other things could you do with your money during that year which might be of value to you? You might think that it's worth $100 to have your whole house cleaned, but if you have to pay $100 in advance for the cleaning job to be done nearly one year from today, that might not seem fair.

Being astute, you discount the value of future cleaning jobs by some amount that makes you feel comfortable parting with your money today in exchange for a series of scheduled cleaning jobs at your house.

In effect, what you have done is exactly the same as what you did when you decided how much Cousin Louie should have to pay you in one year, only in reverse. You've determined today's value of something that will be received in the future. From Cousin Louie, the value today is $1,000, but you'll be getting more than that from him in one year. From the cleaning person, the value is a regular stream of services, each of which has value, but each of which you'll receive in the future.

If you've ever invested in a U.S. Treasury Bond or a Corporate Bond, you've done the same thing. These financial instruments usually agree to pay some amount of money, at regular intervals, called a coupon payment (people used to literally have to take coupons in to get them redeemed) and to pay a large lump sum at the end of all of the coupon payments, which is the return of your investment. The government or the corporation has agreed to give you something of value at specific points in time and you have agreed to lend them money today.

Bonds and loans to Cousin Louie are investments. They have common features, often including the payment of some kind of cash to the investor at various points in time in exchange for money given today. Stocks may pay dividends. Apartment complexes may pay rents. Hedge funds may provide capital gains when you redeem your interest in them. Choosing among these options is the equivalent of choosing between apples, or perhaps more accurately, choosing among apples, kiwis, nectarines, and oranges.

You see, there is a way to convert all of these choices into a common measure of present day value, even though what they give to us in the future may be highly diverse and of varying degrees of uncertainty.

This understanding is key to beginning to align value, our values, and value creation.

Now, let's consider a concept that's even more abstract: the value of something "good." For many people, giving to charities or benevolent organizations is a normal part of their lives. In fact, for many faiths, giving to charity is an expectation. If you are pre-disposed to charitable contributions, either of your time or your financial resources, how do you choose which ones to support and how much to give?

One element of your decision might be an analysis of the value of that charity. (Those running the charity might be interested to know that too.) Charities don't typically sell their services, so we're left with some difficult approximations to make. The value of donations made might provide us with some measure, but often their work is highly dependent upon the volunteer time of its supporters. So, perhaps we need to add to the value of donations some metric of the value of volunteer time. But still, that seems to leave much to be desired in our valuation of something non-commercial. We're really trying to get at our live duck for shoes valuation, but in this case, we're dealing mostly with intangibles, for which we try to find a tangible substitute.

ARE WE ACTING ON OUR BELIEFS?

Value and values are different. The former is an attempt to quantify the worth of something and the latter is more frequently associated with intangible concepts like principles and beliefs. An organization's values, therefore, often go beyond monetary measures and are described by its board of directors, or organizing body, as part of its business planning process or its foundational documents. These may be simple mission statements, which reflect general beliefs, or they may be elaborately developed business plans and conduct policies that describe the objectives of the organization and boundaries of behavior that are allowed in pursuit of those objectives. In any case, the extent to which an organization can fulfill its values may be a more appropriate measure of value. When a company has return on shareholder equity as its only value, then we have no problem reconciling value and values in a monetary fashion. But rarely is it so simple. Still, the objective is the same — to turn the degree to which we fulfill our values into some kind of measurable value.

As individuals, our values are what we believe to be good; to phrase it differently, what is good is often seen by us as being valuable. In other words, it is what forms our belief system. In effect, we use our values to determine the value of a choice. We decide to support a charity by making the decision to part with our time or wealth in support of its mission. Similarly, if the enjoyment or better health I get from eating good-tasting fruit are among my values, that may have signaled my brain to make me walk to the local co-op and buy that tasty Honeycrisp apple. As individuals, we might even have negative influences on our perception of value when we believe that something is inconsistent with our values and beliefs.

Again, our belief systems influence our perception of value when we make a choice. Whether that choice is to substitute charity for consumption of goods or services, investing, or saving, our values collectively determine the value that we ascribe to something. Case closed, right?

Well, it turns out that our values are not quite as constant or pure as we might think them to be. In fact, our values may even change just because of what we see others doing. Princeton Professor Emeritus John Darley has researched how people behave in groups versus how they behave as individuals, and we'll look at some of his work later in this book. For now, just note that one of his findings is that when we see others in a group to which we belong doing things that we might individually find to be against our values, we are more likely to engage in similar bad behaviors, even failing to recognize that those actions are inconsistent with our values.[1] On a more positive side of our changing values, if we hear that one of our friends is supporting a particular charity, that piece of information may influence our choice to support it as well. There is an amplification of actions when we see others doing something, good or bad, and that amplification can change our behaviors and perceptions of value, sometimes radically.

Let's consider four types of organizations whose value we might wish to assess: for-profit businesses, charities, political economies, and self-organized groups without any formal corporate structure (think of a time you got together with some people to "do something"). In this latter case, it may be that some set of values spontaneously, or with some initial leadership, stimulated a collective action by people with similar values. In all four cases, their values can be described, and in all four cases we seek a way to measure the value that each creates and, further, to understand how we might maximize that value.

ECONOMICS AND THE CREATION OF VALUE

To pursue objectives, every organization needs resources like cash, people, connections, or even goodwill (not the accounting kind), all of which can be used in pursuit of our values. In business-speak, these items are called capital. Capital can be described in financial terms like cash, debt, or equity, or we can use common business vernacular like human capital or political capital.

As economics is the study of how people use their limited resources in an attempt to satisfy unlimited wants, we'll group these forms of capital under the umbrella of *economic capital* — a label that tries to capture the simultaneous condition of limited availability and desirability of these resources.

Economic capital, like most resources, is scarce. In other words, those who want it have to compete to get it and if they do not use it well, it can go away, often very quickly. Quite infamously, and over a matter of days during the financial crisis in 2008, companies like Bear Stearns and Lehman Brothers, once among the venerable leaders of Wall Street, effectively disappeared in terms of ongoing operations when key parties to their successful pursuit of corporate values denied them their needed economic capital. Still others in the same business were recipients of additional economic capital from the same key parties, even amid the crisis. Something made these successful firms different from those that failed.

I mentioned earlier how duck and shoe trading was a form of bartering, which helped with the formation of early economies. The study of economics is a social science, meaning it looks at how elements of societies, organized or not, interact to allocate scarce resources and thereby determine their value. If you have attended college in the past 35 years, you have probably had some introduction to economics, most likely through an introductory course in *macroeconomics*.

Macroeconomics, or studies of big social interactions like "the economy," has fallen generally into two major schools of thought. The first, influenced by the writings of Adam Smith and Milton Friedman, are those who believe in something called "The Invisible Hand." In short, this group believes that an open market or trading process is highly efficient and is superior at determining how scarce resources are allocated to maximize the total value of all transactions. In some almost invisible way — hence the name — the availability of information and the rationality of the members of the economy move resources to the place where they can be most effectively used.

The second group tends to believe less in such a "market god" and more in a hierarchical structure of economies, believing that there is a greater role for institutions like governments to play in ensuring that economies produce better results by intervening in how resources are allocated by the market. The writings of John Maynard Keynes are among the most influential for this group, whom I label "The Interventionists."

Neither school of thought has managed to take hold entirely, in part because both seem to fail with great regularity. In its review of the impact of the financial crisis that began in 2007, *The Economist* magazine said, "Of all the economic bubbles that have been pricked, few have burst more spectacularly than the reputation of economics itself."[2] It turns out (and many said this early on) that some of the assumptions behind the effectiveness of the Invisible Hand are simply not found to be true in the real world. At the same time, the notion that a hierarchical structure can be agile and insightful enough to allocate resources in something as elaborate as a large economy challenges credulity even to the untrained person. Picture one person trying to organize all of the activities of even one neighborhood, let alone the entire town, state or nation! Parents, I need only point out how hard it is to keep your children's schedule, let alone get them to do their chores or pick-up their clothes when you tell them to.

A third group has emerged in the past two decades with evidence that they can explain some of the issues facing the Invisible Hand crowd and can make the Interventionist crowd a bit better at what they do. The works of Herbert Simon, Daniel Kahnemann, and Amos Tversky are among the most influential in this group, commonly labeled "The Behavioralists." Behavioral economics looks at how simple factors can bias people's actions, assumptions and thoughts, and can lead to less than perfectly rational behaviors. Further, work in this area incorporates research from the field of psychology on how people feel about risk and perceived risk's effect on their decisions to allocate resources like economic capital.

If you took an introductory macroeconomics course in college, and you paid attention, you probably recognize the Invisible Hand group and the Interventionists. But, unless you studied during more recent times, you are not likely to have been greatly influenced by, or even exposed to, the Behavioralists. The first two groups are quite entrenched. Entrenched entities, by their nature, are resistant to change and, until the middle of the first decade of this century, the Behavioralists had been marginalized by the first two groups. This is one reason you may not have learned of the Behavioralists and may not be fully realizing the value of your work.

Nevertheless, no one set of economists can claim the mantle of full knowledge. Because of this realization and the openness of some economists to new ideas, a fourth school of economics called *Complexity Economics* is emerging. Labels like "Complexalists" or "Complexitists" do not seem to roll off the tongue. Therefore, for now, we will simply refer to their emerging way of thinking as Complexity. What makes the Complexity group unique is their focus on explaining and demonstrating how value is created: how groups of things work in systems and how those systems interact to make more out of a scarce input like economic capital than existed before. It's a blend of economics, psychology, biology, physics, and other sciences, and it is contributing to one of the most important developments in finance and economics, ever.

You know already that our world is full of complicated systems. However, not all complicated systems are complex systems. Complex systems are those that create something that is more than the sum of their parts. A car, for example, is a complicated system. When taken apart, it is just its parts. Don't try this at home unless you really know what you are doing, but if you do, you can see the fuel injector, spark plugs, steering wheel, etc., laid out in front of you and can re-assemble these parts to get the same car with which you started. However, a business or an organization formed for the pursuit of its values produces, through the interaction of human agents with other resources, many intangible innovations and tangible services that go well beyond the sum of its input parts. If you disassembled each part of an organization and put them on the ground in front of you, you would see much less than what you see when you view their output as a whole. Again, don't do this at home because some of the components are people and much like live ducks — they don't divide very well.

The magic here is in the way in which the various agents interact in such complex systems, creating something more that is beyond the sum of the inputs. That "something" is often worth more than the resources used. When it is, their activities have created value.

ONLY ONE EQUATION, I PROMISE

Fear not — read on! This is the only equation you will find in this book. And, since it is an important one, I insist that you endure and have a good look at it!

The equation below is a *present value* equation. Remember when we tried to determine how much it would be worth to us today to have someone clean our house one year from today? We were determining its present-day value or present value. The same thing applied to Cousin Louie's loan, the corporate bond investment we made, and the apple I purchased.

$$Value = U_0 + \frac{U_1}{DR_1} + \frac{U_2}{DR_2} + \frac{U_3}{DR_3} + \cdots$$

Our present value equation has three components that matter. First, the numerator (the bit on top) is the amount of something you get at some point in time (the U's, with each separate time you get something denoted by a sequential number). It may be a series of "somethings" like coupon payments or clean homes, but they come to you at some point in the future. If we change nothing else in the equation, the more you get at each point in time, the higher is their present value today. Suppose our home cleaners offered three grades of service: Ten-Year-Old-Boy Clean, Cousin Louie Clean, or Hospital Clean. For which one do you think you should pay more? You get the picture.

$$Value \uparrow = U_0 + \frac{\boxed{U_1}\uparrow}{DR_1} + \frac{\boxed{U_2}\uparrow}{DR_2} + \frac{\boxed{U_3}\uparrow}{DR_3} + \cdots$$

Similarly, if the "somethings" we get will happen more often, then you will usually be willing to assign a higher value to them. Suppose, if you paid up front, you could have your house Hospital Cleaned twice each week for a year, or the service was still offered weekly, but for five years instead of one. Again, you will be getting more from this service that you value, hence you would usually be willing to pay more for it.

Back to the equation: the three dots at the end, called an ellipsis, suggest that you continue to receive the "somethings" into the future. The more times you expect to receive these, the higher the value of this equation today.

$$Value \uparrow \ = \ U_0 + \frac{U_1}{DR_1} + \frac{U_2}{DR_2} + \frac{U_3}{DR_3} + \overrightarrow{(\cdots)}$$

These first two parts of the value equation are relatively simple. You get more and so you are usually willing to give more. Now comes the tricky part. How do you translate these "somethings" which you get later into something you have today and might be willing to trade for the "somethings" in the future? The method used is called *discounting*. In effect, you always have the choice to take what you have today and invest it to buy things later. Suppose, for example, you thought it a better idea to make an investment today that would give you $100 every time the house was about to be cleaned. You'd be able to pay the cleaning bill, exactly, each time.

But we all know that investments of most kinds are risky. Maybe you'd have more than $100 some times and less another time. However, if you choose to prepay for the cleaning service, you also have risks. Maybe the company won't clean as well if they have your money already. Perhaps they'll go out of business before they give you all of the cleanings they promised. Or, even worse, what if it's a scam and they will never show up, skipping town with your money?

In effect, what we have to do is find an investment that has the same risk as we perceive the risk of the cleaning services to be. We can then translate the value of the cleaning services into an equivalent value of an investment. We can translate cleaning services into ducks, shoes, or corporate bonds — if we can match their risks. In short, we can determine the value of any of these things through the use of this value equation.

One other aspect of this part of the equation is that perceived risk is on the bottom (the denominator, the DR's, or discount rates — they can be different in each time period, so each is denoted with a sequential number to identify them with the timing of the "somethings"). So, if the risk of something goes down, its value will go up and vice versa. If something is without risk (and there is no inflation), then each DR is equal to one and today's value is just the sum of the value of each "something" received in the future. If the perceived risk is large enough (approaching infinite risk), the value today will be close to zero. This understanding of the inverse relationship between perceived risk and value is critical to our analysis and is probably the most underappreciated element in terms of its impact on the value of anything we do or have.

$$Value \uparrow = U_0 + \frac{U_1}{\overline{(DR_1)} \downarrow} + \frac{U_2}{\overline{(DR_2)} \downarrow} + \frac{U_3}{\overline{(DR_3)} \downarrow} + \cdots$$

As you'll see later in the book, value need not be just a monetary measure. Overall, we're looking to understand the extent to which we effectively fulfill our organization's values, which this equation will also allow us to do. Value can gauge both how effectively you use capital — usually a monetary measure — as well as the extent to which you are able to fulfill your beliefs.

Okay, one equation down, none to go. But remember, this is an important equation and we can use it to value just about anything. So don't forget it, okay?

In simple terms, remember these three things about the present value equation:

1. When the amount of the "somethings" you receive grows, the value today increases.

2. When the number of times you receive the "somethings" is expected to grow, the value today increases.

3. When the risk that you won't receive the "somethings" that you expect shrinks, the value today increases.

Effective governance of our human organizations is about making these three things happen.

NOTES

1 For example, see Darley, J. M., Messick, D. M., and Tyler, T. R. (Eds.), *Social Influences on Ethical Behavior in Organizations*, Erlbaum, 2001.

2 "What Went Wrong with Economics, and How the Discipline Should Change to Avoid the Mistakes of the Past," *The Economist*, July 16, 2009

CHAPTER 2

Systems and Networks in Our Lives

Virtually every activity in which humans engage makes the use of systems, usually multiple systems. In this chapter, we'll define several terms that are used when talking about systems. We'll then go into some of the basic types of systems and their characteristics.

SECRET AGENTS

Systems are nothing more than the interaction of various parts, called *agents*, such as human beings, machines, etc. Each one performs some *function* which may be repetitive and constant, or it might be quite dynamic and interactive. The roles of the agents and how they interact will be discussed later. However, starting at this point to view everything you see in the world as an interaction of agents in systems is essential for the development of better governance.

If you are like many people, you start the work day with the purchase of a cup of coffee. At this early time of the day, you may not recognize that your first step into your favorite shop was made possible by an agent who had successfully arrived before you to unlock the door, and perhaps another who has turned on the lights, warmed the water to brew the coffee, etc. As you approach the counter to place your order, someone in the system had already designed and placed signage to make your purchase more convenient. Another agent hired the coffee producer (who had already engaged dozens or perhaps hundreds of coffee growers) to arrange for the shipment of the coffee beans to this particular store at this particular time. And don't forget that all of the shippers had hundreds of agents involved in making sure the shipment was timely and passed through customs properly. When you greet your favorite barista (agent) to place your order, she engages the computerized pricing and inventory system that allows the speedy quantification of the money you will gladly pay for the result of all of the systems interacting properly. She next engages a production and delivery system which puts your coffee in your hands, and you happily march off to engage in the thousands of other systems that affect your day. At this point you've likely turned your mind to other things, oblivious to the multiple systems you have just set in motion to process your payment, refill the inventory you have consumed, and send a signal to buying agents about the popularity (or not) of the kind of coffee drink you are now sipping. Like a domino effect of sorts, the seemingly innocuous act of purchasing your morning cup of java has set into motion a repeating buying system that will deliver to you, and thousands like you, at some point in the future, a cup of coffee, generally exactly to your liking.

I challenge you to think of your morning order in the same way tomorrow and identify how in the world a similar system can deliver a banana from South America to my local gasoline station in Minnesota for just nine cents each! But I digress.

In fact, the interaction of agents in systems has received growing attention in business and academic circles. The purpose of this chapter is to introduce you to some of the basic elements of Systems Theory and Network Theory, an area of applied mathematics and network science that has broad application across our governing of systems. Again, I promise, no more equations. So read on.

Eventually, we will build to an understanding of how complex systems, like coffee orders or businesses, behave. This knowledge will allow us to positively impact the three factors that influence the value of our organizations — the amount of "somethings," the number of times we get the "somethings," and the perceived risk of being disappointed in our expectations about those "somethings." This understanding will allow us to create more value in everything that we do.

SYSTEMS THEORY

In the mid-1900s, the science of systems, or how systems in nature, society, and science interact to produce something of value, emerged as an area of academic study. The origin of this study is often traced to the work of biologist Ludwig von Bertalanffy.[1] In the late 1920s, von Bertalanffy challenged the generally held beliefs of the scientific method that systems were just parts that could be added in a linear fashion to create a whole, and that each part could be analyzed independently of the other parts. The example of a car in the first chapter fits the original belief nicely, but the delivery of a cup of coffee does not.

In systems theory, there is something about the interaction of agents in a system that results in more being created than is put in. It's a bit of magic, in a way, and differentiates businesses, for example, from cars.

A *controlled system* is defined as having a property, which, if a variable in the system moves outside of its normal range for that system, the system will move to bring that variable back into acceptable ranges. Consider a police officer with a radar gun, pen, and citation book at the ready to be a control on the system of roads that we use. This is how the overall system is kept in order, or under control.

When a new piece of information is brought into a controlled system, it causes a change in response to the information. For example, your morning coffee order has *information value* for those planning what to order in the future to meet your demands as well as the demands of other people like you. For reasons that are related to each other, we are most used to and generally most comfortable in controlled systems.

A system that is in balance is said to be in *equilibrium*. However, to be in equilibrium, it does not need to be stable or static, because equilibrium can also occur when part of the system is not changing, but other parts are in a state of change, moving towards equilibrium. In order for a system to continue indefinitely, though, it must be able to be unchanging or moving towards equilibrium.

Systems can provide *negative feedback* to restore variables that are out of line to a level acceptable to the system. Similarly, systems can provide *positive feedback* that drives a variable from its current place, or value, to a larger value in the future. This is an amplifying feedback of a perceived positive behavior, which will generally push that something to its natural limit. A village, neighborhood, or family will usually attempt to correct misbehavior among its youth using negative feedback and to encourage positive behaviors by granting greater authority and responsibility to those in which such good behavior is observed...up to a point.

Positive and negative feedbacks may result in patterns being observed in the system — people go to jail for violating certain rules and people are promoted at work for achieving success. Some of these patterns are learned patterns communicated from others to agents in the system and thus might be described as a *culture*. We often hear about a corporate culture, which simply refers to patterns of behavior that have been sanctioned, knowingly and sometimes unknowingly, by a corporate system.

We next differentiate between *closed systems* and *open systems*. Closed systems have no interaction with other systems, but solely among agents within the system. It is believed that the only closed system with which we come into contact is the universe. If it is actually closed, then it is in a state of entropy, which means that it is continually moving towards greater and greater disorganization. Taken at face value, this is not good. But thankfully, the process seems to be slow, despite everyday evidence to the contrary. And newer ideas seem to suggest that even the universe may not, in fact, be closed.

An open system gets feedback and information from other systems and its *environment*, which contains all systems, and also sends feedback and information to other systems and the environment. All systems in our known world, except with the possibility of the universe as a whole, are open systems. They are changing via the dynamic interaction of the agents in them, as well as through their interaction with other systems. A good example is a political economy. Through feedback from citizens, their control is attempted. Open systems tend to show greater and greater forms of organization.

Information in systems is processed via three functions. The first is the *communication* of information among agents in the system and between systems. The second function is a set of *rules* the system uses to make decisions based on that information. The third function is the means by which systems *transact*. We communicate to exchange information and we transact to exchange things like money, live ducks, or coffee.

One control of our systems is the fact that they must compete with other systems for scarce resources. Adam Smith's Invisible Hand seemed to make systems change based on feedback from the marketplace for resources that multiple systems demanded. Higher prices for a scarce commodity may redirect demand to a substitute product. Another form of control is *intervention* where some guiding hand that is not so invisible makes the corrections to elements within the system that have moved outside of the system's comfort zone. Aggressive actions from a central bank to reduce or increase the supply of credit, or government deficit spending, are examples of this form of intervention.

Systems must be in a state of change in order to remain healthy. The overall health of an organization is strongly linked to its ability to anticipate and adapt to change. Further, in many ways the health of the overall environment is dependent on the transactions that take place within the systems that comprise its environment. When the interventionist control is engaged, those who guide the intervention are well-warned to consider not only how their decisions affect the system on which they focus, but also the other systems with which the system of their attention interacts — think in terms of the law of unintended consequences.

To predict what might happen when variables change, we might engage mathematical models, noting that our models have *error terms*, or random amounts by which forecasts turn out to be wrong. Sometimes the model predicts too high of a value, and sometimes it predicts too low of a value.

Some changes to variables in a system may wind up stimulating an uncontrolled system variable in an unanticipated way that might create *chaos* in the system as a whole. This is particularly true if some parts of a system behave in *non-linear* ways. In other words, they are amplified at each stage of development through some kind of dramatic positive feedback mechanism. In this context, positive is not necessarily good. Rather, it suggests that the value keeps getting larger and larger, growing at a non-linear rate.

You may have heard the famous question posed by Edward Lorenz about the effect of the flap of a butterfly's wings in a complex system: *Does the flap of a butterfly's wings in Brazil set off a tornado in Texas?*[2] This is the idea that the flapping of a butterfly's wings might create changes in the atmosphere that could ultimately modify the path of a large-scale weather pattern. It's a cascading effect that changes outcomes. So, the butterfly flapping in the rain forest of Brazil could change the system of weather in a miniscule manner that impacts other systems, eventually causing a tornado in Texas, or even stopping a tornado in Bangladesh that would have happened if the wings had never moved.

The "Butterfly's Wings" question might seem a bit abstract for the intended practical purposes of this book. However, it is illustrative of the possibility that through the interaction of complex systems, even small changes in one place can result in dramatic changes in another.

Another important notion about the stability and predictability of systems relates to how much we know about them. In systems theory, the less information we have about a system, the shorter the time interval before the outcome of that system becomes unpredictable. Remember the present value equation in the first chapter? To know the value of something today, you have to discount back the value of something you expect to receive in the future. If the outcome is unpredictable or wildly unstable, the risk of being wrong in your expectations might cause you to assign a very high discount factor to it that could potentially render it worthless. If you knew nothing of the cleaning company that offered its services to you in Chapter 1 other than an online ad — no personal references or details — you'd likely pay much less for its services because there would be substantial uncertainty about the company's ability to fulfill its obligations to you, especially far into the future.

NETWORK THEORY

All that has been discussed so far in this chapter is related to how systems work, with some mention of how systems interact. Interactions in systems are succinctly displayed via Network Theory, representing graphically the relationships between agents in systems. In other words (at least a thousand of them), Network Theory is a way to describe systems in pictures.

You are likely familiar with social network sites like Facebook and LinkedIn or recall the network of systems described earlier when examining all of the work that goes into getting your morning coffee to you. Have you ever seen how these look in a picture? Well, Facebook and LinkedIn are a lot like the famous game, "Six degrees of separation from Kevin Bacon," where the challenge is to name an actor, then connect him or her to Kevin Bacon in less than six steps. So let's look at Figure 2.1, which is a graph of some of the people and things connected to Kevin Bacon.

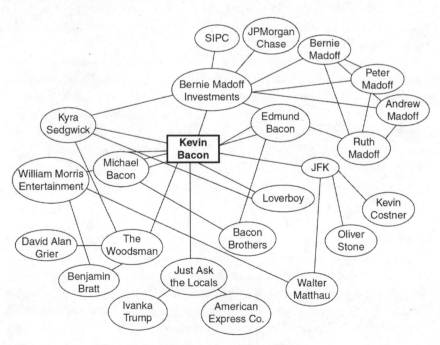

Figure 2.1 The Kevin Bacon Network — Part I
Source: Muckety.com

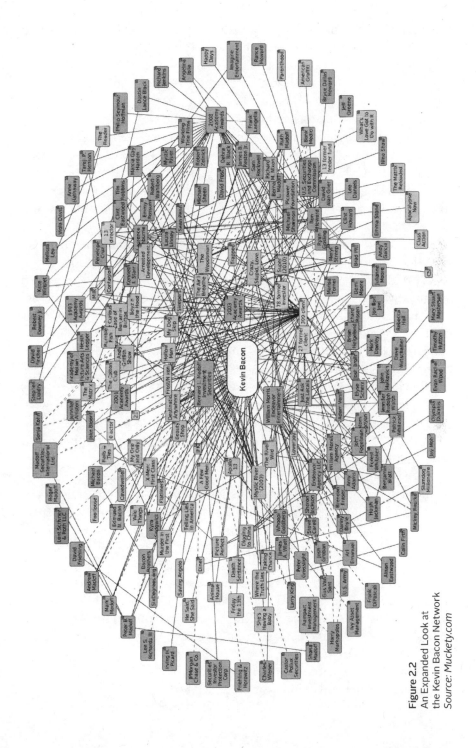

Figure 2.2
An Expanded Look at
the Kevin Bacon Network
Source: Muckety.com

Thanks to this diagram we're able to quickly see just how complicated Kevin Bacon's network/system of relationships is. Figure 2.1 only maps a very small set of those relationships, let alone two or three full degrees of separation from him. If we expand a few more relationships, the chart gets more than a bit unruly.

In Figure 2.2, Kevin is still the center of the world. But we can now see that a growing number of the lines that connect people, groups and companies don't pass directly through Kevin. In other words, these people/groups, each of which is connected to him in some pretty direct way, are able to say things about him that he may never know and can never respond to. He should care about this, for if they say bad things about his movies, people might stop going!

In truth, every one of us has a network of connections that we could map like Kevin's. That's what makes the Kevin Bacon game so intriguing. Now, if we replace any person at the middle of this world and place a company, nonprofit, or other organization, the same thing holds true. Our organizations have complicated and complex relationships with many entities, some of which have relationships with each other. They may say good or bad things about us and we may never know until it is too late to do anything about it.

Some of these agents in systems are people and some are other networks of people. Each agent or network of agents uses their resources to do what they are presently doing, which may include planning for what they want to do later. What they want to do later may be useful information for us and our system.

The trick in using network graphs is trying to find the *power of relationships* to see how they might influence resources, activities, and plans. Some relationships matter more than others, either because we value them more or they have a greater ability to influence how our value is perceived by others. When we look at these relationships, there is information flowing in at least one direction among the agents, as is noted by the lines that connect them. Sometimes information flows two ways and sometimes it circles around through multiple channels before it reaches its final destination. Information is one of the resources that agents have, and as new information flows into their resource pool, it can affect what they are presently doing and what they plan to do later.

Remember the coffee you bought today? Well, Figure 2.3 is a simple map of the system with which you interfaced.

You're somewhere in the middle. What's interesting in this chart?

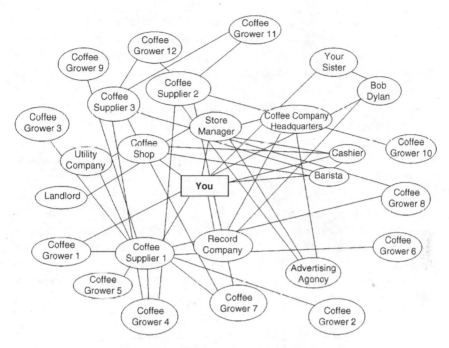

Figure 2.3 The Morning Coffee Network

Well, your sister and Coffee Grower 1 both like Bob Dylan and that's the music that was playing in the store when you arrived. Your coffee purchase funded royalties to the record company that works with Bob Dylan, partially financing the ability for you, your sister, and a coffee grower half a world away to mentally play back the organ riff from *Like a Rolling Stone*, maybe even at the same time!

More interesting to us in terms of governing a system like this is that when you purchased your regular cup of coffee, you sent information to dozens of agents with no further action taken on your part. These agents may have adjusted their behavior based on this information (depending on how powerful your relationship with them is) and may have changed their communication with other agents based on this information. It's unlikely that your single purchase will influence the kind of beans that Coffee Grower 5 farms, but you may influence what the store manager orders next from the supplier, and it certainly affected what the barista did next. In this case, your power over the barista is much greater than your power over Coffee Grower 5.

Tomorrow, if you order something completely new, you might cause a reaction from the cashier who knows you well. He might even start to wonder if everything is okay with you and give you more attention during your order...or not. He might even think some action needs to be taken to bring you back in line with the expectations of the system! Or, the system will be built to respond to your change in a positive manner.

Remember, within our networks, we are communicating and transacting. This interaction affects each system that is part of the network; how our particular system responds is in large part based on how it is structured, or governed. This interaction gives rise to another property of systems in that they may yield information value. Knowing one part of the system may allow us to know something more about another part. Since I can buy Colombian coffee at my local shop, I can infer that the owner of my local shop has some systematic link to a coffee grower in Colombia, and since I can buy bananas here, when it is 25 degrees below zero, my local gas station has some dependence upon transactions with a business in a tropical country.

As you get to know the systems and networks in your life better, you will continue to build towards a better understanding of how your company, non-profit, virtual network, political economy, or neighborhood association, can be of value and how that value might change. You may already be developing a bit of an insight into just how dependent the value of that system can be on other people and systems in your network and how they perceive the value of yours.

That's a great first step!

NOTES

1   Von Bertalanffy, Ludwig, *General Systems Theory, Foundations, Development, Applications*, George Braziller, Inc., 1969

2   Lorenz, Edward, "Predictability; Does the Flap of a Butterfly's wings in Brazil Set Off a Tornado in Texas?," American Association for the Advancement of Science, 139th Meeting, December 29, 1972

CHAPTER 3

The Dynamics of
Self-Organizing Groups

Whether responding to a crisis, taking political action, or mingling at a neighborhood party, humans have the remarkable ability to self-organize. Sometimes these organizations are transient and sometimes they change the world.

Take, for example, the 2011 political uprising in Egypt. A reporter for Gulf News described the epicenter of the protests, Tahrir Square in Cairo, as follows:

> *"This is starting to look like a small city. There's a community feel. Different roles assigned for different people. There's a corner for artists who write slogans, a couple of small makeshift field clinics, a place for people to compile pictures and videos to upload to the Internet. Men take turns to guard the entrances. Some women and men clean the place by collecting garbage and sweeping the streets. Others ensure that everyone is fed. The most interesting part is there is no command structure so far."* [1]

Or consider the response to major floods in North Dakota and Minnesota during the spring of 1997. A research paper written several years later examined the resulting changes in local government hierarchy and responsibilities:

> *"During the 1997 flood, city, county, and state, agencies were all forced to coordinate their efforts daily or hourly. The independence enjoyed by each agency was washed away when the flood reached catastrophic levels...The novel system that emerged during the two weeks that Fargo and Moorhead were besieged can best be characterized as one of suspended rivalries and collaboration via the reputation of neutral agencies...This spontaneous system enabled the southern portion of the Red River Valley to sustain a flood fight that lasted more than three times longer and posted water levels two feet higher than anticipated."* [2]

Anyone who has experienced first-hand or watched media coverage of a major flood or similar disaster has probably seen the spontaneous self-organization of volunteers that so frequently occurs in the aftermath of a catastrophe. Most typically, these groups first organize to provide defense against continued damage — sandbagging lines exemplify this — and next they move to response and recovery.

Parents know what to fear when they leave their normally responsible teenager alone at home while they take a weekend getaway because they have a good sense of what impact a spontaneously assembled group of schoolmates can have.

FROM SMALL, UNCONNECTED BEGINNINGS

What is common among these examples of group dynamics is that people who often have no personal connection to each other organize to achieve some objective without any corporate structure in place to direct them; if hierarchies are already in place, they often change their order spontaneously.

Usually these initiatives begin with the idea or motivation of one person or a very small group. These are the entrepreneurs of society. Not all are business entrepreneurs, but they are all visionaries — people who see things that don't exist and believe that the things they envision are of value. Their passion inspires others to follow their lead, and "something" of value is thus created that didn't exist before.

In the mid-1970s, Bill Gates and Paul Allen, one-time classmates, designed a new programming language for the Altair computer. After some early success, they called their venture "Microsoft" and envisioned to have "a computer on every desk and Microsoft on every computer" — a revolutionary thought, at the time. This ambitious, yet simply stated vision emerged from the conversations between two people with a common interest and a connection made at school.

We all know these two entrepreneurs have done well, but the magnitude of their success is staggering. Early in 2018, Microsoft had a market capitalization of over $700 billion and held more than $140 billion in cash, cash equivalents, and marketable securities on its balance sheet. An estimated 50 percent of computers around the world use Microsoft's operating system and over 120,000 people work for the company.[3] Value for the owners and investors in Microsoft had clearly been created, but one might also argue that their work spurred the creation of value at millions of organizations worldwide whose productivity was enhanced by their innovative business tools. Microsoft has even gone through a re-invention of sorts when former

CEO Steve Ballmer stepped down and was replaced by Satya Nadella. Nadella rallied the organization behind the idea of a continual licensing model and remote computing/storage — something radically different from the original model. The entrepreneurial initiative of the founders and that of Microsoft more recently has led to the creation of an amazing amount of additional value.

Rotary International is another example of positive group dynamics that were initiated by a visionary. This service organization began its life in 1905 as a small business and social club in Chicago, formed by local attorney Paul Harris. He and his co-founders rotated early meetings among their respective offices and the term "Rotarian" was coined to name their group. Their initiative inspired the development of similar clubs in other cities and within 15 years Rotary clubs could be found on six continents. Within 20 years of its founding, Rotary had grown to 200 clubs with more than 20,000 members and the organization's distinguished reputation attracted presidents, prime ministers, and a host of other luminaries to its ranks. As Rotary grew, in addition to serving their professional and social interests, members and local clubs began pooling their resources and contributing their talents to help serve communities in need. This transformation was so successful that Rotary has officially adopted the motto of "Service Above Self" to convey its purpose. Today, Rotary exists in more than 200 countries, counting more than 1.2 million members in more than 32,000 chapters. It is active in local, regional, national, and international service, and community building.[4]

But Rotary International and Microsoft have more in common than just being success stories. In 2009, the Bill and Melinda Gates Foundation, an organization that was created from the personal wealth Bill Gates derived from his Microsoft innovations, pledged more than $350 million to support PolioPlus — a program that Rotary International launched in 1985 with the goal of eradicating polio worldwide. The progress this initiative has made is remarkable. In 1985, polio cases could be found in 125 countries.[5] Today, this disease is found only in a few communities in Afghanistan, Nigeria, and Pakistan. And, to continue the effort towards total eradication, in 2017 the Gates Foundation pledged additional matching grants of up to $300 million to the program.[6] The vision of a mission to eradicate polio is inspiring, simply stated and is now within reach. Undeniably, this joint effort born out of collaboration of previously unrelated groups is of tremendous value.

Microsoft, Rotary International, and PolioPlus are big success stories. What a better world it would be if every initiative could generate the same kind of value. It need not be the case, though. In fact, often we may find ourselves involved in initiatives that generate only a modest amount of value, if any. Some of our initiatives may even fail. However, the opportunity for innovation will continue, and understanding how this is fostered can enable us to be better governors of the systems in which we are involved.

To begin to understand the source of value creation, let's play a couple of games. These concepts can be challenging, and you'll have to do some visualization. But this is essential knowledge, so stay with me.

HOPS, SKIPS, JUMPS, AND LUCK

Scientists researching innovation sometimes use rules-based games or simulations of how agents in systems work with each other. Their work shows how organizations might form and how discoveries can be made. In our first game, we place you somewhere on a big, open, undulating terrain and give you the goal of finding high ground. In this game, if you get to a higher spot, you get more energy and you live longer. That's good! This particular terrain has lots of flat places and lots of higher places — some higher than others — several very high places, and some very deep holes. If you are unlucky enough to step into one of these holes, you will die. It's a diverse landscape.

As in life, if you move from where you are, you will deplete your energy. If you move too far without finding a higher place (and more energy), you'll eventually expend all of your energy and die.

As the game begins, you have a choice to make. If you stay in one place and don't move, you may have enough resources to survive for a long time, yet all for you will remain the same for a long time too. It could get quite boring. If you move, things will change — they might get a little or a lot better, or they might get much worse.

More information may help to guide your decision. There are three ways to move: walk, hop, or jump. Hopping and jumping take more energy than walking, but you can hop farther than you can walk, you can jump farther than you can hop, and you must hop or jump to get up to a higher place. As you might expect, when hopping and jumping to a place, it is more difficult to control the outcome. You will try to land in one place, but you may miss it. You can walk to exactly where you want to go at the same height, but again, you have to hop or jump to get to a higher place.

Good news, though: if you are successful, you are then able to hop and jump farther and with more accuracy. You gain advantage the better you perform.

Eventually, the game ends when one person gets to the very highest place. S/he is the winner, has the most energy, and gets to decide the future rules.

At the start of the game, you and other players are randomly dropped on the terrain. Some players land on flat places and some lucky people land on higher ground.

For an unknown reason — up to this point anyway — some players are perfectly content staying in one place and do not move. Meanwhile, others begin walking, hopping, and jumping. Many of these adventurers fall into deep holes (and die) or slip off of high peaks to which they inaccurately jumped. The stay-put crowd uses the wailing emanating from those who failed as justification for their choice.

Simultaneously, successful hoppers and jumpers express delight with their accomplishments and earned rewards, encouraging other adventurers, and perhaps a few stay-putters, to leap as well. Eventually, the most successful explorers will reach levels of satisfaction that may turn them into stay-putters — things are pretty good at the height they have attained and dying, just now, would have more consequence than it had on the flats. Nevertheless, there are still some jumpers and hoppers who seek even higher heights. Some fall into holes, some succeed, and the process of winnowing continues until one adventurer finds the peak and the game, as it was defined up to that point, ends. Was it you?

RISK, SUCCESS, AND FAILURE

This game is analogous to real life. We have to make choices and these choices will result in good, really good, bad, and really bad outcomes.

This is a good place to define the term *risk*. For most people, risk is characterized by negative outcomes — the "bad" and "really bad." For example, if you buy a stock, it might go down in value. Or, if you cross the street without looking, you might be hit by a car. Taking a step on our terrain and falling into a hole would be really bad — to say the least. In general, people try to avoid bad outcomes. They try to avoid risk.

In truth, risk has both positive and negative connotations and limiting oneself to just the negative consideration of risk can lead to suboptimal decision-making. We'll discuss this in greater detail later in the book. But for now, let's change the definition of risk to be simply an unknown change in value, of some magnitude, from what something is worth today — from its value today. In our first game, if you hop, walk or jump, your energy level will change by some unknown amount, either up or down. Your value in the first game is essentially the amount of energy that you have — remember, the winner had the most. So, moving around changes your value up or down by some amount that is unknown until you move. There is risk associated with your decision to move.

The use of the terms "magnitude" and "amount" in our definition of risk suggests measure. This correctly differentiates risk from uncertainty. Risk, in other words, is something to which we assign a value and that value can be positive or negative.

The first game we played was full of successes and failures — realized risks — both with gradations. Let's categorize the failures as either *partial failures* or *catastrophic failures* — "bad" and "really bad." A partial failure in this game was the failure to have found a higher place when taking a hop or jump, but not having fallen into a hole and not having spent the last bit of your energy. Catastrophic failure would have been anything that ended your ability to continue to play the game. In other words, it would have been your death. The difference between these two descriptions of failure is quite important when we ultimately consider the impact that the possibility of negative catastrophic risks has on value and whether you might just decide to stay home.

THE GAME OF EVOLUTION

Our first game was about you, the value of your energy level, and whether you were willing to take a risk to become more valuable, or even the most valuable player! But the point of this chapter is to look at how groups of people come together to create value, sometimes spontaneously. Do odd games like the one we just played have any connection to the way organizations form or are run in the real world? Is the story helpful enough for you to go wake your boss and tell her to change everything she does right now?

Well, yes, but not yet (read the rest of the book first). There is a parallel in real life that has played out over millennia and you (as well as your boss) are who you are today, in part, because of it. The game is Evolution. It's an ongoing drama of interacting agents that serves as an important allegory for us when considering how to re-govern our organizations.

Most of us are familiar with DNA. It's the chemical instruction manual for everything a living thing does: grow, divide, die, etc. DNA constitutes our human genome and its four different chemical building blocks, called bases, are abbreviated as A, T, C, and G. In the human genome, about 3 billion bases are arranged along the chromosomes in a particular order for each unique individual. Six billion pairs are arranged in a double-helix structure, to which most of us have been introduced in some basic science

class. Among humans alone, there are multiple billions of different combinations of bases. You are your DNA and your boss is her DNA. You are
quite a bit alike, but also very different.

In his highly important book, *The Origin of Wealth*, Eric Beinhocker
describes the work of scientists studying DNA sequences and how the evolution of genes might be traced on a kind of landscape not too different from
the terrain described in our first game.[7] It's a useful illustration of how an
evolutionary process might contribute to the success of a system — in this
case our living world — which is made up of millions of interdependent
agents and systems that usually work quite nicely together. The evolution
of DNA has much to do with this successful interplay.

Beinhocker directs his readers to the work of researchers like Daniel
Dennett, Stuart Kaufmann, Sewall Wright, Jim Crutchfield, and John Holland when discussing an exploration of something called a *fitness landscape*.[8]
The fitness landscape is a terrain that is made up of all the possible DNA
sequences, each represented by a narrow piece of terrain, like a small rod of
earth. The height of each rod is determined by the fitness of the particular
DNA sequence for life. The better the DNA sequence in terms of its fitness
to survive, the higher the rod associated with it will be. Does it sound a
bit familiar?

As an example, the DNA sequence that gives us mouths with which
to eat is useful and greatly increases our chance of survival. There may be
some sequences that are so much better than the rest that future gene pools
could be dominated by them because their likelihood of being passed on to
future generations is so much higher. As an illustration, nearly all people
have mouths, some bigger than others!

There are multiple billions of possible DNA combinations and, hence,
multiple billions of these rods on the fitness landscape. Most of these DNA
combinations are genetic nonsense and don't generate a living thing. In such
a case, they have no value and their height is zero — they make up the flat-
lands. In fact, most of this unimaginably large landscape has a height of zero.

Beinhocker further notes that on this fitness landscape, the DNA combinations are arranged in such a way that they are just one letter apart. For
example, the sequence AGCCT is next to CGCCT, which is next to GGCCT,
etc. So, right next to the rod that is you are all of the 36 billion variants of
you that differ by just one letter. Walking from where you are today in the
game would be like changing one letter in your DNA sequence. If you hop,
this would be like several letters changing and seeing if you have reached
a higher place, stayed just about the same, or fallen into a hole.

While the rods near the one on which your DNA stands are likely to be close in fitness to each other, a long distance away from the starting point there might be 10,000 letters changed in the DNA sequence. At such a distance, there is a higher likelihood that the height of the rod will be much different than the height of the rod at the starting place. Imagine this change to be like taking a big jump, or multiple hops, in our previous game. You might wind up in a really great place, or you might wind up dead.

When a small change in the DNA sequence has a large positive impact, it might open the way for even more fitness-improving alterations. This is like the previous game in that success makes you more likely to succeed again. In Beinhocker's words, such large increases in height from small DNA changes are fast routes up a mountain, or *portals* to a better place — really, really big jumps.[9]

The rules of this game are like our first one, except that the value perspective is not that of one person trying to maximize her energy level. Rather, each agent in this game is represented by a DNA combination and the game is about maximizing the "fitness" of the overall landscape — the value of the overall system of interacting agents. The more fit the system, the more valuable it will be. In this way, earth can be viewed like any company or human organization seeking to increase its value.

Our first game was about individuals and individual outcomes. This game is about some collective system.

But how does a non-thinking system decide to take jumps, to walk about, or to stay put? In this case, the process occurs through changes in the agents that make up the system. The history of life on earth shows that the length of DNA sequences has been growing over time as living creatures become more complex. For the game, this means that fitness landscape is continuously expanding as the number of possible DNA combinations grows. Some will be more fit than others.

Beinhocker tells us that the history of earth's "landscape" shows that it also bucks and heaves — for example, if an asteroid hits the earth or there is some other dramatic change in the environment, it may have massive implications for the probability of survival of some existing DNA combinations.

Some of the bucking and heaving that Beinhocker describes is also a result of changes in other living things on the landscape. For example, when living creatures are interdependent — the success or failure of one impacts the success or failure of the other — a dramatic change in the fitness of either can stimulate a cascading change in the fitness of the other. One way to visualize these sometimes random changes is to view them as a cloud of poisonous gas that rises and falls occasionally across sections of the terrain. If an agent is at a level on the terrain below where the gas reaches, that agent will cease to exist.

Consider the case where each new generation of a living creature would have only a single letter change in DNA — akin to taking a step in our game. If that step is to a higher ground, then the next generation is likely to take another step in that same direction — keeping that one letter change and changing only one more in the next generation. If there is no change or a drop in height, the next generation will try a step in a different direction. This way of moving and learning is called an *adaptive walk*.

The problem with limiting movement to adaptive walking steps is that since the steps are very small, it is highly likely that an agent will find a local peak in the terrain — where all steps around go lower — and will stop there. This may be an insufficiently high peak to survive one of the waves of poisonous gas. This risk is mitigated by the fact that the DNA of a next generation is likely to be much more than just one letter different and might even be vastly different from its parents — these are like hops and jumps in our first game. By hopping or jumping, agents can avoid being trapped on local peaks and might find substantially higher places before the cloud of gas reaches them. In a way, by changing multiple letters in our DNA, the environment takes risk, which may change its value higher or lower.

Even though we know that agents might experience a partial or catastrophic failure with each new generation, movement about the "landscape" is necessary to survive because of the rising and falling gases. You have to take risk. So, there is a continuous incentive to keep agents on the move if the system is to survive.

The game of evolution goes on continuously with less-fit agents disappearing and portals to new heights being created as new generations of agents come about. The process is one that focuses on both the survival of the system and the increase in its overall fitness — an increase in its value.

This is life.

THE MEANING FOR ORGANIZATIONS

In the first game, one person could win and subsequently set the rules for the future. We may think of this result as the game reaching a kind of equilibrium. But in the real world, such is likely to be just a temporary equilibrium. As our self-organizing protestors in Cairo showed, others in the game can grow tired of an arrangement where one person sets all of the rules, ultimately taking risks (hops and jumps) to change the rules as a group. In the game of evolution, because of the bucking and heaving of the landscape, there is no top that is permanent and so the system has to be continuously improving.

These games have relevance for the evolution of organizations and systems within which we operate. The agents in organizations may be groups or networks themselves, some of which have self-organized. Group members may help each other to be more successful or avoid catastrophic failure. Further, dynamic changes (portals) can occur through communication and transaction. Collaboration allows for a greater chance of success and those who collaborate well are likely to survive. Good examples may be copied and bad ones may be remembered for their failures. In sum, the organization becomes more valuable because its collection of agents improves.

Chapter 4 examines a type of economic evolution that follows this description in greater detail, allowing us to continue our movement to a higher place on the governance fitness landscape.

We began this chapter with an example of self-organization from Egypt. This political uprising was inspired by a riot that had occurred in Tunisia just a few weeks before. The Egyptians heard the passionate screams of success and felt inspired to walk, hop, and jump to what they perceived to be a higher place, even though it carried negative risk. At the very moment I wrote this section of the book for the first edition, news broke that the protestors had achieved their primary demand that their President, Hosni Mubarek, resign. One joyful protestor in Tahrir Square said "Everything now seems possible!"[10] That uplifting message of success was being heard in neighboring countries. As we have since witnessed, Egypt was only off to a new temporary equilibrium and more chaotic episodes followed there and elsewhere. Where Egypt and other countries will ultimately wind up — at higher or lower elevations on the fitness landscape — is not yet known. The changes they stimulate will continue nearby and likely also in places we have not yet even considered, affecting some organizations that have not yet found sufficiently high ground.

As I wrote this second edition of the book, a similar movement was under way. Students from a small high school in Florida had self-organized in response to a tragic shooting at their high school in which 17 people were killed. Just five weeks after that event, through their use of networks and systems, hundreds of thousands of protestors — many of whom were high school aged, were rallying to force better and more reasonable controls on guns in the United States. But these rallies were not just in Florida. They took place in venues across the country — in an estimated 390 of the country's 435 congressional districts, and in non-U.S. cities like London, Copenhagen, Madrid, Paris, Rome, Tokyo, Sydney, Brisbane, and Berlin — a total of more than 800 so-called "sibling marches," all organized by students.[11, 12]

On the technological front, new processes and relationships are rapidly emerging via blockchain and related, networked technologies. These are leading to massive wealth creation, destruction, and great uncertainty about their eventual impact on the existing order.

Self-organizing groups have amazing power.

NOTES

1   "Anti-Mubarak activists pour into Tahrir Square," *Gulfnews.com*, February 4, 2011

2   Sellnow, Timothy L., Seeger, Matthew W. and Ulmer, Robert R., "Chaos Theory, Informational Needs, and Natural Disasters," Central States Communication Association Annual Conference, 2000

3   Readers of the first edition of this book might be shocked to note the differences in these values from the time it was published in 2012: market capitalization: $200 million, cash on balance sheet: $40 billion, employees: 90,000.

4   Rotary International

5   Ibid.

6   Tindera, Michela, "Gates Foundation and Rotary Pledge Additional $450 Million To End Polio," *Forbes*, June 12, 2017

7   Beinhocker, Eric D., *The Origin of Wealth: The Radical Remaking of Economics and What it Means for Business and Society*, Paperback; Harvard Business Review Press, 2007, pp. 202–212

8   Sewall Wright, see citation in Ibid.

9   Beinhocker credits Jim Crutchfield of the Santa Fe Institute for the use of the term "portals."

10 Live broadcast, Al Jazeera English TV, February 11, 2011

11 Shear, Michael, "Students Lead Huge Rallies for Gun Control Across the U.S.," *The New York Times*, March 24, 2018

12 Winsor, Morgan, and Eccleston, Jennifer, "March for Our Lives takes place around the world, from London to Berlin to Sydney," *ABC News*, March 24, 2018

CHAPTER 4

The Emergence of Complexity Economics

I studied economics as a graduate student at Northwestern University, near Chicago. As an undergraduate at Miami University in Ohio, I chose economics, mathematics, and statistics as the focus of my studies. Building on these and the interest in markets that my father's gift of Texaco stock had stimulated, I began my career on the trading floor of the First National Bank of Chicago — or First Chicago, as it was referred to in those days — working for the bank's futures subsidiary.

In the 1980s, money was flowing into the financial markets and seemed likely to do so for the foreseeable future. On the job, while I pined on about macroeconomic variables and Federal Reserve policies, others taught me about the "technical" measures of market behavior. Some of the smartest traders were trying to predict the markets using all manner of charts and tools. Big money was being made and lost, and careers were catapulted or stunted based on one's fortunes in "beating the market."

My first real trading mentor knew about the emotions of trading and how to best understand human responses to gains, losses, and risk. He taught me how these feelings would influence the trading behaviors of others and how to spot such in the movement of prices. The message was this: in order to succeed, you need to master an understanding of your own emotions and those of the collective market, not to know about changes in the "money supply."

Much of my on-the-job experience conflicted with my academic course-work in economics and I knew from these real-world experiences that something was missing from the teachings of the day.

TWO SCHOOLS IN CONFLICT

The "Chicago School" of economics in the 1980s was all about efficient markets, rational behavior, random noise, and market-clearing prices that eliminated the potential for profit. Emotion management and price charting techniques were self-inflicted delusions. The proof of this statement was a tautology — if they were not, everyone would be using them and the profit from such information would immediately disappear. How do you argue with such reasonable logic, especially as it was being taught by some of the smartest academics in the world?

Still, I watched, learned, and experimented in the markets. Sure enough, it seemed to me that the markets were not as random as I had been led to believe and patterns did seem to emerge in the behavior of prices. I clearly felt emotions and they often led me to make irrational trading decisions. It remained very challenging to make money off of patterns and emotional intelligence, but the sense that what I had been taught about the efficiency of markets was not accurate gained greater and greater hold over my thinking. And it turned out that the trading methods my mentor had taught me worked so much better than should have been possible. They were also much more closely aligned with the actual behavior of market prices than was economic theory.

To this day, the concept of efficient markets still has a strong hold on economics — especially in introductory courses taught at the university level. But it is wrong to continue this belief in its absolute form and people are making bad decisions because of their blind faith in "the market."

A new school of thinking about economics and markets has emerged and is beginning to upset all that we have believed over the past four decades. Finally, we have a better way to understand markets. But it doesn't end there. This new way of looking at economics can help us understand much of what constitutes all of our economic interactions and how they have come to be. The influence of emotions is real. Markets are not always random and efficient, if ever. Patterns of behavior can be found to consistently emerge. And some people will indeed make a lot of money from their businesses, their investments and, frankly, sometimes their dumb luck. All of this becomes clearer with this new way of thinking called *Complexity Economics*. We'll explore this subject in more detail shortly. But first, we have to understand some of the reasons why we need a new way of looking at things that fills in the gaps I first noticed on that trading floor more than 30 years ago.

WHAT'S WRONG WITH TRADITIONAL ECONOMICS?

Assume that Traditional Economics is wrong. If the argument against the way in which economics has been taught began like this, you would rightly dismiss any conclusions from the reasoning as not squaring with reality. Lots of very good work has come from the study of economics and resultant applications. But the problem with much of the Traditional Economics approach to markets and economies is just this — making simplifying assumptions that do not square with reality in order to prove a theory to be correct.

For example, in order to find a price that balances the supply and demand in the market, we have to assume cost-free, full, and perfect access to relevant information. We also have to assume that each economic decision we make is the result of an instantaneous complex calculation of present and future values of that particular economic decision and all possible substitute decisions at all times in the future.

Take the example of buying an apple. If this assumption is true, you know the exact impact that single purchase will have on the quality of your retirement life and have calculated with exact accuracy the trade-off between pleasure now and pleasure later and the decision that pleasure now is best derived by buying a specific apple right now, balanced by the benefit you will receive from reduced medical costs in the future that come from eating healthy food and knowing that you would rather eat that apple now than give to a charity that will buy an apple for a starving child. Further, despite its firm red cover, you know this apple to be sufficiently worm-free on the inside and the exact degree of its deliciousness. You know of all future political upheavals, budget deficits, and weather patterns that might affect expectations of your future life. You know your entire career path, your success, and your future well-being relative to others. Not only are you able to make these calculations with immediate effect, but so can everyone else at the same time, resulting in a stable equilibrium price for the apple that perfectly clears supply and demand.

After all of that, you'd more likely be thinking, "Just give me the @#&* apple! I'm hungry."

In *The Origin of Wealth*, Eric Beinhocker retells the story of a multi-day gathering of ten high-powered economists and ten high-powered physicists, biologists, and computer scientists at the Santa Fe Institute in New Mexico in 1987.[1] Nobel Prize winners were present on the economics team. Larry Summers, famous for his work at Harvard and in the Obama administration was there. A future chair of the economics department at the University of Chicago — *The* Chicago School — was also in attendance. The team of physical scientists included academics of no lesser standing in their respective fields. According to Beinhocker's retelling:

Each side presented the current state of its field and then spent ten days debating economic behavior, technological innovation, business cycles, and the workings of capital markets. The economists were excited by the physical scientists' ideas and techniques, but thought the scientists were naïve and even a bit arrogant about economic problems. On the other side, the physical scientists were impressed by the mathematical virtuosity of the economists and genuinely surprised by the difficulty of economic problems.

But what really shocked the physical scientists was how to their eyes, economics was a throwback to another era. One of the participants at the meeting later commented that looking at economics reminded him of his recent trip to Cuba…shut off from the Western world for over forty years by an economic embargo…the streets are full of Packard and DeSoto automobiles from the 1950s…kept running on salvaged parts and the odd piece of Soviet tractor. For the physicists,…it looked to them as if economics had been locked in its own intellectual embargo, out of touch with several decades of scientific progress…the Packards and DeSotos were the equations and techniques that the economists had plundered from physics textbooks a hundred years earlier…missing entirely the revolution in physics that has taken place since that time.

Beinhocker relates how the physicists were also shocked by the way the economists used simplifying assumptions in their models. That modus operandi is okay in science — as long as it doesn't contradict reality — and those assumptions need to be tested to be sure they don't affect the answers given by their theories. The economists insisted that these assumptions were needed to allow them to solve their problems. Without making them, nothing could be done, they stated. The physicists were reported to have bluntly replied, "If the assumptions are not reality, then you are solving the wrong problem."

Colloquially, this problem is referred to as the "garbage in, garbage out" problem.

Beinhocker then quotes Milton Friedman, another Nobel laureate and University of Chicago economist, as saying in an essay that unrealistic assumptions in economic theory simply do not matter, so long as the theories make correct predictions. In other words, so long as garbage doesn't come out, it really doesn't matter what went in and how it got there.

In essence, the assumptions required to make the traditional neoclassical model of economics work describe incredibly smart people facing very simple situations. In reality, people tend to be relatively simple, but have to deal with incredibly complex situations.[2] While there is much good that has come from the study of economics, some of its core conclusions and assumptions do not reflect the reality of our world. The view from the top down may look right, but it really takes building from the bottom up to see how things work, and that is where Complexity Economics has real strength.

BUILDING AN ECONOMY

Countless theories on economic analysis begin by assuming the existence of an economy. How does it help to "assume an economy?" If we are trying to build a successful organization, or any economy, from the ground up, it's not very helpful for us to make the assumption that an economy exists and then just move on. Imagine a budding entrepreneur bringing his business idea to the hit TV series *Shark Tank* and beginning the pitch for investment capital with these words: "Assume my business has sales of one million dollars." Fans of the show can imagine the look on the faces of two of the shows stars, Kevin and Daymond, when they hear this opening. Let's just say, it wouldn't go well for our very assuming entrepreneur.

What is more useful in understanding economics and the value found in an economy is to gain a better understanding of why economies exist in the first place and, as science would dictate, how they work and how they have evolved. As you'll learn, or may already understand, businesses are just small economies. We simply put a different boundary on them when defining the level of their success.

With the knowledge of how businesses or economies come to be, perhaps we can build better from the bottom up rather than attempting to deconstruct only from the top down.

One of the most intriguing aspects of economic theories and models has been their use as predictive tools to describe expected outcomes. And, as noted above, it seemed that Milton Friedman felt the models used in his work were pretty good at doing just this. That was a top down view, though. For example, it was a widely held belief in the 1980s that the growth of the money supply in an economy could be a predictor of the rate of inflation in that economy. But as it turns out, such information works sometimes and to some degree of accuracy, but not often enough or well enough to be truly helpful or profitable.

If we begin to look at the economy from the ground up, perhaps we'll arrive at a place that satisfies more thoroughly our desire to know how the value in economies comes about, and recognize that similar rules likely apply to our own organizations, which are also little economies. Further, it would be better if we could do this without making simplifying assumptions that do not square with reality.

Well, thanks in large part to the Santa Fe Institute, this kind of study has been happening over the past 20-plus years, emphasizing the interaction of various scientific disciplines and making use of recent and substantial advancements in computational power. The most intriguing work being done in Complexity Economics involves the study of agents in networks and systems with a little evolutionary theory tossed in. This work has been able to show how complex economies, with both good and bad features of observable real economies, can emerge via relatively simple decision-making mechanisms like those which people actually use in their daily lives.

In his book, Beinhocker describes the outcome from computer simulations of a world similar to that in the games described in Chapter 3. Instead of a fitness landscape of DNA, though, Beinhocker tells us of research conducted by Joshua Epstein and Robert Axtell where agents (people) are dropped onto a landscape that contains two mountains, one made of sugar and the other made of spice — higher places on the landscape.[3] Each agent is given a random endowment of sugar and spice and is required to find more of each in order to survive. Some agents are lucky enough to be dropped right on top of either the sugar or spice mountain, while others are unfortunately dropped in the middle of nowhere — not unlike the variety of conditions under which people enter the real world.

In this computer simulation, agents are required to have some sugar and some spice — think of this as a metaphor for the "food pyramid" that dictates our dietary guidelines, our source of energy, or as simply "food and water." With the dual requirement of sugar and spice, landing on one mountain, or finding one mountain after moving about, is not enough. Each agent has to find a way to obtain both sugar and spice. Agents are neither smart nor dumb. They simply are able to move around the landscape, expending energy as they move, seeking the sugar mountain, the spice mountain, or someone with whom they can exchange one for the other. Their movements are based on their ability to see forward — each is randomly assigned a certain degree of acuity — and if they succeed in finding sugar or spice, or trade for whichever they lack, they gain energy and can continue to move.

To make the game even more realistic, the researchers created a rule that allowed agents with sufficient amounts of sugar and spice to procreate, creating generations of agents. So, if two agents of the opposite gender meet on the landscape and both have enough resources, they marry and have offspring. Their offspring get some of their parents' sugar and spice, as well as some of their ability to see forward and move about, and the game continues.

What is fascinating about this game is that after thousands of computer simulations several features of real economies seem to magically emerge. First, trading begins, as was expected. Next, intermediaries appear, traveling between sugar and spice mountains, allowing those who have landed in great spots to stay there and enjoy their wealth, while others engage in multiple transactions bringing the resources from the other mountain to them. In effect, a supply chain emerges from the interaction of agents.

Commercial banks arise too, as those with excess lend to the needy. Wealth inequalities also emerge with distribution patterns strikingly similar to what we see in our world today. There is a very high concentration of wealth in a very small number of families and that concentration of wealth grows over time. Substantial "poverty" also appears, and those born into poverty tend to stay in poverty. This agent-based simulation also generates market bubbles and market crashes, phenomena which should not occur in a rational world, but which do happen in reality.

In short, by giving agents in this game access to resources, defining boundaries of their movement, giving them basic requirements to survive, mobility, some ability to exchange, and the ability to have children, a real economy emerges, and it looks a lot like what is seen in real life. Hence, the simulation not only satisfies Milton Friedman's requirement of having a good output, it does so without needing to assume lots of things that are out of synch with our reality.

THE BOUNDS OF RATIONALITY

The assumption of full information in the traditional macroeconomic model is not its only shortcoming. Assuming that people behave in a perfectly rational manner is also a requirement to get the results the theory claims to derive. But in reality, perfect rationality is not something we humans possess.

As will be examined in more detail in Chapter 6, people tend not to be very good at making some decisions, showing both helpful and unhelpful biases that can be traced to evolutionary roots. For example, the well-known fight or flight reaction to surprises is now hard-wired in us to be a reflexive process and not a cognitive one. It has been built into our bodies through evolution as a way to survive.

For instance, fighting a 500-pound lion would be a bad decision, and this action would not be repeated by any future offspring. On the other hand, running from one would only be successful if you were quicker than the beast. So, the offspring of someone who successfully evaded a lion would likely be smarter and faster than those born to a parent who thought himself a good match for a large animal with very big teeth.

Lions are not the only threat humans have faced over time and not the only influence on the likelihood of any particular person's (agent's) survival and ability to procreate. Like the computer simulation, hominids, from which humans have evolved, have been dying early or living and having off-spring for hundreds of thousands of generations, or hundreds of thousands of generational iterations. Because of this selection process, what we are today is a vast improvement on what humans were when we first stood up and noticed lions coming towards us from a greater distance than before.

Rather than assuming perfect rationality of people in economies, agents in Complexity Economics are assumed to make decisions using rules of thumb. For example, "I saw a lion eat my friend Thor. Next time I see a lion, I will not stand around for long." Or, "That apple looks really good and I'm hungry. I think I'll buy it."

Over time, we learn what kinds of decisions tend to work out well and which ones tend to be less than ideal. We learn, for example, that putting a hand on a hot stove is bad. We might even share this information with others, allowing them to learn from us without ever having enough, pardon the pun, first-hand experience themselves to be fully informed, or fully rational, about why it makes sense to keep hands off a hot stove. We build up libraries of this knowledge and when we don't have information, we may observe the decisions of others and use those decisions as information to guide our own choices. We even pass along much of this information to our offspring, making each generation, generally, more knowledgeable than the one before it.

It turns out that while we don't have access to perfect information, our brains are very good at recognizing patterns from partial data and can complete those patterns with some degree of accuracy using our stored knowledge and experiences, as well as by observing the behavior of others nearby.

Herbert Simon coined the expression *Bounded Rationality* to describe the notion that when individuals make decisions, they are limited to the information they have, by the cognitive limitations and processes of their mind and a limit on the amount of time they have to make a decision.[4] His work has greatly influenced the understanding of behavioral economists, as well as those working on Complexity Economics. Bounded Rationality is real. Complete rationality is not. And Bounded Rationality is at play in the agent-based models used in Complexity Economics.

NOT SO TIMELY OR STABLE

This brings us to two additional challenges faced by Traditional Economics — time and equilibrium. In the models we have used over the last several decades, all market adjustments take place immediately. Equilibrium is found at a market-clearing price and we stay there until some random exogenous shock causes the supply or demand curves to shift, immediately causing a change in prices upon which a new equilibrium is reached. One thousand new workers arriving by boat to apply for ten jobs at the docks will likely lower the price paid for the workers to fill those openings.

Economies and prices are always moving around and are never at a full equilibrium. For example, on May 6, 2010 the price of a share of global advisory firm Accenture was around $41, valuing the entire company at more than $25 billion. A share purchase is a decision to pay a price for partial ownership of that $25 billion company. If $41 was a rational and fully informed price, such a purchase appeared rather incorrect when within five minutes, the value of the company had fallen to less than $10 million, or $.01 per share. No news about the company had been released and no major economic surprises were revealed; yet any investment made five minutes before was now worth over 99 percent less.

Accenture, it turns out, was one of the victims of the now infamous Flash Crash, when massive selling in several specific stocks occurred and demand for them virtually evaporated. Over a period of about 15 minutes, more than $1 trillion in total stock market valuation on the New York Stock Exchange was temporarily erased, then returned.

Such rapid price volatility was unprecedented and essentially a statistical impossibility according to traditional economic theory. But it was not impossible according to Complexity Economics, as the buyers' behavior had been driven by the interaction of agents in a system. A massive flow of selling — in essence a pattern which investors had never seen before — felt a lot like a lion charging at them and the flight instinct kicked in. This was exacerbated by the vision of others doing the same thing. In other words, the buyers ran and hid in their caves and prices fell until the lion looked more like a kitten (prices were so low, the risk of loss had been greatly reduced). By the end of the trading day on which the Flash Crash had occurred, the price of Accenture was back above $41 and all of its pre-Flash Crash value had been restored.

While the recovery from the Flash Crash was fast, it was not instantaneous.

Information flows with time lags and people respond to the new information, often through relatively slow cognitive processes that are based on their experiences with old information and how that information has changed. Take the challenge that most retailers face in determining their product mix. They have experience in what has sold well in the past and have likely adjusted their inventories to meet that expectation. Then, one day, they unexpectedly sell out a product and are forced to order more before they had planned to do so. Now, they must decide whether the surge in demand is temporary or is likely to be sustained. If it's the latter, the question becomes one of guessing how long the higher demand will continue. They must adjust their orders to the distributor based on that expectation and the distributor will, seeing a surge in demand from this retailer, subsequently need to decide if that increase will continue from this particular retailer, if it will be mimicked by others and, if so, for how long. The demand from the distributor is conveyed to the manufacturer who must then decide on the use of fixed capacity to produce more of the item in demand, or whether the demand is surging enough to warrant an expansion of production capacity. None of these things can happen instantaneously, particularly the choice to add production capacity. If you imagine that at any point in this cycle these expectations are not met, there will likely be a cascading effect in the opposite direction, resulting in an unstable, non-equilibrium setting that shows substantial oscillations with respect to the passage of time.

The kinds of behaviors described above are not uncommon in natural systems where non-linear dynamics like those that drove the Accenture stock price or the manufacturer's production capacity abound. Traditional Economics has assumed that most economic processes are either linear — or straight-lined — and dynamic, or non-linear and static. But it turns out that most economic processes are both non-linear and dynamic, which means that they will sometimes generate wildly positive and negative outcomes that seem highly improbable or even practically impossible if you assume a traditional view of the economy. In fact, very few economic processes are either linear or static.

Non-linear dynamic systems have two key features that will affect how we understand their behavior. First, the outcome of a non-linear dynamic system is highly dependent upon the conditions under which it begins. This is referred to as *sensitivity to initial conditions*. For example, a very heavy rain storm might cause flooding if the ground on which it fell was already densely saturated. Under normal conditions, the same amount of rainfall would have mostly been absorbed by the ground without impact to those in flood-susceptible areas.

Second, non-linear dynamic systems are known to be *path-dependent*, meaning that their value today is a function of their value at previous time periods. For instance, the quality of a return shot in tennis is a function of the quality of the serve made by the opponent. A better serve will likely increase the variability of the return of service, while a weak serve may well lead to a strong and controlled return — to the dislike of the server.

Another example of a path-dependent system is a bank savings account. If you put money away at the bank, that investment pays interest. The value of that bank account in three years is going to be a function of how much interest it earned this year and how much interest it earns in the second year. More interest is paid in the third year if there is a larger balance in the second year, and the second-year balance will be larger if the interest rate in the first year is higher.

THE ROLE OF NETWORKS, EVOLUTION, AND SOCIAL INTERACTION

Complexity Economics explains the non-linear dynamic behavior of economic processes by looking at how networks affect economic interactions. A common property of dynamic and non-linear systems is that they tend to follow patterns, moving from relative stasis and random-like behavior, or a kind of equilibrium — "peace and quiet," to dramatically higher or lower levels, and then back to temporary states of stasis. Patterns in the movement of stock prices match this description quite well. In fact, a mathematical approach to modeling market volatility is based on this idea. The concept also nicely fits the pictures on my trading floor screen back in 1986 and the patterns we still see today in all kinds of markets.

These phase transitions occur between what is referred to as *punctuated equilibria*. Niles Eldridge and Stephan Jay Gould are credited with coining this phrase. In their review of the biological record on evolution, these two researchers found the evolutionary process did not follow a nice linear pattern of improvement in species that had been expected by the theory of the day. Rather, they found that relatively calm periods were interspersed with periods of major innovation and major collapses or extinctions.[5]

The parallels are striking. But as you read further, you'll understand that they are not surprising.

Evolution has a role in how our economies function. In many ways, one of the effects of markets is to spur economic evolution as fit business concepts thrive, while others are filtered away by initial lack of demand or innovation that deems them not fit enough anymore. Economic stresses may also be viewed like periods of mass extinction in nature. Innovations such as new technologies spur periods of rapid ascent, but also create new relationships and dependencies that may threaten or help economies to grow. Radical innovation by competitors is akin to a poison gas that just rose to your level.

Networks, as discussed in Chapter 2, are systems of agents, connected in some ways, either directly or indirectly. Kevin Bacon, like most of us, is separated from nearly everyone else by less than six steps in the network of all human beings. All of our organizations, for-profit, nonprofit, virtual, political, or social, are a lot like Kevin Bacon, with both internal and external systems that connect them to hundreds, thousands, or even millions of other systems, some of which matter greatly for their success or extinction. Further, our economy is made up of resources and individuals engaged in activities that are nearly all interconnected in some way. How individual systems work within the bigger economic system will affect its success at growing or its risk of extinction.

This evolutionary process is an aspect of market economies that works to a great positive effect. "The market" is very powerful. It just doesn't work as cleanly and nicely as we have been taught in our Traditional Economics courses.

WHAT'S NEXT?

As we move into the next section of the book, we'll begin to explore the role that perceptions, communications, and risk have in generating dynamism to the value of our work, both positively and negatively. Those in our networks and in networks to which we are linked have a profound influence on our value. We must be armed with an awareness of their potential to influence our value and apply that understanding to our governance efforts. To get there, though, we first have to let go of some of our standard thinking on how economies work. Complexity Economics is a major step in the right direction.

A summary of some key takeaways regarding Complexity Economics versus Traditional Economics, and what makes the former better, include the following:

1. Complexity Economics focuses on how agents interact in systems and the wealth that emerges from such interactions — it doesn't assume an economy; it shows how economies emerge.

2. Complexity Economics allows agents to make reasonably rational

decisions based on limited, or bounded, amounts of information — they are not required to be perfectly rational.

3. Computer simulations using the agent-based models of Complexity Economics result in economies that look a lot like the real world — without the need to make unrealistic assumptions to get there.

4. Complexity Economics shows how economic adjustments can take place over time — following evolutionary processes.

NOTES

1   Beinhocker, *The Origin of Wealth*, Harvard Business Review Press, 2007, pp. 46–48

2   Paraphrase of statement by Leijonhufvud in "'Towards a Not-Too-Rational Macroeconomics," in D. Colander (Ed.), *Beyond Microfoundations: Post Walrasian Economics*, Cambridge University Press, 1996, pp. 39–55

3   Beinhocker, *The Origin of Wealth*, Harvard Business Review Press, 2007, pp. 80–88, citing Epstein and Axtell, *Growing Artificial Societies*, Brookings Institution Press, MIT Press, 1996

4   Simon, Herbert A., "Bounded Rationality" in J. Eatwell, M. Millgate, and P. Newman (Eds.): *The New Palgrave: A Dictionary of Economics*. Macmillan, 1987, and Simon, H.A., "Bounded Rationality and Organizational Learning," *Organization Science* Volume 2, No. 1: 125–134, February 1991 and Simon, Herbert A., *Economics, Bounded Rationality and the Cognitive Revolution*, Edward Elgar Publishing, 1992

5   Gould, Stephen J., and Eldredge, Niles, "Punctuated Equilibrium Comes of Age," *Nature*, Vol. 366: 223–227, November 1993, and Gould, Stephen J., *The Structure of Evolutionary Theory*, Belknap Press of Harvard University Press, 2002

PART TWO

Looks Matter

"It's better to look good than to feel good. And let me tell you something, darling, you look mahhhvellous!"
— Billy Crystal, American Comedian, doing an impression of actor Fernando Lamas on *Saturday Night Live*

"Reputation is only a candle, of wavering and uncertain flame, and easily blown out, but it is the light by which the world looks for and finds merit."
— James Russell Lowell, American Poet

"No man ever looks at the world with pristine eyes. He sees it edited by a definite set of customs and institutions and ways of thinking."
— Ruth Benedict, American Anthropologist

CHAPTER 5

The Enterprise and Those Who Influence Its Value

At the top of a stone arch sits the most critical part of its structure, the *keystone*. Without this element, any shifting weight or pressure on the columns will cause them to collapse. However, with the keystone in place at the apex of the intersecting columns, the archway becomes one of the strongest and most enduring structures we know. This product of simple human engineering allows the shifting weight to be distributed down to the sturdy base, making it possible for the structure to be both resilient and strong.

Keystones exist in many other forms as well. We know that in nature certain species are critical to the health of their overall environment. The honeybee is one of those species, believed to be responsible for pollination of as much as 30 percent of food crops in the United States.[1] The extinction of these particular insects could easily result in a catastrophic collapse of other species that depend on them for the successful cultivation of food. When the consequences of this kind of demise through the food chain would be substantial, the species is referred to as a keystone species.

KEYSTONES, VALUE, AND SYSTEMS

An archway and nature are both systems. A keystone in these systems has a value that is directly related to the value of the overall system to which it belongs. Taken as a standalone, a keystone may have only modest value. But, as part of a system of interacting elements, its value grows. And, when that system interacts with other systems in a large environment, the keystone may have an enormous impact on the value of the whole system, and thus becomes even more valuable itself.

In Chapter 1, we began our study of the value of organizations. As a standalone, without interaction with other elements of society or the economy, an organization will not be a keystone and will generally have a lower value than if it interrelates with its environment in a positive way.

Conversely, the value of that organization also depends on how elements within the environment interact with it. It can be assumed that some of those elements are keystones to its value and, therefore, their absence, or a reduction in their interaction with that organization, will greatly reduce its value.

Taken from another perspective, if your organization is a keystone element to other organizations, its perceived value by the owners or beneficiaries of those other systems will increase. That's good.

In this chapter, we consider some of the common interactions of organizations with those who care about them and affect their value. Successfully governing our organizations demands careful attention to those entities in our environment. We must understand whether the partial or full absence of one of those elements, or even a change in their perception of our organization, might have a catastrophic impact on its value.

What are the keystones in our networks and what drives their willingness to be part of our network or system? Every governing body should be able to answer this question.

THE ORGANIZATION'S SOCIAL NETWORK

All organizations have a social network that might be illustrated something like Figure 5.1.

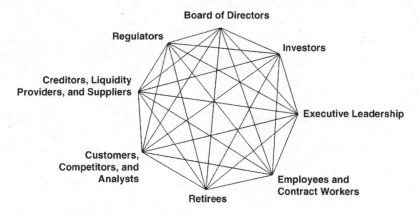

Figure 5.1 The Forces of Change on Organizational Value

The lines in Figure 5.1 represent lines of communication and show that the various entities that affect our organization's value can often communicate outside of our internal networks and may influence our value without our being aware of it. Let's take a closer look at who they are and why we should care about them.

CUSTOMERS

We begin with the most obvious members of our organization's social network: our customers. The meaning of the word "customer" changes based on what our organization does. In a for-profit entity, customers (clients) are those who pay us for our goods or services. In a social network, customers buy into our idea for a party or neighborhood gathering and thereby make it a success through their participation. At a nonprofit or charitable organization, users of the entity's services are sometimes referred to as clients or customers. However, in this context, it would be more accurate to define customers as those who support the organization — donors or organizations that purchase or fund the goods and services for use by the ultimate beneficiaries.

In political organizations, the customer is the voter or a donor (although it may sometimes seem more accurate to describe the politician as the customer of the voter, especially when the "voter" is a corporation).

In the end, a customer is someone who exchanges something of value that she already has for something of perceived value that our organization offers, and they are critical for our ongoing survival. Dipak Jain, former Dean of both the INSEAD School of Business and the Kellogg School at Northwestern University, said "the single biggest risk any company faces is that it does not know what its customers' needs will be in two years' time."[2]

Earlier in the book I mentioned the rapid demise of Bear Stearns — a story that illustrates the importance of customer sentiment. In the midst of the financial crisis of 2008, this leading Wall Street investment bank was fending off rumors that it was in need of cash or liquidity. Liquidity crises can be swift and violent, often precipitated by first-mover actions and fears of being left behind when running for the exits of a failing company.

Even though Bear Stearns executives felt they could survive the storm, a major hedge fund, who was a key customer of the company, announced that it was shifting more than $5 billion it had on deposit with them to its competitors. They were not the last. One veteran Bear Stearns employee was quoted as saying on that day "Our cash is flying out the door. Our clients are leaving us." Quickly, the company burned through billions of dollars in cash and was struggling to find financing for ongoing operations.[3]

When the company ultimately was purchased by J.P. Morgan Chase, within days of the withdrawal of large customer assets, the price paid was $10 per share, down from more than $130 per share just five months earlier. The impact of the loss of key customers, during a particularly bad time in the markets, wiped out most of the value of the company and its other customers were left with a counterparty that was different than they had experienced to that point in time.

INVESTORS

For nonprofits, an investor might be someone who regularly donates his time to the organization's cause. Or, it might also be someone who endows a large gift to a university, museum, or community group. In the for-profit sector, an investor is a provider of working capital in exchange for partial ownership of the entity. This can be a person who buys as little as one share of publicly traded stock, a pension fund that owns millions of shares of a company, a venture capitalist who invests to build upon early growth of an entrepreneurial venture, or even one company that forms a long-term partnership with another organization.

In politics, the investors are those most likely to perceive their ability to curry favor with politicians. John Keating was famous for his role in the Savings and Loan crisis of the 1980s when five United States' Senators were accused of improperly intervening to halt a regulatory investigation of Keating's financial institution. When asked whether he thought his donations to various politicians had helped him advance his business interests, he answered, "I want to say in the most forceful way I can: I certainly hope so."[4]

Investors lose the use of their money for an extended period of time when they invest in our organizations. They expect some material increase in the value of their investment for this loss of use. The extent to which they expect to be rewarded is driven by their perception of an organization's current and potential value and they tend to be focused on the very long term.

EXECUTIVE LEADERSHIP, EMPLOYEES, AND CONTRACT WORKERS

Within the system that is our organization, there are usually people who have been engaged to provide their particular expertise in exchange for a regular salary, consulting fee, commission, or other forms of incentive compensation. Employees, including the executive leadership, and contract workers can generally be described in the same way regardless of whether the organization is political, social, charitable, or for-profit.

Key employees are those whose participation in the organization is viewed as highly valuable, perhaps because of a unique skill or owned intellectual property. In some cases, the loss of these key employees would greatly affect the organization's ability to function as it had been, especially if these people work in small partnerships, start-up companies, or at asset management firms where they are responsible for the management of a successful fund. Investors in these companies will often ask for their money to be protected from the departure of these keystone employees by requiring either *Key Person Insurance* or a special clause in their investment agreements. Employees, executives, and contract workers are managers, sales people, line workers, risk managers, accountants, auditors, financiers, marketers, human resource experts, etc. The list goes on and on, particularly at large, complex organizations where there are many specialized roles to fill.

Employees and contract workers make the decision to exchange what they have of value — their time and talent — for a monetary reward, which they perceive to be of equal or greater value to what they have given to the organization. In many cases, they too are making a long-term assessment of the organization's potential worth, both in terms of their individual reputation — having worked for a highly regarded and successful company or for one that failed or committed fraud — and the monetary value of any future raises and deferred compensation they might receive, such as retirement benefits, stock options, etc., or, in the case of contract workers and consultants, the possibility of an extended contract for services.

BOARDS OF DIRECTORS

Board members are often thought of as the top-of-the-house governors of our systems, since they determine the strategic objectives of an organization, as well as the rules by which those objectives are to be pursued. They also hire and review the chief executive of the organization. Their critical function, both as individuals and collectively, has prompted the courts to define specific legal responsibilities of board members to the organizations and, where appropriate, to the organization's investors. In the United States and Canada, for example, board members are obliged to show a *Duty of Loyalty* and a *Duty of Care*. The former demands that they use their role as a member of the board for the good of the organization and not for their personal benefit or the benefit of some other organization. The latter requires that they do their homework and provide sufficient guidance and oversight to protect the interests of investors.

The Duty of Care and the Duty of Loyalty are considered key duties, which, if not adequately fulfilled, could result in the potential failure for the organization and personal liability for the individual board member. These will be discussed further in Chapter 14.

At political organizations, the board may be a group of large donors, or established and well-connected politicians who seek to maximize the chances of success for their particular party, or, if the entity is narrowly focused, the success of advocacy for specific issues. If one considers elected bodies as the governors of political systems, then these would be Members of Parliament, Senators, Representatives, etc.

Social organizations tend not to have legal structures in place. Hence, the "board of directors" might just be a group of people who came up with the idea for a party, service, or activity. On the other hand, some neighborhood associations or special interest groups, which organize both politically and socially, may have a very formal board of directors to govern their activities.

Board members are often compensated in terms of moral gratification, as in the case of service to a nonprofit, or financial rewards, such as stock and cash. Good board members can have an enormously positive impact on the success of a company. But, they must feel comfortable that the risk to their careers, and perhaps to their financial well-being, is limited and manageable or they will politely decline to become part of that system.

SUPPLIERS

Large and complex organizations rely on the efficiency of their suppliers in successfully delivering key ingredients to their process in a timely manner. The whole concept of just-in-time delivery is based on the ability of external parties to bring us what we need, when we need it, in sufficient quantities to meet our current demands. Your coffee shop has this process down pretty well, when considered from your perspective. You can get a small, large, or extra-large coffee any day without too much disruption to the system or to your day. You can even change what you buy at the last second, without a dramatic impact. At the same time, the coffee shop has a critical reliance on the delivery of cups, beans, electricity, and water, to name just a few ingredients of a happy and productive you. The loss of any one of these could greatly affect your day.

Just as you might not be able to function without coffee, charitable organizations have a dependence on volunteers to regularly supply their time to deliver meals, care for the elderly, watch children in a nursery, or even to sing a song in church.

Political organizations rely on enthusiastic volunteers to supply their time, but they also need materials for political signs, newspapers, magazines, and a website to supply advertising space, as well as politicians to provide their ideas and commitment to serve, if elected.

Political economies are usually much better off if they engage in trade with other systems, many of which supply to them unique talents, raw materials, or products which they can produce at a comparative advantage.

Finally, social organizations are almost entirely dependent on the supply of volunteer time. And, for parties, the flow of snacks and beverages is often the keystone to success.

From the supplier's perspective, each will likely need to make some infrastructure investments to meet a specific customer's needs. Therefore, each must make a decision regarding the potential value of a client — your organization, for example — weighed against the cost of committing their scarce human and financial resources to serving you. They also have to consider the risk that you might not honor your agreements with them.

As an example of the influence that suppliers can have, take the case of Eclipse Aviation. This company was founded in 1998 to serve a growing market in personal aviation through the design, production and delivery of very light jets that were foreseen to be in use as some of the first Air Taxis. In 2006, the company won a prestigious award from the National Aeronautic Association "for the greatest achievement in aeronautics or astronautics in America." Past recipients of this award include Orville Wright, Howard Hughes, Chuck Yeager, and the crew of Apollo 11.[5]

By the following year, though, problems began to emerge with its relationships to suppliers. The provider of the tail assembly for the flagship airplane filed suit against Eclipse, claiming the company had not paid for parts that were delivered. This precipitated a public feud between Eclipse Aviation and the supplier — only the latest in a series of battles with former suppliers.[6]

Eclipse Aviation's CEO was replaced in mid-2008 amid concerns about the company's progress. Within one month, despite the company having announced plans to increase production in the following year, one of the company's suppliers announced that Eclipse would actually be reducing its production and another, the one who had sued Eclipse earlier, was reported to have closed the production plant it used to supply Eclipse with its tail sections.[7] At the end of August 2008, Eclipse was reported to have held a meeting with 90 of its suppliers to gather support for the company, but instead found that most had already put the company on credit watch for non-payment of invoices and were requiring cash-in-advance payments.[8]

Customers soon followed the lead of the suppliers by demanding return of their deposits and disastrous events snowballed. Late in November 2008, Eclipse Aviation filed for bankruptcy protection and eventually went through a sale of its assets.

CREDITORS

Differentiating creditors from investors — both of which provide financial capital — is important. As noted above, investors tend to take a long-term view, providing working capital they do not expect to be returned to them for a long period of time. Creditors, on the other hand, provide short-term as well as long-term financing in the form of debt and usually on terms that require the payment of interest and principal back to them in regular installments until all of the financing has been returned. Do you recall the loan that Cousin Louie requested in Chapter 1? If you agreed to lend him the money, you became one of his creditors. Or, when you agreed to pay for cleaning services in advance, you became a creditor to that cleaning company. Have you put down a deposit on a Tesla product? Congratulations, you are now one of their creditors.

Creditors can provide working capital quicker and sometimes less expensively than investors. They can also pull away their working capital faster than investors, often with disastrous effect on the organization that subsequently has to locate cash to meet ongoing business needs. Investors usually have the rights and responsibilities of owners, but creditors will only have these rights if things go very wrong, meaning their debt cannot be repaid and they lay claim to the organization's assets.

One instance where things went wrong for creditors was the case of Connaught, a social housing maintenance provider in the UK. After severe problems were discovered at the company, the creditors of Connaught were forced to step in to protect their interests and put the company into administration — similar to bankruptcy. Losses of roughly 70 percent of the capital the creditors had provided to the company were expected because of the company's problems.[9]

For an entrepreneur, a credit card company may be a critical creditor in the early days, as the company may not be generating sufficient cash flows to offset start-up expenses.

Creditors to political campaigns can include suppliers, who hand in their invoices, expecting to be paid at a later date. An example might be a small-town restaurant in Iowa that regularly feeds the campaign team prior to the Iowa political caucuses. Sometimes, unsuccessful candidates enjoy the pie, but don't pay the bill.

Whenever creditors consider engaging an organization, they have to make a decision about the expected value of that organization as a client versus other opportunities into which to put their scarce resources. They generally care less about your ability to succeed as an organization beyond expectations than about your ability to pay them back their principal and accrued interest completely and in a timely manner. If they feel comfortable with your organization, they may also consider doing other business with you in the future or through your affiliate business channels. Still, they really don't want to become investors in your organization as that, like the case with Connaught, is usually a sign that things have gone very badly.

In short, creditors care greatly about your ability to be around for just long enough to pay them back.

REGULATORS

Whenever our organizations have the capacity to impact society in some significant way, we can expect our political leaders to regulate how large that impact could be. For example, if we burn coal to generate electricity, regulators might care about the sulfur we emit through our smokestacks and would regulate how those emissions are "scrubbed" to prevent acid rain. Or, if our company sells investments to the public, the government might want to have regulatory measures ensuring that people are not being deceived.

As some publicly traded companies have misrepresented their financial condition to their investors and creditors, it is a relief to know that when they are caught by regulators, the market punishes these companies severely. In their 2006 paper, *The Cost to Firms of Cooking the Books*, Jonathan Karpoff, D. Scott Lee and Gerald S. Martin, conducted a comprehensive study of nearly 600 companies targeted for enforcement actions in the U.S. by the Securities and Exchange Commission between 1978 and 2002. Their data show that the "reputational penalty" from lost sales and higher contracting and financing costs for misconduct, averages more than seven times the penalties imposed through the regulatory and legal system.[10] For every dollar that a company's misrepresentations had added to its market value, the market took away that dollar, plus more than three dollars more! Further, of this lost value, nearly 90 percent was estimated to be due to the degraded reputation of the firm.

Restaurants have to keep the food they serve at a certain temperature so that it doesn't foster the growth of bacteria; manufacturers are not allowed to put certain substances in their products that might cause us harm. Regulators are also supposed to protect us from groups that prey on our sentiments via false-charity fundraising that often follows natural disasters, and to regulate land use near our homes so that a sulfur-emitting smokestack doesn't suddenly appear in our neighbor's backyard.

Regulators are also supposed to protect us from members of the political system who put their own personal interests over those of the public, which they are intended to serve.

Some people find regulations and regulators to be an inefficient part of our economies. And, sometimes they are. But, they also play a key role in value generation by their influence on other parties mentioned above and by their ability to affect whether we can do business at all. Government, after all, is just a large assembly of "us." Regulators are engaged by our representatives. They especially care about the extent to which any organization might externalize losses or costs — forcing loss or imposing costs upon others outside of an organization — as had been the case in the United States with sulfur dioxide emissions.

ANALYSTS

Equity analysts at investment banks and brokerage firms have been derided for their overly optimistic biases towards publicly traded companies. There are many reasons why such a bias might exist, including the potential conflicts of interest present when other parts of their firm do business with the company being reviewed. Yet, their work is still important, especially for retail investors trying to decide how to allocate their investment capital.

Because it is such a rarity, when an analyst actually issues a "sell" rating on a company, that rating can have a significant impact on the cost to that company of raising working capital from investors and creditors.

Not all analysts work for investment banks. Most, in fact, work directly for investors or creditors. When considering a large investment in a company, a pension plan or hedge fund might spend hundreds of hours conducting due diligence on the prospective recipient of their capital before making a decision.

Nonprofits are sometimes rated by third parties for their efficiency in use of funds and many philanthropists will use these ratings as guides to determine whether to take an interest, or to give, to a particular charity.

Politicians are often rated by groups that have special interests or core political beliefs to promote. The rating by these analysts could affect their ability to raise funds, both positively and negatively.

Therefore, the opinion of analysts can have a large impact on the value of our organizations because they influence the decisions of those who provide the capital for investment, growth, and the daily activities of our organizations.

Consider the impact that analysts had on a company called American Superconductor. On mostly positive sentiment from analysts, the company and investors saw its stock price rise from around $7 per share in late 2006 to nearly $45 per share late in 2010. Around that time, though, an analyst from Deutsche Bank issued a downgrade of the company, which effectively ended the rally and even seemed to initiate the start of a slow and steady decline in the company's value.

On April 6, 2011, the company announced that its largest customer had refused to accept a shipment. As a result of this refusal of delivery, American Superconductor was forced to lower its revenue forecasts, saying that it expected to report a net loss for the company's operations. Following that announcement, additional downgrades were announced by equity analysts and the stock was quickly trading below $13 per share, reflecting a decline of nearly 50 percent in the market value of the company in one day.[11]

RETIREES

Perhaps this is a surprising category to include in this list, but we can imagine why retirees care about how we are doing, especially if their pension plan is underfunded. Consider retirees to be similar to employees, but who based their employment decision on the provision of deferred benefits. In many ways, they are like creditors who are receiving their principal and interest payments, and like investors because they may sleep better, and enjoy retirement more, if they perceive that the company has long-term growth prospects. They may even own some company stock.

Retirees can also be quite vocal and create perception problems for all of the other groups mentioned above, driving a change in the value of our organization through those other channels.

CASE STUDY: ICELAND AND THE CREDIT CRISIS

Systems are more than just organizations. As mentioned earlier in the book, organizations are really just small economies, meaning that larger economies, even the economies of entire countries, are just systems that have the same kinds of internal and external members to their network. In the lead-up to the financial crisis that began in 2008, the country of Iceland experienced enormous growth in its banking sector, and generally in the wealth of its citizens — external agents loved Iceland! Just prior to the global financial crisis, the wealth of an average Icelander was among the highest in the world.

Within a few days in October 2008, however, nearly 85 percent of the Icelandic banking sector collapsed as creditors refused to continue to provide liquidity to the banks.[12] According to *The Economist* magazine, at the time, the collapse of Iceland's banking sector was the biggest, relative to the size of an economy, that any country had ever suffered.[13] Just two months after the onset of the crisis, *The Economist* noted, "Almost no other private creditor [besides a Chinese manufacturer of fireworks who wanted to ensure that

Iceland's annual show went on as planned] is lending them anything."[14]

In just a few days after the crisis began, equity prices in Iceland had fallen by more than 95 percent from their historic high in mid-2007 — a time when the party was going at its best — and within two years, the wealth of an average Icelander had plummeted so drastically that the country's ranking of per-capita income slipped from the fifth in the world to the 29th place.[15]

HOW WE LOOK AFFECTS OUR VALUE

Consider the value equation in the context of this chapter. When we talked about it in Chapter 1, we noted that reduced expectations of risk increased the value of an organization or financial asset:

$$Value \uparrow \; = \; U_0 + \frac{U_1}{DR_1 \downarrow} + \frac{U_2}{DR_2 \downarrow} + \frac{U_3}{DR_3 \downarrow} + \cdots$$

This happens because a lower risk premium is demanded, which pushes the value of the denominator — the bottom part of the equation — down. The converse is equally true. When expected risk increases, the risk premium goes up, and the value plummets. You are willing to pay less for something that is more likely to disappoint you.

$$Value \downarrow \; = \; U_0 + \frac{U_1}{DR_1 \uparrow} + \frac{U_2}{DR_2 \uparrow} + \frac{U_3}{DR_3 \uparrow} + \cdots$$

As a rational investor or partner with someone, you would make this adjustment so that any economic arrangement you have with them is fairer to you. Your adjustment is designed to compensate you for greater anxiety about the deal or to substitute for the higher return you could earn on assets that were once viewed as being riskier, but that you now perceive to be of equivalent risk to this one.

In the end, how all of these external and internal entities perceive our value is in large part driven by how they perceive the risk of investing in us, partnering with us, contributing to us, giving us credit, or allowing us to do our work. When they decide whether to support our activities or not, each of these parties is making a determination about our value to them, or to the constituency they serve. If we sully their perception of us, it has a high cost. If one of these entities is a keystone part of our network, the value of our organization can come plummeting down, just like an archway that loses the keystone of its structural integrity.

As noted, our network consists of internal and external parties. We may consider the collection of the two groups to be the environment in which our internal network operates. The stories in this chapter are all examples of reactions to events that caused an ex-post, or after the fact, re-assessment of risk by members of our external network. We focus mostly on the members of our external network in the remaining chapters of Part II. As we'll see, if there is a fear that negative risk surprises are even possible, it can also greatly impact our value today. This awareness is critical for the effective governance of our organizations.

If we can move to a point where the perception of our organization improves, particularly if we can remove any perception that our activities present the possibility of a large, negative surprise to our partners and investors, it will dramatically increase our value. That's one piece of news that's worth waking your boss about!

NOTES

1   Roach, John, "Bee Decline May Spell End of Some Fruits, Vegetables," *National Geographic News*, October 5, 2004

2   Conversation between the author and Dipak Jain, when Prof. Jain served as the Dean of the Kellogg Graduate School of Management, Northwestern University, 2007

3   Kelly, Kate, "Fear, Rumors Touched Off Fatal Run on Bear Stearns," *Wall Street Journal*, May 28, 2008

4   "A Man of Influence: Political Cash and Regulation — A Special Report; In Savings Debacle, Many Fingers Point Here," Nathaniel C. Nash with Philip Shenon, Special to *The New York Times*, November 9, 1989

5   National Aeronautic Association

6   Trautvetter, Chad, "Tail Supplier Sues Eclipse," *Aviation International News*, December 1, 2007

7   "Eclipse Aviation Announces Job Cuts," KOAT-TV Albuquerque, August 22, 2008

8   Metcalf, Richard, "Collateral Damage," *Albuquerque Journal*, June 22, 2009

9   Gray, Alistair. "Connaught banks to take hit on loans," *Financial Times*, April 7, 2011

10 Karpoff, Jonathan M., Lee, D. Scott and Martin, Gerald S., "The Cost to Firms of Cooking the Books," *Journal of Financial and Quantitative Analysis*, April 1, 2009

11 Hackley, Randall, and Roca, Marc, "American Superconductor Loses Half Its Market Value After Order Cancelled," *Bloomberg*, April 6, 2011

12 Matthiasson, Thorolfur, "Spinning Out of Control, Iceland in Crisis," *Nordic Journal of Political Economy*, Vol. 34, 2008

13 "Cracks in the Crust," *The Economist*, December 11, 2008

14 Ibid.

15 International Monetary Fund

CHAPTER 6

Our Human Behavior

In Chapter 4 we discussed revelations from the emergence of Complexity Economics as a new area of economic science. These insights help us understand how economies and economic transactions come to be. Within that discipline, there is some account of behavior that is inconsistent with the assumptions made in traditional economic models. But, the impact that emotions and cognitive biases can have on the decisions that agents make is more widely found in the sciences of *Behavioral Finance* and *Behavioral Economics*. Further, the way in which agents interact in complex systems also has a foundation in *Game Theory* — more on this concept will be discussed at the end of this chapter.

In Chapter 5 we examined several key groups of people whose behavior can affect us. They are either part of the system that is our organization or belong to systems that interact with our organization. To varying degrees and in varying ways, they all have an interest in, and perception of, our success and how we might contribute to what they value. The people and groups we identified can, therefore, affect the value of our organizations today and in the future. They may decide to exchange something they have of value for what we offer, or not. They also influence others who are making similar decisions. Because of this potential impact on the value of what we do, we should want to better understand what drives their behavior.

For us to achieve this clarity, it might make life simpler if people behaved in a manner that was consistent and rational. But, we know that some people will make the decision to start a business during a recession; some will decide to run for political office, and others will give away their time without compensation via a volunteer activity in their community. Each person making these decisions — engaging in these behaviors — sees a certain value in what he or she is doing that others do not — at least enough potential value to part with something they have now, such as time or money. This chapter explores behaviors and perceptions by examining Behavioral Economics as well as other psychological influences on our way of making decisions.

To discover all of the value we can offer to others, we really need to understand why people do the things they do and what drives their perceptions of fair value.

VOICES IN BEHAVIORAL ECONOMICS

Because so many of the assumptions behind Traditional Economics seem to be difficult to reconcile with the way in which people actually make choices, there is a growing degree of receptivity to newer ideas that challenge the strict assumptions in these models — particularly those regarding rationality around making economic choices. How our minds reach a state of action is an element of the study of human psychology. So, it seems natural to have an intersection between the social sciences of Economics and Psychology.

Among the most well-known psychologists who have applied their knowledge to economic decisions are Amos Tversky and Daniel Kahneman. The latter was awarded the 2002 Nobel Prize in Economics for his work on this area, now generally referred to as Behavioral Economics.[1] Professor Kahneman won the prize for his work on *Prospect Theory*, which looks at how people make risk-based decisions. We discuss this in more detail later.

Herbert Simon, whom we mentioned in Chapter 4 as the person who coined the term *Bounded Rationality*, is also known for his work in this domain. He was awarded the Nobel Prize in Economics in 1978.

Richard Thaler is a professor of business at the University of Chicago. He has written numerous articles and texts about cognitive biases in our decision-making. He even started an investment company that is designed to take advantage of the mental mistakes investors make, which cause stocks to be mispriced — or incorrectly valued. He is the co-author of the well-known book, *Nudge*, which attempts to tell us how to improve decision making.[2] Professor Thaler was awarded the Nobel Prize in 2018.

But, the importance of human psychology in economic decisions is not new. Adam Smith — revered by the Invisible Hand crowd — is best-known for his 1776 book *The Wealth of Nations*.[3] Seventeen years earlier, however, he wrote *The Theory of Moral Sentiments*, in which he examines the nature of, and motives for, morality — with morality being based on psychological motives. This text is thought to have driven many of the concepts that he included in his later, more famous text.

Even John Maynard Keynes, revered by Interventionists, believed that people made decisions only as rationally as they could, leaving room for the influence of psychology, experience, and beliefs to affect people's behaviors.

Maurice Allais won his 1988 Nobel Prize for rigorous mathematical work in economics. Yet, he is also known as the creator of the Allais Paradox, which shows that theories which assume people seek to maximize their expected utility functions — what gives them value — do not hold for many decisions made under risk and uncertainty.[4] His paradox links our review to the issue of how choices are framed, or *Framing Theory*, which Kahnemann and Tversky also developed and which we discuss in more detail below.

Of more recent note in this area is the popular text *Animal Spirits*, written by Professors George Akerloff (2001 Nobel Prize winner) and Robert Shiller (2013 Nobel Prize winner), which promotes the idea that emotions influence economic decision-making.[5] The authors emphasize how our emotions may stimulate abnormally large swings in the value of things like stocks, cryptocurrencies, and homes.

In short, we have at least six Nobel Prize winners who see validity in the concept that psychology has an influence on economic decision-making, particularly when there is uncertainty or risk. Since uncertainty and risk are almost always present, it is highly likely that an understanding of how people's behaviors are influenced by their perceptions will be meaningful for the governance of our organizations and our effort to create value.

Let's look at the key biases and behavioral influences that guide us when we make economic decisions, starting with Prospect Theory, then briefly examine some of the ways our minds work that make us human.

THE VALUE OF UTILITY

Expected Utility is a term used to describe what a consumer, for example, expects to gain in benefit from the outcome of a game or from some consumption decision — it's a "something." If I eat a Honeycrisp apple, I have a sense for how good it will make me feel and for how it could improve my health. Similarly, if someone tosses a coin and tells me that I will win 50 dollars if the coin lands on "heads," I can calculate what my likely payout would be from repeatedly playing this game and determine its worth.

The view of Prospect Theory is that our risk-based decision-making is a two-stage process. First comes *editing*, in which we order possible outcomes according to some experience-based technique we have developed. We decide which outcomes are roughly identical and use this as a reference point — better outcomes are viewed as gains and worse outcomes are viewed as losses. In the second stage, *evaluation*, we review possible outcomes and the probabilities of those outcomes to decide how much value or *utility* we would get from them if realized — ideally, choosing the one with the highest utility for us. The end result is the prospect of utility, or value, being gained from our decision.

This end result is a bit different from what is normally predicted by *Utility Theory* in Traditional Economics. Under Prospect Theory, people tend to over-weight losses with respect to comparable gains, to be risk-averse with respect to gains of moderate probability and losses of small probability, risk-seeking with respect to losses of moderate probability and gains of small probability, and to respond to probabilities in a non-linear manner. All these tendencies have implications for the perceived value of our organizations, because what we might normally expect people to do when faced with the risk of doing business with our organizations — or investing with us, working for us, etc. — is not what they actually do.

YOU DECIDE

To arrive at personal prospects, we may use our experience or knowledge, called *heuristics*, to solve the problem. These heuristics allow us to make sense of what we are seeing and experiencing — or so we believe. Heuristics are designed to allow us to make quick decisions. For a fly, a local air disturbance or moving shadow might indicate that it is about to be eaten or smashed. So, it will move away without putting much thought as to why. If Thor, who was eaten by a lion in Chapter 4, had developed a similar set of heuristics, he might have lived for another day. Thor's friends, though, subsequently had that heuristic to help them stay away from hungry lions, so Thor did not die entirely in vain.

More commonly, people refer to heuristics as "rules of thumb," "educated guesses," or "common sense," even though not all parties agree about what makes sense in all situations.

It turns out that while Thor would have benefited from not being eaten by a lion, not all of our quick responses are the correct ones. In fact, the way situations are presented to us can affect how our heuristics work and even cause us to make bad choices. Therefore, the form of presentation of a situation, or the *framing* of the situation or choice, is very important.

Take, for example, the following choice that has been given to people in controlled experiments:

You're the director of public health in a small town and, due to a recent outbreak of some virus, all 600 inhabitants are expected to die if you do nothing. You have uncovered two options for action and must choose between them. With option one, 200 people in the town will be saved. If you choose option two, however, there is a one-third chance that 600 people will be saved, and a two-thirds chance that no people will be saved. Which would you choose?

In reported studies, roughly 70 percent of the people given this choice picked option one — the certainty of saving 200 lives.

However, when the same options for taking action are worded a bit differently, decisions change. Now, if you choose option one, you are told that 400 people in the town will die. With option two, there is a one-third chance that nobody will die, and a two-thirds chance that 600 people will die.

When worded this way, roughly 80 percent of people choose option two, even though the expected outcome of the first option in both scenarios is exactly the same and the expected outcome of the second option in both scenarios is exactly the same. The re-framing of the question from one that focused on how many people will live to one that emphasized how many will die, dramatically changed the choice people made. If people were perfectly rational, there would be no change from one framing of the choice to the next.

There are dozens of similar studies that show the significant impact of framing, and people in the marketing profession know this well. However, such widespread awareness is not present in our board rooms.

But the biases and unexpected behaviors don't just come about because of framing.

WHAT ARE THE CHANCES OF THAT HAPPENING?

People also tend to overreact to *small changes in probability* of events happening, especially if they thought that something was impossible or highly improbable. For example, if you live in an area not known for earthquakes — maybe one that never had an earthquake before — and one day the dishes rattle and the pavement cracks from a seismic event, your view of your locale will likely change quite radically.

If you believed that walking through your neighborhood at night was very safe, but one day someone is mugged and badly beaten one block away from your house, you are likely to overreact and expect that there is a much higher possibility that your neighborhood is unsafe than is actually the case.

This bias is particularly relevant to organizations that have earned a high degree of trust from those in their network, because a violation of that trust might have higher than expected negative consequences for that organization's value. If you recall from the last chapter, the markets tend to punish firms found to have been dishonest in their accounting by many multiples of the magnitude of their misdeed. Most of this is due to the loss of reputation among investors and is reflected by a higher risk premium being assigned to the expected cash flows from that company.

RUN FOR THE HILLS

If this loss of faith is substantial enough, or sets into motion some additional triggers (we discuss these in Chapter 8), there may be a mass movement away from the company, called *herding*. Herding is an instinctual reaction to a threat and usually comes about because members of the herd are seeking protection and make quick decisions to follow others who are close to them in their network.

Herding can be beneficial as well. In short, herding can come about when one of our heuristics is that the people in our network are trusted and we see them taking some action, which we had not previously considered to be necessary. We may act at first in the same manner as they do and ask questions later. Did someone see a lion?

DRAGGING AN ANCHOR

What if people know very little about our organization and what we are doing? The starting point for value determination by new or prospective members to our network will, in part, be driven by what others networked to these prospects think, and various descriptors about us. What we do and what people think about other organizations like us will matter. In fact, humans have a bias towards *anchoring* a valuation based on a piece of information that may or may not be relevant to our particular case.

Take, for example, banks during the subprime financial crisis. Not all banks issued subprime loans and not all banks had exposure to subprime loans. Yet, any institution that was called a bank was painted with a higher risk profile because of defensive herding and expectations of risk that came from information discovered about other banks. As risky financial institutions' exposures were discovered, the risk assessment of even "good" banks was anchored at a higher level because of the realized riskiness of the banks that did have sub-prime exposures.

Anchoring also shows up in other places that are less relevant to our governance purposes but demonstrate its effect. If you ask a random group of people what the average temperature is in Singapore and give them no other information, their answers will have a different mean and greater variability than if you begin your question by saying something like "The average temperature in Hong Kong is 73 degrees Fahrenheit." In the latter case, the answers for Singapore's average temperature will tend to be closer to 73 degrees, which is, in fact, a figure below the average low temperature for all months of the year in Singapore.

I COULD LOSE HOW MUCH?

Perhaps the two most important biases that impact our organization's valuation by others relate to the discounting of future expected "somethings," or utility, that a person would get from partnering with us as a customer, employee, donor, investor, etc.

The first of these biases is *loss avoidance*. This term refers to people's strong tendency to prefer to avoid losses versus acquiring gains. In fact, some studies have shown that if the possible losses and gains are large enough, there may be a preference for avoiding losses that is as much as two-and-one-half times as big as the preference for receiving large gains. As investors, if we thought there was a chance that we'd lose half of our money, we'd only make that investment if we felt there was an equal chance of gaining more than 125 percent. Otherwise, we wouldn't feel adequately compensated for our negative risk. This is the behavior of an average individual and is not true for every individual. Some people love risk, while others have an even greater aversion to loss than is described above. But, the average person is of high importance to us and the work of our organization.

AND JUST WHEN WOULD I GET THAT?

The second critical bias that affects our value today relates to the timing of things we value and how we discount future rewards to a present value. In our value equation, we show that our future utility is being discounted back to a value today using *exponential discounting*. Or, a more straightforward way to say this is the value of a "something" in the future declines in a consistent manner for each additional unit of time between now and when it is received. However, evidence from the science of Behavioral Economics shows that people actually use something different that reveals their preferences — a time-inconsistent model of discounting called *hyperbolic discounting*.

In hyperbolic discounting, valuations fall very rapidly for small delay periods — there is punishment, so to speak, for getting something tomorrow that we expected today. This might take the form of the stock market driving down a company's price by what seems to be an extreme amount for reporting earnings below expectations, even if the company says that it will be back on track next quarter. Or, we might vote someone out of office because that person failed to deliver on his promises quickly enough.

Hyperbolic discounting also tends to value future rewards much more highly than in the typical exponential discounting method. Companies that are expected to deliver excellent long-term results — perhaps, because they are well-governed — will be rewarded more handsomely via a hyperbolic discounting effect than would be expected via exponential discounting. If we like a politician and she has a long track record of decency and good work, she may be re-elected by a wide margin even if she has not delivered anything extraordinary recently.

One experiment that reveals the presence of hyperbolic discounting asks for a person's preference between receiving one dollar today or three dollars tomorrow, versus receiving one dollar one year from today or three dollars in one year and one day. A significant number of people choose to receive the lesser amount today but accept waiting one extra day, one year from now, to receive three dollars instead of one. Both instances involve one-day delays to receive an extra two dollars. So, the rational decision would be to make the same choice in both cases, but people still highly discount a one-day delay from today more than one in the future.

EVERYWHERE, BIASES

Below are listed several more interesting biases that may affect our organizations, their performance, and their perceived value:

> *The Overconfidence Effect* — We are far more confident of our abilities than is usually warranted. For example, most of us think we are above average drivers, which cannot be true. Or, when asked how confident we are in our answers to questions, we may indicate 99 percent confidence, but be wrong 40 percent of the time. This overconfidence effect is an issue of great importance when governing the decisions of senior management and boards of directors. One antidote is found in the form of Network Governance, which is discussed in Chapter 14.

> *Projection Bias* — "It's not my fault, he made me do it" are words familiar to many parents. Sometimes our children deny responsibility for their actions, especially ones that they expect to result in punishment. Well, it's not just our kids who are in denial. The phenomenon of projection bias is found in most of us. It is a defense mechanism in which we deny our own attributes, thoughts, and emotions, and

imagine or project the belief that others have those feelings or are responsible for the bad things that have been done. We might blame another person for a failure of our own making, which can be an impediment to advancing our organizations.

Self-Serving Bias — Not surprisingly, people may also be biased towards attributing their successes to personal factors. We tend to take credit for our success, but deny responsibility for failure. We may also tend to interpret information presented to us in ways that is most supportive of our views.

Confirmation Bias — We tend to find evidence from the past that supports our views today and discount or ignore research and opinions to the contrary. We generalize, when we should not.

Groupthink — Within deeply cohesive groups, members may validate each other's thoughts and ideas without any external input or evaluation. Further, groups that are suffering from this phenomenon may actually prevent contradictory views from being expressed and considered; those voicing contradictory feelings may be punished by the group, reducing the willingness of others to challenge the group's consensus. In many ways, a group suffering from Groupthink is like a closed system, which tends towards greater and greater disorganization. Executive committees and boards are subject to this bias but steps taken via Network Governance in Chapter 14 can help combat it.

Illusion of Control — This is the tendency to overestimate our ability to control things around us. Throwing dice with extra emphasis or after giving them a good-luck kiss is an example of this bias. If we receive positive feedback — the roll of the dice is what we wished for — the effect is enhanced; if the feedback is negative — a loss of our bet, for example — we discount it.

Endowment Effect — People tend to value things that they already own more highly than those they do not. If my house has fallen in value by 30 percent, I would still tend to believe that it is worth more, as it was in the good old days before the real estate bubble burst. The same is true for a stock in our portfolio of investments that has decreased in value since it was first purchased.

Disposition Effect — In some ways, it is similar to the endowment effect on our perception of value. Investors tend to be more likely to sell investments that have increased in value rather than those that have dropped in value. The action of realizing losses stimulates a feeling of *regret*, which we try to avoid, even to our own detriment.

Sunk Cost Fallacy — If you paid for a non-refundable ticket to an event and then changed your mind about attending, you may still use the ticket because you don't want it to "go to waste." If it is likely that you will not enjoy the event, attending it is an irrational behavior — it brings you negative utility — and it would keep you from doing something you enjoy more. In our organizations, we may commit more of our scarce resources to make an initiative work because we have already invested so much into it, throwing good money after bad.

Money Illusion — People tend to think of the value of things in nominal terms and not in terms of their purchasing power or "real" terms. Sometimes it is difficult to raise prices on products or services, even if there has been general inflation. However, when there is general inflation, people tend to be willing to accept increases in their salaries that are lower than the inflation rate, even if they would be unwilling to accept a cut in pay in the absence of inflation. Nominal values, it seems, are like anchors and provide us with a benchmark or rule of thumb by which to judge value. Why do we tolerate a Federal Reserve target of two percent annual price inflation instead of zero?

Status Quo Bias — People tend not to want to change things. "Life is pretty good, why change now?" Or, "We've always done it like this and things have worked just fine." The Status Quo Bias may be a result of loss avoidance in combination with the endowment effect.

Survivorship Bias — Our studies are more likely to focus on cases where organizations did well, as there tends to be more data available on those. We do not tend to incorporate positive evidence from failures, even though that evidence may be helpful, simply because it is more difficult to find.

Tunneling — Similarly, we may be more likely to gather data and inferences from a few sources that are well-organized or easy to access rather than from those which take more work or effort to gather. Wikipedia is a beneficiary of this bias, while the readers of high school term papers may not be.

Gambler's Fallacy — This is the belief that patterns observed in random processes imply that future observations will be more likely to be the opposite. For example, if a coin is tossed 10 times and comes up "heads" every time, the gambler's fallacy is that it is now more likely that the next toss will be "tails," even though the likelihood of "heads" or "tails" is the same with each toss. It is important to note, though, that if the coin is not fair, or if the distribution of future outcomes is not the same as was expected, there may be information value from observations that were believed to be unlikely. Maybe the coin that has landed on "heads" 10 times in a row is not a fair coin after all.

Mental Accounting — This bias attempts to describe the process where people evaluate possible outcomes, like income they might receive from an investment. People will tend to categorize assets as belonging to current income, current wealth, or future income. The way a person subjectively categorizes a transaction that should result in an expected outcome will determine the amount of utility he expects. This affects the numerator in our value equation. For example, I might gain more utility if I believe that an investment will yield income today than one that creates wealth today which I cannot spend.

You'd think we might understand ourselves better with an awareness of these biases, but we really don't seem to change very much.

I CARE ABOUT YOU

Our evaluations and biases are not just about things we might consume or acquire. We also have feelings towards others that should not exist if we are locked into the world of Traditional Economics. These feelings have implications for how we share information in our networks and how we respond to information given to us.

There is evidence that cooperation in systems can be a multi-stage process where one member of the network or system will actually take an action that temporarily reduces its well-being because it expects a form of *reciprocal altruism* from other members of the network when they face a similar situation. A vendor might not charge a customer for a larger order than they expected — even if the customer made the mistake — under the belief it builds the strength of the relationship and the customer might be more likely to forgive a future error made by the vendor.

Reciprocity can cut both ways, however, and negative actions might be met with negative reactions just as easily as positive actions are met with more favorable responses. Positive reciprocal actions may be altruistic, or they may simply be calculations that result in a higher expected value from the relationship.

In Chapter 2, we discussed how controlled systems might take actions to bring a member of the system back in line with the system's culture. This is a form of negative reciprocity. In 2009, Elinor Ostrom was awarded the Nobel Prize in Economics for her work on *Governance of the Commons*. We'll discuss her work more extensively in Chapter 15. For now, it is important to note that in order for public goods like a commons to be managed well, the potential for negative reciprocal actions by those benefiting from the commons seems to increase the positive contributions of others to successful management of that common good.

There is also evidence that we have a sense of *fairness* embedded in our decision-making processes. Not everyone cares for others, but generally we do. In some studies that show this behavior in action, two people are told that they can split a certain amount of money that will be given to them by a third party. The challenge is that only one of them gets to decide what share of the gift each will receive. She gets to be the dictator. Still, both have to agree to the terms, or no gift is given.

It would be rational for the member who is not in control to accept any share given to him, even if it is just one dollar, because one dollar is better than none. However, the data show that a value of "fairness" will kick in whenever the share of the person deciding on the allocation is "unfairly" large. The other person will even forgo any gain to punish the dictator, if he feels that the proposed allocation is unjust.

OUR EVOLVING THOUGHTS

So, maybe we're not as coldly rational as we need to be to efficiently clear markets. Or, maybe we are pretty smart and generally make good decisions based on our knowledge — being as rational as we can be. Now that we know we are also biased — in some cases to the extent of making poor decisions — is there any hope that we will use this information to change for the better?

One school of thought about our mental processes looks to the impact of evolution on our minds. *Evolutionary Psychology* argues that, in many ways, our minds are like our bodies. They are modular — having different modules, which have evolved over time to serve certain functions that solve problems from our human ancestral times. Some of these problems include the need for communication, the detection of potential cheating among group members, and perception regarding things to rightly fear.

One of the more interesting beliefs from this area of study relates to reciprocity and how people interact with others to whom they are not genetically related, but who they may encounter more than once. This may occur if an individual is part of a group or network (like one of our organizations), or is part of the environment in which our organizations work. If someone will remember a bad act and punish a person for that in the future, this will positively affect that person's desire to cooperate with other group members.

In Game Theory, the famous *Prisoner's Dilemma* tells the story of two people believed to have been involved in a crime, but for which there is insufficient evidence to convict either one. They are separated by the police and each is told that if he agrees to testify against the other and the other remains silent, he will be set free. But, if he does not cooperate and his accomplice agrees to testify against him, he will face a substantially harsher punishment. For both suspects, the optimal outcome is keeping quiet. However, if there is a chance that one person will agree to testify against the accomplice, the optimal outcome is no longer possible and the best choice for each suspect is to agree to testify against the other. The fact that they cannot communicate with each other is key to this sub-optimal outcome being the likely choice each makes.

However, if two suspects expect to see each other repeatedly in the future, the outcome of the game changes. In this iterative Prisoner's Dilemma, when players may encounter each other again, cooperation with each other — silence — can be a sustainable strategy. It need not be a game about going to prison to be a Prisoner's Dilemma. We face choices about how to interact with other agents throughout our day. How we behave towards each other — cooperating or working against each other (*defecting* in parlance of game theory) — depends on our relationship.

Robert Axelrod, who has researched and written about the *evolution of cooperation*, organized a tournament back in 1984 to test strategies for playing the iterative Prisoner's Dilemma.[6] He invited game theorists to write computer programs of any degree of complexity to play other computer programs in a round-robin format. The results of the tournament showed that greedy and self-serving programs tended to do poorly while more altruistic strategies did better.

In fact, the winner of the tournament was one that simply cooperated on the first iteration of the game and then responded in the next iteration by doing to the opponent what it had done on the previous move — called a "tit-for-tat" strategy. In this strategy, if both parties always cooperated, both always did very well. But, a violation of mutual cooperation was met with a quick response of non-cooperation. It was an incredibly simple rule followed by the program and it showed remarkable resilience.

Looking at the best strategies overall, the following programmatic behaviors were found to be most helpful in securing the biggest benefit:

1. Be nice — Don't defect before your opponent does.

2. Retaliate — Strike back if your opponent is not as nice as you are.

3. Forgive — Retaliate for only a short time to see if your opponent will subsequently be nice to you.

4. Be clear — Be transparent in your strategy so that the other player can recognize it and adapt.

On the 20th anniversary of this first tournament, though, things changed.[7] A new entrant, or more accurately, a large number of new programs from one entrant, discovered that if it could distinguish "friends" (other programs from the same entrant) from "enemies" (those entered by others), it could systematically adopt strategies that cooperated with friends and defected from enemies. The ones finding enemies became self-sacrificing, knowing that such behavior would also drag down the enemies. The programs that found friends greeted each other with permanent cooperation and sailed to the top of the final rankings. Because of the iterative nature of the game, such success may have reflected a kind of evolution of altruism via natural selection. They may also reflect the high value of communication. Technically, communication is not permitted in the pure form of the Prisoner's Dilemma, but these programs communicated, in a way, by exhibiting particular behaviors that would allow friends to recognize each other through those actions — a kind of dance, if you will, that was unique to their group of entries.

Some theories of evolution emphasize *kinship*, the degree to which people share genetic code or how closely clustered they are on the fitness landscape. These theories hold that kinship will drive a behavior similar to the one exhibited by the winner of the 20th anniversary of the Prisoner's Dilemma tournament. Some members of a clan or family may make self-sacrificing decisions to increase the probability of the closely related genes' likelihood of survival. Perhaps Thor threw himself to the lion to protect his brothers in the hunting group? And, in nature, worker bees will sacrifice their lives when the hive is attacked in order to protect the queen. Even grass and plants have been shown to collaborate more closely underground with plants to which they have a genetic relationship.[8]

Axelrod believed that cooperation could emerge without any central authority or hierarchy.[9] He also thought that the foundation of cooperation was not trust, but, rather, durability of the relationship between players in the game.[10] We'll examine the role of trust in networks in Chapter 9, as there is other evidence that trust matters.

Finally, Axelrod compared games in which there was only one winner with the real-world scenarios involving a vast range of situations and relationships. In the reality-based situations, he found evidence that success was not achieved by conquering others, but by finding ways to elicit their cooperation.[11] This is an interesting and highly important insight for us as we seek to govern our organizations and recognize the impact that the behavior and perceptions of those in our system have on their desire to cooperate with us and, subsequently, on our value.

NOTES

1   Amos Tversky would have almost certainly been a co-recipient of this award had he been living. However, the Nobel Prize is never awarded posthumously.

2   Thaler, Richard H., and Sunstein, Cass R., *Nudge: Improving Decisions About Health, Wealth, and Happiness*, Penguin Books, 2009

3   The full title is *An Inquiry into the Nature and Causes of the Wealth of Nations*.

4   Press Release, The Royal Swedish Academy of Sciences, October 18, 1988

5   Akerlof, George and Shiller, Robert, *Animal Spirits: How Human Psychology Drives the Economy, and Why It Matters for Global Capitalism*, Princeton University Press, 2009

6   See, for example, Axelrod, Robert, *The Evolution of Cooperation: Revised Edition*, Basic Books, 2006.

7   "New Tack Wins Prisoner's Dilemma," *Wired*, October 13, 2004

8   See, for example, Fleming, Nic, "Plants talk to each other using an internet of fungus," *BBC.com*, November 11, 2014.

9   Axelrod, Robert, *The Evolution of Cooperation*, Basic Books, 1984

10 Ibid.

11 Ibid.

CHAPTER 7

The Human Reaction to Risk

In our Value Equation, a higher level of perceived risk increases the denominator in the equation, or the discount factor, and lowers the value of that good or service to us today. In Chapter 6 we discussed how people's perception of risk, and thus value, can be biased by many factors, including the risk of large losses, discounting that varies with time, and the introduction or realization of risks that were never considered possible up to that point.

In this chapter we build on an understanding of the impact that risk has on value by identifying some of the factors that cause us to believe that risk exists, how we try to cope with the presence of risk, and how we react to risks that are either nearly or actually realized.

THE PERCEPTION OF RISK

People considering an economic interaction with our organizations are assessing the value of a current, future, or ongoing relationship with us. A critically underappreciated element to the discount factor they use to arrive at that value is the perceived risk we present to them. In other words, they consider the risk that the amount of utility actually received in the future might be different from what is expected today — that we might disappoint them. Do you recall the cleaning company that offered to clean our house for the coming year? The uncertainty we felt over the viability of the company made us less likely to do business with it; on the other hand, we'd be willing to pay more if we had greater confidence in the company's ability to deliver all services as promised. The success of companies like HomeAdvisor and Angie's List, which was acquired by HomeAdvisor in 2017, is evidence of the value of this kind of knowledge.

Small risks matter somewhat for how we discount the value of engagement with an organization. However, it is the possibility of catastrophic risks that matters most when we make these decisions. The possibility that the cleaning company would fail to ever provide its services has a greater impact than the possibility that its workers might not clean as well as we expected. By the same token, a material possibility that a bridge could collapse will keep us from crossing it.

When people perceive the possibility of a catastrophic loss should a risk be realized, they tend to be afraid of it. This fear impacts their sense of value dramatically, especially if they don't understand the source of a risk or the risk itself. Columbia Business School professor Elke Weber has developed three approaches to describing how people arrive at a perception of risk and their reaction to its possibility of being realized. She calls these the *axiomatic, socio-cultural, and psychometric paradigms*.[1] We need to pay attention to all three of these sources of influence on how people perceive the risk of associating with our organization.

> *Axiomatic paradigms* focus on the way in which people subjectively transform objective risk information about a possible event — for example, data on a "100-year flood" — into how the realization of the event will impact them personally. If you live in a town near a river, you'd mentally conjecture what a relatively rare "100-year flood" would do to your home and the impact it would have on your daily life.

> *Socio-cultural paradigms* focus on the effect of group- and culture-level variables on risk perception. Some cultures find that certain risks require attention, while others pay little or no attention at all to these same risks. This can be true inside of a business with a risk-loving culture or an organization, which has never experienced failure of a large magnitude from any of its decisions. If those around you don't fear the effect of the flood, then maybe you'll think that you shouldn't either. Cultural differences in trust of institutions, whether corporations, governments, or markets, may also drive a different perception of and reaction to risk under this type of paradigm.

> The *psychometric paradigm*, on which we focus in this chapter, looks at people's emotional reactions to risky situations and how perception affects their judgment of the riskiness of events beyond their objective consequences. This paradigm is characterized by two factors or *risk dimensions*. The first is called *Dread Risk*, which is invoked when someone believes that he lacks control of a situation with perceived catastrophic potential. The second risk dimension is

called the *Risk of the Unknown*. This is the extent to which the risk is judged to be unobservable, unknown, new, or delayed in producing harmful impacts — we might believe that there is more negative risk to come and we are not sure of the amount.

In Chapter 6 we discussed the concept of loss avoidance, noting that the negative sentiment towards large losses was, on average, about two-and-one-half times greater than the positive sentiment towards equally large gains. Minimizing the possibility, or perceived possibility, of a catastrophic loss, or addressing the elements that create fear from those perceptions will have a considerable positive impact on the value of our organizations by reducing the impact of loss avoidance on discounting. This is true for businesses, charities, and even entire political and economic systems like cities, states, or countries.

Paul Slovic and his colleagues at Decision Research have developed a way to describe these risk perceptions and to measure their impact on individuals, industry, and society using a dread/knowledge spectrum that is represented in Figure 7.1. While their work primarily focuses on the impact of physical risks like earthquakes and diseases, it's fairly easy for us to see how these apply to financial risks as well.

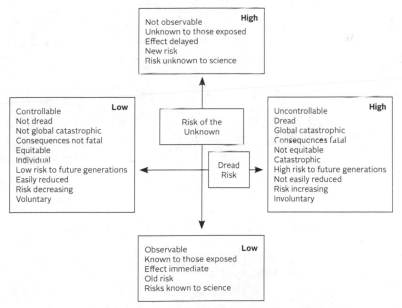

Figure 7.1 The Dread/Knowledge Spectrum
Source: Slovic, Paul and Weber, Elke, Perception of Risk Posed by Extreme Events, prepared for discussion at "Risk Management Strategies in an Uncertain World," April 12-13, 2002.

The Dread Risk factors capture aspects of the described risk that speed up our heart rate and make us anxious as we contemplate them. A perceived lack of control over exposure to the risk, with consequences that are catastrophic, may have global ramifications, or affect future generations, are good examples of these factors in terms of physical risks. Being hit by a bus is a more personal issue of similar magnitude, while the closing of the company for which we work would also be disastrous for some employees, as well as for the investors, creditors, and suppliers to that company.

The factors listed regarding the Risk of the Unknown capture the degree to which one's exposure to a risk and its consequences are predictable and observable — or not. Our response to such a possible risk is based on how much is known about it and whether the exposure is easily detected. Are you more likely to fear a tornado at night when you cannot see or one that occurs during the daytime when you can seek visual confirmation? Will you be more likely to donate to a charity that makes details of its programs available or one that tells you nothing of the results of their efforts to date?

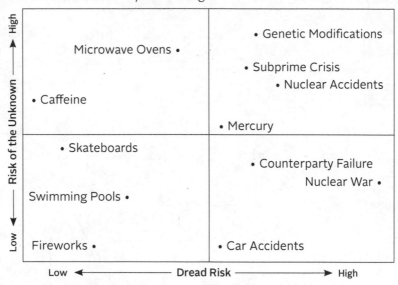

Figure 7.2 Dread Risk and Risk of the Unknown Dimensions
Source: Adapted from Slovic, Paul & Weber, Elke, Perception of Risk Posed by Extreme Events, prepared for discussion at "Risk Management Strategies in an Uncertain World," April 12-13, 2002.

Research has shown that the public's risk perceptions and attitudes are closely related to the position of a risk on a chart that has Dread Risk and Risk of the Unknown as the two axes. The higher a risk's score on the Dread dimension (the farther to the right on Figure 7.2), the more people want to see the risk reduced, and the more they are willing to see strict regulation to achieve the desired reduction in risk. Similarly, they will lower their perceived value of the entity presenting the risk in order to compensate them for any costs to offset or control that risk.

In the Risk of the Unknown dimension, a risk that is not observable or is unknown to experts pushes the risk to the top half of Figure 7.2, increasing our fear of its realization. If we only know of the cleaning service from an online ad, there are many unknowns. Risks that are in the upper right quadrant of the Figure 7.2 are, therefore, the ones most likely to be feared by us, and to trigger our desire for loss avoidance and its consequent effects on how we perceive value.

Both Dread Risk and Risk of the Unknown are addressable. In fact, we may only need to address one of the sources of these risks to minimize their impact on how people perceive the risk of our organizations. A familiarity with a risk lowers the perception of its "riskiness." People may acquire familiarity with a risk through transparency and communication or through daily exposure to it, like a daily commute by car to work. Driving to work is dangerous compared to a lot of other things, but people still do it semi-willingly every day.

The purchase of insurance and the seeking of shelter during a storm are examples of actions we may take to remove the fear that the risk being realized will result in a catastrophic loss. The colloquial American expression "don't bet the farm," means that we shouldn't take risks that could wipe away all we have. In investment portfolios, people are urged to diversify so that if one investment falls in value, that loss won't materially impact one's way of living.

Understanding the sources of Dread Risk and Risk of the Unknown as they are perceived by those who influence our value is a centerpiece of good risk management and a good governance framework. It can also be a way in which we unlock hidden value in our organizations.

PROCESSING RISK

Still, sometimes things go wrong even if we work very hard to manage our risks. It is, therefore, important for us to understand how the people in our system are going to respond to the realization of a negative risk. Let's walk through an example:

A shrill voice of warning shrieks from behind you. In front of you a city bus brushes by so closely that you are literally within an inch of losing your life. Within milliseconds you assess your well-being and the narrowly avoided disaster. Your next response is to offer effusive thanks to the person who just saved your life. At least that is your initial next response. How this incident affects you and your decision-making going forward gives us another important insight into peoples' general behavior following negative risk events.

Paul Slovic and Elke Weber have studied the human reaction to negative risk events — like the bus that almost hit you — and have discovered that people have two types of natural responses.[2] The first is a survival instinct that is hard wired into us. As time passes, though, there are changes in our behavior and perception regarding similar situations that we encounter; as a result, the impact of the realized risk slowly fades away and may even cease to be a factor affecting our behavior. In the case of the bus, we are certain to look very closely for a bus when we resume our attempt to cross the same street and may look more carefully at every street crossing for some time. Eventually, though, the potential danger posed by buses fades from our minds.

The reactive way that we process risk information was developed as an evolutionary response system related to our knowledge and experience. This experience or association-based processing enabled humans to survive during a long period of evolution and remains the most natural and most common way to respond to a threat.[3]

This is called an *affective paradigm* that relies on images and associations linked by experience to emotions, both good and bad — in other words, heuristics. It transforms uncertainty and a threat into emotional or affective responses. For example, running from the lion or jumping back from the street when someone screams at us both count as affective responses. We also use feelings like the ones mentioned above to tell us whether it's safe to walk down a dark street or to drink strange smelling water.[4]

The second paradigm for processing risk is one that comes into play after the initial danger has passed, or after we have become more comfortable that the risk no longer presents the possibility of being immediately catastrophic. This process is analytic and rule-based. As a result, it is slower and requires awareness and conscious control.[5] The process has usually been taught to us and its appropriateness of use for a given situation needs to be obvious. It does not get triggered automatically like the response that we have when directed to jump back from danger.[6] For instance, our attention to passing buses may begin to wane after crossing numerous streets without seeing another bus in dangerously close proximity, and we rationalize that the event was a one-off occurrence and no longer deem it necessary to expend mental energy on this fear.

To illustrate the difference between these two processes, Professor Weber uses the example of how a mind responds to the question "Is a whale a fish?"[7] The first process immediately says that the whale sure looks like a great big fish, while the second process says that it cannot be a fish because it is warm-blooded.

While these two processes work simultaneously, when they are in conflict, evidence strongly suggests that the affective, or emotion-based system, will prevail. This difference matters significantly for our value-maximizing goals.

Consider the case of a publicly traded company that relies on banks and others to provide it with critical overnight liquidity to run its business. If the liquidity provider sees a 40 percent decline in the company's stock overnight, the affective response of that partner may be to immediately assume there is trouble and to cut off further credit to it. If the company depends on the relationship with the liquidity provider, that stock price decline could trigger additional problems for it in terms of paying suppliers, etc. Up to this point, the analytic process of that liquidity provider had indicated that partnering with the company was prudent and further expansion of the relationship might even have been possible. The fear that the drop in stock prices has been correlated with deterioration of the company, though, triggered a reaction in the domain of the Risk of the Unknown and immediately overrode the analytic process. This override would have occurred even if the original analytic conclusion continued to be the correct one.

In the example above, a visceral reaction like fear or anxiety is treated as an early warning and indicates that some risk management action is in order and motivates us to execute that action.[8]

We see this kind of behavior in financial markets where foreign-exchange rates overshoot levels that equate purchasing power, or in cases like that of Bear Stearns and the country of Iceland, which we discussed earlier in the book. Similarly, when stock and bond prices react to news or changing market sentiment, they will move down on bad news far more quickly and violently than they will increase on good news. Such behavior can easily be associated with the dominance of the affective process.

QUANTIFICATION AS A COPING MECHANISM

Since risk and uncertainty make us uneasy — we naturally prefer to move further down on the Risk of the Unknown factor chart — we may attempt to turn subjective risk assessments into objective measures, or quantifications.

In effect, we attempt to convert uncertainty, which is not measurable, into risk, which is believed to be measurable.

Let's look at the liquidity provider mentioned above. When considering the advisability of an unsecured $20 million line of credit to a company, the provider may look for a market-based estimate of the company's probability of default in the credit default swap market. However, in the absence of complete transparency of the receiving company's financial data and business plans, the liquidity provider does not know the actual probability that its customer will default on the loan (in fact, neither does the market). But, the market data gives the liquidity provider a metric that makes the lender think it knows this probability of default and it thus becomes more comfortable assigning a value to the line of credit.

People rarely have sufficient time or resources to evaluate the effectiveness of large charities in doing their work. So, they will often rely on efficiency or effectiveness ratings from companies about which they may know even less. Still, the fact that a numeric rating has been assigned seems to give people greater confidence in their evaluation.

Paul Slovic and Elke Weber both note that much of social science analysis actually rejects the concept of measuring uncertainty, arguing that "objective characterization of the distribution of possible outcomes is incomplete at best and misleading at worst."[9] Risk, they say, is "a concept that human beings have invented to help them understand and cope with the dangers and uncertainties of life."[10] Nassim Taleb has become quite famous for his jeering of the quantification of risk in his books *Fooled by Randomness* and *The Black Swan*, which we discuss further in Chapter 13. Another interesting perspective on this can be found in Luca Celati's less-known, but still excellent text, *The Dark Side of Risk Management*.

The assignment of numbers to that which is not measurable creates its own risk, with realization of the error impacting us much in the same way that an earthquake can disrupt our faith in the stability of the ground on which we stand. We saw this happen during the financial crisis of 2007–09, when estimates of the risk of loss from borrower defaults were found to be wanting and the markets greatly overreacted.

LOOKING TO THE EXPERTS

In addition to seeking comfort in quantification, we also look to people or institutions with specialized skills or better information to help us. In a severe storm, we turn to a meteorologist and her radar. The term *expert* is used to refer to a person or a group with an actual or perceived information advantage regarding a risk. When risks are complicated, new, or not well understood by the public, experts may be relied upon by the public to address the fear we have from that risk's position on the Risk of the Unknown factor. Risk managers are considered to be experts in the quantification of uncertainty and the management of risk. Doctors are considered to be experts in the analysis and management of illness. Regulators or scientists are expected to be experts in the fields of their focus. In the example of the liquidity provider above, the market for credit default swaps was, in fact, a proxy expert.

If we believe that experts are in control, we may become more neutral about our concerns.

Should our expert prove to be wrong, though, we may alter our response to the realization of risk, overshooting its actual place on the Risk of the Unknown factor and perhaps even believing it to be of increasing risk and greater dread. If our experts let us down, we are likely to amplify our affective or emotional reaction. Further, there will be reduced trust in experts like markets, governments, and companies, which will only return once the long analytic process can manifest an assessment that the risk is not growing.

LESSONS FOR GOVERNING OUR ORGANIZATIONS

In short, people don't like negative surprises. (That, in itself, is not a surprising statement!) They want us and our organizations to be experts in our fields. If we violate their trust, they will punish us for a long time. Some surprises may lead to cascading problems, which we discuss more in the next chapter.

From a governance standpoint, our boards and executives must be cognizant of anything our organizations are doing that scores high on the Dread Risk or Risk of the Unknown factors and do what they can to address these issues. This is especially important for any risks that are perceived to have catastrophic potential. Value will be unleashed by addressing these issues of perception and reality.

NOTES

1   Weber, Elke, "Risk: Empirical Studies on Decision and Choice," in *International Encyclopedia of the Social & Behavioral Sciences*, Elsevier Science, Ltd., 2001

2   Ibid.

3   Ibid.

4   Ibid.

5   Weber, E., "Who's afraid of poor old age? Risk perception in risk management decisions," in *Pension and Design Structure* by Mitchell, Olivia S., and Utkus, Stephen P., Oxford University Press, 2004

6   Weber, E., "Experience-based and description-based perceptions of long-term risk: Why global warming does not scare us (yet)," *Climatic Change,* Vol. 77, 2006

7   Weber, E., "Who's afraid of poor old age? Risk perception in risk management decisions," in *Pension and Design Structure* by Mitchell, Olivia S., and Utkus, Stephen P., Oxford University Press, 2004

8   Weber, E., "Experience-based and description-based perceptions of long-term risk: Why global warming does not scare us (yet)," *Climatic Change,* Vol. 77, 2006

9   Slovic, Paul, and Weber, Elke, "Perception of Risk Posed by Extreme Events," prepared for discussion at *Risk Management Strategies in an Uncertain World*, April 12–13, 2002

10 Ibid.

CHAPTER 8

Social Amplification and Tipping Points

In Part I of this book we discussed how complex systems of agents in networks interact to create things that didn't exist before. Ideas, products, services, political systems, and even festive gatherings can emerge when connected agents interact around some common interest. These relationships add value to our organizations by providing something useful to those who interact with us (utility) — the top part of our Value Equation.

$$Value \uparrow \; = \; U_0 + \frac{\textcircled{U_1}\uparrow}{DR_1} + \frac{\textcircled{U_2}\uparrow}{DR_2} + \frac{\textcircled{U_3}\uparrow}{DR_3} + \cdots$$

Sometimes these interactions lead to something really big. Mark Granovetter, a professor of humanities and sciences at Stanford University wrote about big interactions as early as the 1970s, calling their starting points *thresholds of collective behavior.*[1] His work inspired the likes of Malcolm Gladwell, whose book *The Tipping Point* was a *New York Times* bestseller, bringing that expression into the mainstream lexicon. Both authors examine phenomena where the interactions among people reach a tipping point to such an extent that actions which are subsequently taken surprise us and perhaps even those taking them; products and ideas take-off as fads, or "go viral" — a relatively modern reference to the spread of interest or adoption that mimics the dissemination of a viral contagion.

Roger and Jeanne Kasperson, along with Paul Slovic and others, take a look at a darker side of amplification, especially of negative risks. Their *Social Amplification of Risk Framework*, or SARF for short, conceptualizes how people's fears and communication about risk events can lead to dramatically larger negative consequences than those that resulted from the initial loss.[2] If you'll recall from the last chapter, people sensing a possibility of a catastrophic loss brought about by something our organizations are doing will reduce the value of what we can do for them by raising their estimate of the risk associated with our activities; in other words, increasing the denominator in the Value Equation.

$$Value \downarrow = U_0 + \frac{U_1}{\widehat{DR_1} \uparrow} + \frac{U_2}{\widehat{DR_2} \uparrow} + \frac{U_3}{\widehat{DR_3} \uparrow} + \cdots$$

It is helpful to think of tipping points as social amplifications. In governing our organizations, we need to understand how these positive phenomena develop, and to encourage them. Likewise, we need to understand the process and potential impact of negative amplification, so that we can structure our organizations to deal with those phenomena most effectively.

Let's turn up the amplifier and see what happens.

AT THE THRESHOLD

Professor Granovetter is well known for his work in three areas related to the interaction of people within networks. First, his threshold models of collective behavior examine what kinds of triggers need to be in place for the interaction of individuals in a group to stimulate mass behavior. Second, he studies the role and varying impact that *Weak Ties* and *Strong Ties* in networks have on the expansion of ideas and behaviors beyond small groups of people. And, finally, the overall social interaction of agents in networks and the impact on economic behavior is reflected in his work on *Embeddedness*, which we will reference in Chapter 9.

Let's begin with a common question about crowd behavior: what causes a riot? For a moment we'll focus on this negative crowd behavior and note that there is an equally important behavior mirrored in the positive realm. People are not generally pre-disposed, *en masse*, to violent protest or action. In fact, each of us likely has a different, but generally high, trigger point at which we might join some kind of riotous actions. The idea behind modeling thresholds of collective behavior is that while most of us believe we would not be likely to riot, actions of group members around us might trigger surprising behavior in ourselves.

Referencing Granovetter's conceptual development, consider a group of 100 people with each one having a trigger point to engage in riotous behavior of one more than the next person. In other words, one person will riot spontaneously by himself, another person will require that at least one person be rioting before she will join, etc., up to the last person who would only riot if 99 others were already doing so. If you asked group members individually whether they would be likely to join a riot, most would likely say no, thinking that even a threshold of 20 or 30 rioting people is highly unlikely to draw them in. But, in fact, every member of this group will riot because the independent, spontaneous rioter triggers the threshold in the one who needs at least one other rioter to join in, who then triggers the threshold for the one who needs at least two rioters to join in, and so on, until the 100th member of the group has turned the situation into a complete mass chaos. In this case, the threshold for collective behavior was one.

Now, if the distribution of triggers for riotous behavior changes even slightly so that there is no one member of the group who will join in after just one other does, then no riot will occur and just that first spontaneous, independent rioter will take action — and likely suffer the consequences alone as well.

Granovetter's work helps explain why identical environmental conditions do not always lead to mass behavior and how mass behavior can surprisingly come about because of the structure of a group. Even in the presence of a large grievance, mass protest will not arise every time. Similarly, on the positive side, the adoption of a revolutionary new product or idea by some will not necessarily lead to mass adoption by a larger group. The outcome depends on the distribution of trigger-levels, or thresholds, among group members.

Those distributions among group members are not necessarily random, but they can be. More likely, though, groups of people will have some connections to each other that are either strong or weak. A family member, in most cases, would be considered to be a Strong Tie. Or, a business partner, member of the same church committee, fellow board member, or next-door neighbor might also be a Strong Tie. A street gang is likely comprised of people with very strong ties to each other and thus, tends to be a closed group — keeping secrets, taking collective action at a low threshold, and protecting each other. Boards of directors and executive committees may display similar behavior if their group mindset is similar or develops in a closed way.

Weak Ties are those to which we have a tangential or informal connection. The children of your next-door neighbor will likely be at the same school as your children, but so too will the children of parents living several blocks or even miles away. You may have no other interaction with those parents other than at school events. You know each other and will recognize one another (most times) in other settings. Still, you are neither close associates nor close friends. Your link is weak compared to that of your Strong Ties.

Weak Ties are important for the integration of information from outside of a group, as well as for the dissemination of good ideas that come from within a group. Imagine a start-up company that never told anyone about its ideas because its employees never interacted with other people. They might discover the secret of long life, but no one would ever buy their product. Or, consider that this start-up's product had high levels of externalities, meaning that it had a high negative impact on people outside of the company. Without any interaction with those external agents, they would never know that, taking into account its impact on the environment of all people, the product was not as good as they had believed.

If the product is really good, though, and this start-up's employees began to tell their casual acquaintances about it, the product might become the "next big thing." Have you ever told a friend about some food that was "to die for?" Well, if you are not an American, you may think that reference a bit strange. But, as one of your new Weak Ties, I'll tell you it's actually an endorsement! People, generally, like to talk and they use their networks to share and to receive information, both good and bad.

Strong and Weak Ties can help us prevent the emergence of groupthink, as was described in Chapter 6. Strong Ties are helpful if they bring information to a group that contradicts that group's way of seeing the world. Part of this is driven by the implicit trust that we have in our Strong Ties. Weak Ties, though, can also have an influence, either by delivering information to Strong Ties outside of our group, or if a sufficient mass of those Weak Ties conveys the same message to us. For example, Apple Inc. doesn't know most of its customers, but the company is at least a Weak Tie to all iPhone users. Feedback from those users, either through transactions, lack of transactions, or other forms of communication (such as customer feedback), impacted the subsequent designs and functionality of all ensuing iPhone models.

Flash® is a product of Adobe Corporation that, among other things, allows for the delivery of multimedia via websites. As of the first edition of this book, the technology behind Flash® was not being supported by one of Apple's other successful products, the iPad. It was noted then that if enough iPad users demanded Flash® compatibility from Apple, it would eventually happen. Conversely, if a high number of iPad users demanded that websites stop using Flash®, Adobe would pay attention. The strength of ties between website owners and the Weak Ties of Apple and Adobe to their clients drove the eventual outcome. The question was what the threshold trigger at Apple, Adobe, and various websites would be, and which would be reached first. In 2017, Adobe announced that it was working with various technology firms, including Apple, to stop distributing and updating Flash® by the end of 2020.[3] The threshold was reached.

GETTING TIPSY

Malcolm Gladwell used tipping points as a term to describe the point at which a group's threshold trigger is reached such that it stimulates mass behavior. Like Professor Granovetter, his writing looked at negative amplification processes as inspiration for how positive outcomes on a large scale could also materialize. In his case, he used the spread of a virus or disease as an example of how ideas and new products might catch hold of large groups of people.

Consider measles in a classroom of children. Once one child brings that disease into the room, it spreads rapidly to almost every other child in the room who has not been immunized, and then it dies out quickly. It only takes one small change in the environment — the arrival of one child with measles — to cause a mass change in the situation of the entire group.

The origin of mass protests in the Middle East during 2011 are often traced to the act of Mohammed Bouazizi, a fruit vendor in Tunisia who set himself on fire to protest what he perceived to be repeated unfair treatment of his business by the Tunisian government. Clearly, the environment was one where the threshold for action was low and the sensitivity to a small change in the environment was high. Governments have been toppled and millions have had their lives changed because of the actions this one person triggered.

Gladwell looks at networks in a slightly different way than Granovetter does. Rather than focusing on Weak and Strong Ties, he describes three types of people who need to be present in order for a tipping point to be reached and for a product or idea to go viral.

Connectors are the people in the world who bring others together. They may be Strong or Weak Ties to hundreds or even thousands of other people. They often cross social lines and mix with a variety of groups who share Strong Ties among their membership. Online Connectors have large groups of Facebook friends or connections on LinkedIn. Face to face, these are the people who introduce you to others at parties or when you are new to an organization, a small town, or neighborhood.

Mavens are people to whom we look to connect us with new ideas or information. They initiate word-of-mouth epidemics and are likely to be highly trusted by other members of their networks. They may

be trusted because they have access to special or unique information or may have a track record of successfully sharing information
that is timely and helpful. Online Mavens may be trusted websites
that review technology from an expert point of view, or they may
be a collective assessment of quality of a product shown on Ama-
zon.com or similar shopping site. Face to face, these can be the
people who are known to show care and to do careful research
before spending money. Or, they may be the first adopters of new
technology, to whom we look for advice before spending our time
and reputation.

Salesmen are those who sway our ideas with their words. We like
them, want to act on their suggestions, and mimic their actions.
Okay, we don't like all salesmen. But, the concept of a salesman is
someone who can move your opinion to an action. Suppose one of
your Maven connections has just purchased a car with driverless
technology. You're not sure that you want to adopt that technology
just yet. So, you seek additional advice, perhaps from an expert
website or by calling a support line. The words that you hear are
from a salesman, using words to turn a previous potential action
into a real action.

Gladwell and Granovetter are getting at the same concepts, using
different terminology. But, the general idea is that a social connection
between people is required to stimulate mass behavior.

WALKING ON AIR

When Gladwell's three types of people interact in an environment that is
susceptible to change, big things can happen. In his book, he reviews the
case of Airwalk Shoes, suggesting it to be representative of the phenomenon
he describes.[4]

Airwalk is a shoe company based in San Diego that started as a specialized shoe maker for skateboarders. It is named after a well-known skateboarding move — the Airwalk. In the early days, styles and construct of the
shoes attracted extraordinarily loyal customers among the skateboarding
crowd. Within a few years of its founding, the company was generating
nearly $13 million in annual revenue.

With the objective of becoming an international brand, they expanded
into products for surfing, snowboarding, mountain biking, and bicycle
racing, and engaged an innovative advertising company to create their

brand image. They sponsored professional competitors in the sports which they serviced and launched a grassroots campaign to meet the buyers for youth-oriented shoe stores. Within three years, their sales shot up to $175 million annually.

The professionals who adopted the Airwalk shoes and whose skill and "cool" reputation were sought by their fans, were Mavens, Connectors, and Salesmen all in one. They brought the new idea of Airwalk to a larger crowd. The advertising agency had its own in-house Maven as well — someone who knew "cool" when she saw it. She networked with different groups of kids around the country to find out what was emerging as a new trend and rode the wave of those viral movements.

Gladwell tells of the downside of a viral expansion as well. When Airwalk went mainstream, it lost the edge of coolness that caused its message to be spread. Sales collapsed and the tipping point reversed.

LETTING OUT THE AIR

The collapse of sales at Airwalk was not as much a negative realization of risk as the loss of positive amplification effects. Amplifications of real losses can and do occur, and they are often embedded in industry-specific or broad societal costs that such amplifications impose.

Consider the impact on the nuclear energy industry from the problems experienced at Three Mile Island in 1979 and Chernobyl in 1986. Due in large part to the resultant fears and increased regulation that followed these disasters, no new nuclear power plants were built in the United States over the next three decades. Almost 40 years after the Three Mile Island incident, the high costs of attaining operational approval for a nuclear power plant cast doubt on the ability of the nuclear industry in the U.S. to ever have any kind of renaissance.

In response to the 2011 earthquake in Japan and subsequent damage at the Fukushima nuclear power plant, the German government announced that it intended to phase out all of its nuclear power plants by 2022. At the time of their decision, nearly 25 percent of Germany's energy supply was being derived from nuclear reactors. Unless substitutes are quickly found, the supply of energy to German consumers will necessarily drop while the demand is more likely to rise. In response to the potential of negative risk, short-term financial cost will be borne with near certainty by all energy consumers in Germany, and investors in nuclear power technologies may experience large losses.

THE SOCIAL AMPLIFICATION OF RISK

The threshold research of Professor Granovetter showed that amplification doesn't always occur, even if two situations appear to be very similar in nature. The Kaspersons' and Slovic's work explains the process and necessary conditions for a realized negative risk to be amplified by magnitudes of the initial loss.[5] SARF is highly relevant for the discussion of governance of our organization's value as it impacts both the potential realization of utility by those in our network and their perceived risk of our organization's ability to meet their expectations for delivering utility. It can, therefore, impact both the numerator and denominator of the Value Equation in ways that reduce our value today.

In the SARF model, the extent to which amplification occurs is determined at two stages — when information is transferred and when people respond to that information. Gladwell discusses the roles that Connectors, Mavens, and Salesmen play in the communication of information, while Professor Granovetter highlights how Weak Ties and Strong Ties affect the quality or strength of information. The conceivers of SARF define *Information Sources, Transmitters, Receivers,* and *Signals* by the roles they play in communication and potential amplification. In their framework, an Information Source is a person, group, or organization that sends out a message full of Signals to Transmitters and Receivers. Transmitters are also Receivers, but differ from Receivers in that they pass along their interpretation of the message to other Transmitters and Receivers. At each point of transfer, there is a potential for distortion and amplification. The game of "Whispers" is a classic example of this process, where a person starts a rumor and asks the person to whom they tell it to pass it along down a line of people. Each person receiving the message is asked to do the same until the last person re-tells the rumor to the person who started it — usually resulting in great laughter when the original message is compared to the final message delivered.

The actualization of amplification will depend, in part, on how people and groups are influenced by the biases and heuristics we discussed in Chapter 6. Public perceptions and responses, the authors argue, are a function of the interaction between these biases, our economic interests, and the values of the culture in which we operate. For example, the Information Source has an intended message. However, that message is processed and received by Transmitters who make use of their own experience, knowledge, and ambitions to determine which parts of the message should be emphasized, de-emphasized, or ignored as the message is passed along.

When the message reaches a Receiver, it may not carry the same signals that were intended by the original Information Source. Further, how it is received will be a function of the heuristics of the Receiver, some of which may cause a reaction that was unintended or unanticipated by the Information Source. This problem grows more severe as the message is passed along multiple times.

Some types of Transmitters have more influence and are referred to as *amplification stations*. Scientists who assess risks, the news media, opinion leaders in social groups (akin to Mavens), public agencies, personal networks of peers (akin to Strong Ties), and the institutions responsible for the management of the risk being considered, are all viewed as critical amplification stations. Receivers will link a message with the quality of the source of the information and draw inferences from the credibility or economic motives of that link. These inferences may make the message more important or influential, and thus more likely to be acted upon. Consider a message received from an independent Nobel laureate regarding a potential nuclear risk versus the same message being provided by a spokesperson for the nuclear energy industry. They may deliver the same message, but the respective Signal value of each message may be quite different to the Receiver.

Statements that are repeated multiple times tend to increase their believability and the potential for amplification. This effect is enhanced when multiple sources repeat the same message. Political parties have learned this lesson well as is evidenced by "talking points memos" issued to a large array of public figures who reiterate the same message through different media outlets. The message has no more truth to it than if it had come from their political party headquarters directly to Receivers. But it will seem more believable because Receivers and Transmitters hear it being affirmed by many sources and through a variety of outlets.

In the SARF model, the second major stage of amplification, response, is driven through four major avenues. The first is a result of quick heuristics — much like the automatic response to a cry of warning from behind you — and group values. Sometimes behavior by other group members will increase one's fear of some risk. With increased fear comes the possibility for heightened, or amplified, reaction.

Second, a risk might become a social issue. Political parties have also discovered that they can generate greater responses when they polarize voters via something people fear. The campaign of former Massachusetts Governor Michael Dukakis for President was damaged when opposition groups aired an advertisement showing a frightening picture of Willie Horton, a convicted felon who had been given a weekend release by Governor Dukakis and subsequently committed additional horrific crimes. Pushing this imagery was a way to associate the election of Governor Dukakis as President with increased risk of being a victim of crime oneself. And more recent efforts to create a fear of immigrants and people of differing religious beliefs by connecting them to greater negative economic and physical risks have been highly impactful.

Third, a risk event may have some kind of signal value that the risk is new, more serious than was previously believed, or not well understood. If the risk is realized in a situation that is not understood, seems to be uncontrolled, or not being managed well, it is likely to result in a greater response from Receivers. Recall from the previous chapter that this condition is akin to being in the realm of Risk of the Unknown.

Finally, there can be a very negative branding or stigmatization of a place or group associated with a risk event. Usually this is some form of negative imagery, like dying animals, people losing jobs or homes, or mass destruction. These images are in the realm of Dread Risk. People typically respond to negative stigmatization via loss avoidance. If loss avoidance is present among those whom we wish to draw into our network, it means that we have to offer more in order to earn their commitment. If we are trying to attract capital, either from investors or creditors, we will have to pay more for it, or spend more of our resources to attract donors, voters or people to attend our parties, reducing our ability to do other things. If the stigmatization grows, we may have no access to economic capital at all.

Through the transfer of information — communication — and the response of Receivers, amplification of negative risks can occur. When it does, the societal or industry-specific costs can be seen in secondary impacts like rioting, reduced business sales or property values, increased insurance costs, changes in public acceptance or trust, political and social pressures, and requirements for greater training, as well as education and certification for those dealing with risks. Realized or nearly-realized risks also create enduring mental perceptions that affect how future information is processed — for example, nearly being hit by a bus affects how you cross the street in the future.

If positive feedback mechanisms like those discussed in Chapter 2 are present in the system, secondary amplifications can drive third-, fourth- and fifth-order impacts, and more. These events may even become out-of-control or chaotic, resulting in unpredictable outcomes.

CASE STUDY: THE MADOFF AFFAIR

In 2008, a multi-billion-dollar investment firm run by Bernie Madoff was discovered to have been nothing more than a giant fraud. The story of Madoff and Madoff Investment Securities highlights both sides of an amplification story.

Positive amplification (gathering of new assets for his funds) originated through messages transmitted by Mavens, Strong Ties, and Amplification Stations. That message: Madoff had a sterling reputation. The trust he earned within his social and professional circles allowed him to easily raise funds for his investment firm. An article from Bloomberg chronicles some of the ways in which this happened:

> Madoff. . .got a boost in his early years from accountant Saul Alpern, the father of his wife Ruth. Alpern referred friends and their relatives. . .A recruiting circuit for Madoff associates included clubs in Palm Beach, Florida, and Long Island, New York. They exploited an atmosphere of trust to rope in investors. . .Madoff's name was synonymous with "bank," David Arenson wrote in [a]blog. Most of Arenson's family had Madoff accounts, which "radiated out through the guest population, through our distant relatives and the distant relatives of guests. . ." Arenson said in an interview, "Madoff had wormed his way into the system to such an extent that we felt comfortable with him."
>
> Cynthia Arenson came to Madoff by following her parents, who were "best friends" of Alpern, she said. Her father was a retired attorney, and his friends were retired teachers. Joyce Greenberg, a retired Houston stockbroker, said she and six other family members gave money to Madoff because her stepmother's first cousin, Carl Shapiro, had confidence in him.
>
> [R]ecruits became unpaid solicitors for Madoff, either by expressing confidence in him or by taking a more active role.[6]

Word of mouth was further amplified because there was an additional positive feedback mechanism in place. Investors were consistently receiving above-market returns on their investments and were eager to talk about it to their friends.

Madoff Investment Securities was a Ponzi scheme, using new investor money to provide the "above market" returns to existing investors. As with all Ponzi schemes, the flow of new money finally was insufficient to pay "above market" returns to existing investors and the game stopped.

Now that the fraud has been uncovered, there are second- and third-order costs being socialized, even impacting companies that had nothing to do with Madoff. Investment firms now face increasing regulation of their activities, to the point that it is substantially harder for small investment companies to bring new ideas to the market. Allocators of investment funds face substantially larger costs to perform due diligence on investment managers they might hire, reducing returns to their customers. Investors are less willing to commit capital to innovative ideas or projects that they don't completely understand because they don't want to be the victims of a fraud. As a result, the cost of capital, for any company that relies on external investors or creditors, has gone up relative to where it would be had the Madoff fraud never been allowed to occur.

PROBABILITY AND IMPACT ARE NOT ENOUGH

If people's risk perceptions change in such a way that they view our organization as more risky, that will lower our organization's value. Similarly, if there is an amplification effect that increases regulations or internal costs of executing our corporate vision, the amount of utility that we can deliver to our investors may decline, increasing our cost of capital and reducing the value of what we do.

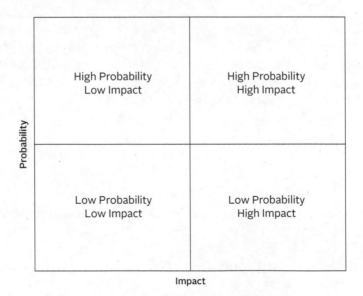

Figure 8.1 Typical Risk Assessment Grid

But perhaps even more significant is the implication that amplification of negative risks has for organization-wide risk management. Typical organizational risk assessments will focus on the probability of something going wrong and the expected impact of that negative risk if it were to be realized. For example, what is the probability of a flood near our computer and data storage center? If that center is flooded, what will that cost our firm?

By multiplying these two values, it is believed that an expected loss can be derived from a risk to which an organization might be exposed, allowing known risks to then be prioritized. This kind of two-dimensional assessment has even been promoted through widely adopted risk management frameworks like that from the Committee of Sponsoring Organizations or COSO.[7] This method is usually represented by the grid shown in Figure 8.1 with varying risks plotted in one of four quadrants.

The challenge that amplification brings to this type of analysis is twofold. First, these types of risk assessments tend to direct resources toward risk events with an obviously high possible impact on the organization. Low impact events are often ignored, especially if they are low probability events. Lurking in those low impact events are some that, through the processes described in this chapter, can become amplified and result in more substantial losses than were expected.

"High probability / high impact" events will tend to get immediate attention, while "low probability / high impact" events will either be ignored, because they are considered too remote or be addressed through insurance, capital provisions, or other forms of risk-transfer like financial market hedging programs. Some "low probability / high impact" events may have their potential impact greatly underestimated if their potential for amplification is not understood. If this occurs, the organization may have insufficient insurance or capital reserves to cover the losses, which could be severe enough to end the organization's existence — prematurely truncating the utility that it delivers.

$$Value \downarrow = U_0 + \frac{U_1}{DR_1} + \frac{U_2}{DR_2} + \frac{U_3}{DR_3} + \overleftarrow{(\cdots)}$$

THE REAL IMPACT

Amplification, by definition, is a self-feeding mechanism that can be triggered by the failure of risk management processes to incorporate the potential for amplification of risks. One of the steps that Receivers take in assessing the value of a message they receive is whether there are experts responsible for the management of the risk who understand it and are capable of dealing with it. When there is a realization that the experts misunderstood the risk, there is a penalty applied by Receivers and they will become even more defensive towards that risk. One example of this is the 2007–09 financial crisis where it became abundantly clear that experts had failed to understand the potential for amplified losses on subprime loans to impact their organizations. The amplifications became so large that the entire global economy was believed to be under threat — high Dread. When high Dread was combined with a lack of confidence in experts — high Risk of the Unknown — the climate for amplification grew even more volatile. Ultimately, a few hundred billion dollars in losses on subprime mortgages were amplified into tens of trillions of dollars in lost wealth and economic activity, scarring confidence in capitalistic economic and political systems.

Companies, political economies, non-profits, and neighborhood organizations are all potential beneficiaries of positive amplification effects and potential victims of negative risks that become amplified. Good governance of these organizations requires an understanding of, and appropriate action toward, the sources of each amplification that are critical to their respective missions.

NOTES

1   Granovetter, Mark, "Threshold Model of Collective Behavior," *The American Journal of Sociology*, Vol. 83, No. 6, May 1978

2   Kasperson, Roger E., Renn, Ortwin, Slovic, Paul, Brown, Halina S., Emel, Jacque, Goble, Robert, Kasperson, Jeanne X., Ratick, Samuel, "The Social Amplification of Risk: A Conceptual Framework," *Risk Analysis*, Vol. 8, No. 2, 1988

3   Estes, Adam Clark, "Adobe is Finally Killing Flash (For Real, This Time)," *Gizmodo*, July 25, 2017

4   Galdwell, Malcom, *op. cit.*, pp. 193–215

5   Kasperson, et al, *op. cit.*

6   Sandler, Linda, and Dodds Frank, Allan, "Madoff's Tactics Date to 1960s, When Father-in-Law Was Recruiter," *Bloomberg*, Jan. 29, 2009

7   See "Guidance on Enterprise Risk Management," Committee of Sponsoring Organizations of the Treadway Commission, coso.org

CHAPTER 9

The Role of Trust in Networks

To increase the value of what we do today, the Value Equation shows that we need to do the following:

1. Increase what others expect to receive from us (utility) each time we interact.

2. Increase the number of times that others can expect to receive something of value (utility) from us.

3. Reduce the risk that they'll be disappointed by the reality of interacting with us.

Ideally, these three conditions can be achieved simultaneously through more effective governance (which is the point of this book).

Up to this chapter, we've focused on how innovation happens within systems and complex networks — how we invent and deliver things of value or utility to others — and on the perception that other agents have of our organizations and the risk that we'll disappoint them; in other words, what drives sentiment and, particularly, what causes large movements in sentiment among those in our network. Beginning with the next chapter, we'll focus more purposefully on the second factor in the Value Equation. But, before we do, we have to consider a highly important contributor to the success of all that we have outlined so far — *trust*.

Trust is a necessary component in the relationships in our lives, as well as in the systems in which we engage. Complex systems like our business, our coffee shop, our friendships, our state, provincial, local, and national political economies, and digital economies, can be highly dynamic entities, generating amazing results when agents within them are allowed to successfully interact. As we've seen all too often, though, they can also be very unstable, damaging, and even highly inefficient when things go wrong.

Trust plays a key role in determining which outcome we realize through our specific efforts and that's why this is a critically important chapter in the book.

HOW DO I TRUST THEE? LET ME COUNT THE WAYS

Articulating the meaning of trust is difficult, because trust is a feeling. Alex Todd, formerly the Chief Executive Officer of Canadian advisory firm Trust Enablement, defines trust both as "a person's willingness to accept (and/or increase) their vulnerability" and "acceptable uncertainty."[1] In our Value Equation, acceptable uncertainty is quantified by the risk premium we demand in order to feel adequately compensated for the risk we perceive or for the lack of trust we feel. Our absolute and relative choices help us gauge how much trust exists in a given relationship.

If you donated to a charity this week, you indicated a positive trust in that group. If you voted for a politician, relative trust had an impact on your choice. If you decide to drive a car, fly in a plane, walk across the street, or take a drink of water, your action will be influenced by your trust in people, technologies, and systems that are in many ways outside of your control. Your decision to engage in these activities shows that you have confidence in others to manage their part in the system well enough for you to entrust your health, safety, and comfort to them. Your trust level, in other words, has passed a threshold of acceptability.

Where trust is absent to any degree, people can substitute contracts, policies, laws, and punishment as forms of governance and assurance. Higher insurance premiums and greater regulatory hurdles are examples of how a lack of trust is manifested. To the extent that trust is present, people tend to grant greater freedom, like revolving lines of credit, access to willing volunteers, and the authority to make independent decisions.

Trust may also be measured by the degree of detail in contracts, policies, and laws required for two parties to agree to exchange things of value. Required specificity is inversely related to the amount of trust that exists between interacting agents. The level of our trust affects what we demand in return for engaging in transactions with others or for giving them the liberty to act independently.

EMBED WITH TRUST

Traditional Economics would have us believe that individuals in networks act in an individualistic, self-interested fashion and social interactions have no effect on the economic decisions we make. In reality, our economic relations are actually embedded within our social relationships. Professor Mark Granovetter's "embeddedness," which was mentioned in the last chapter, is the degree to which individuals or organizations are enmeshed in a social network. People will guide their choices, in some part, based on past interactions with other people they know. For example, we use our Strong Tie relationships to assess uncertainties with those only tangentially related to us. If a friend recommends a new product or a restaurant, we're more likely to give it a try. If we like the food and service, greater trust and a strengthening of ties will be established over time as long as we have repeated, positive experiences with this new entity. In other words, trust is enhanced when expectations are met and undermined when they are not.

One effect of embeddedness is that our organizations can be the beneficiaries of higher trust from those in our network. When this is the case, transacting can be less expensive and we can more effectively use our scarce economic capital, generating more value through our work. Our lenders may reduce the cost of borrowing, our customers may respond with shorter sales cycles, those who need our social services may be more willing to seek us out, we may increase employee retention, enhance the value of our brand, or reduce the need for expensive attorneys.

This effect of embeddedness impacts more entities today because small organizations, and even some larger ones, are creating virtual corporations by stringing together outsourced service providers to fill roles that may have previously been considered only as in-house operations. Legal counsel is often sought externally. Customer service may be provided in another country. Web design and marketing may come from a creative agency thousands of miles away, where subcontracted workers answer your emails while wearing shorts in the comfort of their own home. A lack of trust or social regulation can make external market transactions like these more expensive, as greater due diligence, legal contracting, and audit of performance will be required.

Alternatively, our connections can reduce our expected risk of hiring these distant entities. Social networks in which we are embedded can provide a check on the abuse of trust. If a charity or third-party service provider abuses a trusting relationship, it could lose donors or customers, and its damaged reputation might make it difficult to serve its targeted clients. If the negative consequences of a loss in trust are known in advance to significantly increase the cost of doing business, embeddedness will serve as a powerful self-regulator of dealings in a network.

TRUST ME AND DO AS I SAY

Social embeddedness is reflected in the economic impact of our influence on others and theirs on us. If you recall the scene in the local co-op when I purchased the Honeycrisp apple, I was influenced by someone who confidently grabbed a Honeycrisp as I deliberated my options. His confidence and the fact that he shopped at the same store helped drive my value decision. He was loosely embedded in my network, but it was enough to push me across a threshold of decision.

Like the relationship between the confident shopper and me, internal and external agents in systems are impacted by the levels of trust we display in each other. All else equal, the overall level of trust we have in someone determines how much any information they provide will affect our decisions, or how much influence they have over us.

In Figure 9.1, the connection between three agents in a network is depicted. Lines connecting each agent represent communication channels and potential avenues of influence via trust. In this figure, Agent A is connected to both Agents B and C, but Agents B and C do not share any direct connection.

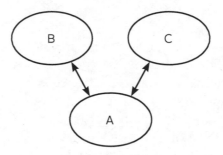

Figure 9.1 Connected Agents

From this depiction, Agent B and Agent A will be able to influence each other, but Agent B can only influence Agent C through Agent A. Agent C has a similar relationship to Agent A as does Agent B.

Figure 9.2 is a slight modification of Figure 9.1, using the thickness of the line connecting agents to represent the amount of influence one might have on the other. Influence might come through a large economic relationship or through increased trust, as is the case in this example. Agent B is more influential on Agent A than is Agent C. This figure also suggests that Agent A is similarly influential on Agent B.

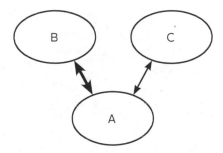

Figure 9.2 Connected Agents with Differing Levels of Influence

If you are Agent A, consider the choice you face regarding an expensive purchase like a car or whether to buy shares in a publicly traded company. Figure 9.3 shows that if your two connections provide you with different advice, the one who has the most influence over you, in whom you have the most trust, will drive your choice.

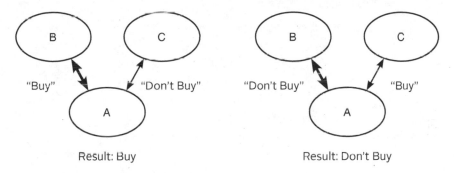

Figure 9.3 Impact of Influence on Decisions

Likewise, if you were trying to sell a product to Agent B and Agent C, you would be likely to have more success, all else equal, influencing Agent B than Agent C.

In Figure 9.4, the complexity of the relationship among agents is increased by the interaction among agents who are not directly connected to you (Agent A). Your ability to convince Agent C to buy something from you is also influenced by your connections to Agents D, E, F, G and H. However, your connections to them are only through Agent B. So, even if Agent B and Agent C have no direct connection, how you treat Agent B will influence your success, or lack thereof, with Agent C.

Likewise, if you treat Agent C badly, or if he is not satisfied with your product or service, you may suffer in the end. That's because he has a

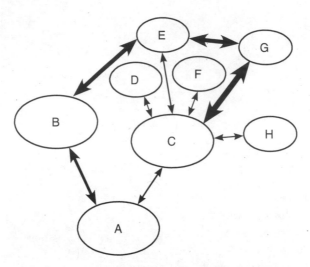

Figure 9.4 Complex Relationships among Agents

particularly influential relationship with Agent G as well as a relationship with Agent E. Agent G also has an influential relationship with Agent E. Since Agent E has an influential relationship with Agent B, if they hear bad things from both Agents C and G, they are more likely to amplify the negative message when communicating with Agent B. In fact, the relationship between Agents E and B is more influential than the one you enjoy with Agent B. So, a poor relationship with Agent C might also cost you the business with Agent B — which you had assumed was independent. This is a form of social regulation.

IF ONLY YOU'D COOPERATE

We know that cooperation among agents is required for things of net value to emerge from complex systems. Efficient cooperation requires trust. Cooperation, as a strategy, was the first move made by the "tit for tat" program, which won the original Iterative Prisoners' Dilemma tournament. And, the program that ultimately beat the "tit for tat" program in a subsequent tournament, found a way to cooperate with other "friendly" programs once it established that it knew them. In other words, cooperation happened once trust had been established between two independent agents (computer programs) that were able to communicate with each other.

An amazing story from World War I helps illustrate how cooperation can emerge even in the most unlikely circumstances. During extended trench warfare, frontline soldiers were known to refrain from trying to kill the enemy during certain times of the day, allowing them to conduct "private business."[2] As long as their restraint was reciprocated by the other side, the place and time of this temporary truce was respected by all.[3] Warring soldiers, who otherwise were ordered to kill each other, developed cooperation because trust was established and re-enforced with each successful venture to the safe zone. Further, since the battle had no pre-determined end time, there was no benefit received from non-cooperation.

DOES OUR RELATIONSHIP NEED TO BE THIS COMPLEX?

The larger a network, the more able it is to bring in new information and ideas. Therefore, larger networks have a greater potential to stimulate innovation. In fact, the potential for innovation increases exponentially as the size of the network grows. At the same time, if the average number of relationships each agent has is greater than one, the number of interdependencies and communication channels within the network grows even faster. With even small changes in one part of a large network, the effect can amplify very quickly, with both positive and negative results.

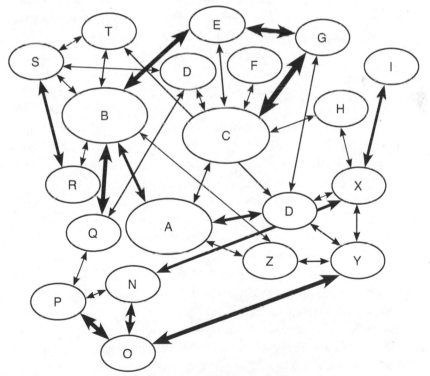

Figure 9.5 Dense and Complex Network

Businesses and political economies are large complex networks. History shows they are able to generate large innovations and also to experience dramatic collapses. Markets are also large and complex systems. The markets for stocks, homes, and even tulips have experienced rapid innovation and advancement, as well as subsequent collapse.[4] Empires that over-extended their reach have experienced the same cycle.

Figure 9.5 shows what is referred to as a *dense network*. Note the highly interconnected nature of the agents in this system, some with Strong Ties (thick lines) and others with Weak Ties (narrow lines). Agent A is the centerpiece of this network, but there is a large volume of information that affects Agent A flowing outside of her direct awareness or control.

Too much interconnectedness within large networks can become inhibiting and can even stimulate negative amplification. Stuart Kaufmann of the Santa Fe Institute calls these *complexity catastrophes*.[5] That's because overly dense networks are less responsive and less able to adapt to changes. They become brittle and breakdown easily.

Take, for example, the case where one unit of a business wants to launch a marketing program for its newest product. In an overly dense network, the marketing department has to check with the legal department, finance department, and the sales department before making any changes to the company's advertising campaign, and each of those groups needs to check within its network for concerns before they can report back. The amount of time it takes to make a decision can be lengthened substantially, particularly as iterations of change follow feedback from each group. The newest product may never realize its potential as the dense network makes sure that its internal connections are all satisfied and cares little for whether the product is still "new" when it reaches the market.

There are two things that can be done to increase the likelihood of success and to address the downside challenges of large, highly connected networks. The first is to add hierarchies and the second is to increase the trust among agents. Hierarchies have generally been derided as stagnant and bureaucratic. However, they can also be constructed to be networks within networks, and adjusted in size so that the negative aspects of overly dense networks don't arise.

Hierarchical organizations, as depicted in Figure 9.6, tend to have fewer Weak Ties and more strong ones. There is more trust among agents because they tend to know each other well and have fewer relationships to manage. Influence is strong and transaction costs are low.

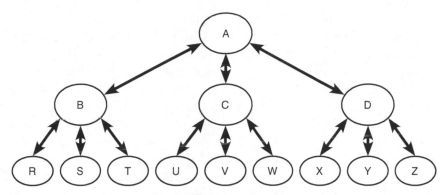

Figure 9.6 Hierarchical Network

But networks that are comprised only of those people who know each other well are also less likely to innovate — they tend to isolate people within silos and they suffer because new ideas are not brought into the discussion as easily. As an example, recall the problems of groupthink discussed in Chapter 6. Further, messages that move up and down a hierarchical structure have more opportunities to be distorted or lost via biases or intentional manipulation.

Because of these issues, large hierarchies are, paradoxically, also inherently less stable than systems that have diverse relationships of both Strong and Weak Ties. The key to success with a larger system is that the size of hierarchies must be managed carefully and they must be socially connected to other hierarchies.

The overall success of social, business, and political networks is driven by three factors:

1. The number of agents in the network.

2. How connected the agents are to each other.

3. The level of trustworthiness among agents.

The vast majority of social networks are a blend of friends, family, and casual acquaintances. Most business networks involve employees, consultants, regular customers, and third-party service providers. Inevitably, a well-governed business network needs to be constructed as a blend of Strong and Weak Ties in a complex system that has embedded hierarchies of appropriate size.

In *The Tipping Point*, Malcolm Gladwell cites the "Rule of 150," suggesting that the most effective network or group size is about 150 people. In effect, with this "rule" he is trying to identify the ideal size of a hierarchical structure. The figure is also called "Dunbar's Number," which British anthropologist Robin Dunbar suggested to be a theoretical limit to the number of people with whom one can effectively maintain social relationships.[6]

However, Gladwell's analysis is invariant with respect to trust, and academic studies have shown that when trust increases, so too can the most effective group size. It turns out that with trust present, complex networks can remain stable even with five or six average connections per person in the group, a fairly high level of density. With three to five levels of hierarchy not uncommon in organizations, the "Rule of 150" seems to be a good approximation for an average effective group size when trust is present, although there can be quite a bit of variance around that median. Without trust, or at low levels of trust, the largest size at which an organization can be effective collapses to as few as 15–20 people. When this occurs, the potential for innovation drops dramatically as far less information is exchanged with members of the internal and external networks. The organization, therefore, incurs an opportunity cost from the loss of trust.

As we know that any message from the top of a hierarchical structure will pass through various transmitters, whose biases and personal agendas will reshape the message each time, we should expect some of its accuracy to be lost every time it is told and, because of time constraints for the message to be compressed — one cannot tell another person everything they know or it will consume all of their time. By some estimates, 15 percent of the value of a message is lost each time it passes from one transmitter to another and at least 50 percent of the message is compressed.[7] So, when the information has been relayed even three times, more than 90 percent of the original message will either be missing or incorrect by that point. This is another constraint to the levels of hierarchy and why excessive levels of hierarchy seem to lead to less effective operations — remember the game of Whispers we mentioned in the last chapter?

I UNDERSTAND THAT YOU NEED MORE SPACE

Trust enhances the ability of our organizations to create larger and denser networks of connections than would be possible in its absence. Larger networks, as demonstrated above, have greater opportunities for innovation and the creation of value. While most organizations begin with a small hierarchical structure, networks within that hierarchy become too dense and they need a bit of sub-hierarchy, or networks within the network, to maintain effectiveness, efficiency, and stability.

Trust gives us a greater ability to distribute accountability and the autonomous management of these sub-hierarchies. As will be discussed in Part IV of this book, the ability to distribute authority within a complex organization is critical for adding value — it makes the pursuit of corporate objectives even more likely to be successful.

HOW CAN I EVER TRUST YOU AGAIN?

Even with trust, there are human failings and manipulations. Trust can only have an ongoing presence within an organization if its breach meets with enforcement mechanisms. The "tit for tat" program would always punish the other program if it abused the assumed trust with which the program began.

Markets, it turns out, are also very effective at meting out punishment for violations of trust.

In an online presentation to the Professional Risk Managers' International Association (PRMIA), Professor Ingo Walter of New York University's Stern School of Business talked about the relationship between reputation and value of publicly traded financial service firms.[8] In this particular case, reputation is used as a synonym for trust. Using a variation on the Value Equation, he emphasized the impact of lost reputation on the denominator in the equation via an increased risk premium.

Among the cases he cited was Salomon Brothers — at one time, one of the most highly regarded firms on Wall Street. It was accused of violating Treasury auction rules in an egregious manner and to its own financial benefit. When the news broke of their misbehavior in 1991, the company's stock price fell by one-third.[9] This incident, which was a breach of trust with the markets, was a driving force behind the ultimate absorption of Salomon Brothers into Travelers Group several years later.

Professor Walter also discussed the early 1990s case of JP Morgan and Banesto, in which JP Morgan suffered a very minor loss in book value, or net asset value, but a more substantial loss in its market value. In this case, it emerged that JP Morgan's role in a special purpose vehicle related to Banesto was rife with conflicts of interest. In short, at a time when JP Morgan had a stellar reputation for work that benefited their clients, the relationships didn't look very good to other clients. Academic work analyzing the impact of this news showed that despite a loss of just $12 million in JP Morgan's book value from this event, overall more than $1.2 billion in market value was lost, roughly 10 percent of the total value of the company and 100 times the size of the loss from the actual incident.

In 2011, Goldman Sachs agreed to pay $550 million to settle securities and fraud charges from the SEC.[10] The impact on the value of the company from this single event was estimated to be approximately $21 billion, or 22 percent of the company's market value. Until the financial crisis of 2007–09, Goldman Sachs enjoyed a reputation on Wall Street much like that which Salomon Brothers had in the 1980s and early 1990s. That is no longer true.

In a study of more than 300 cases of news that impacted the reputation of financial services firms, Professor Walter and his colleagues found that within 10 days of the release of the news, market values of those companies had fallen by an average of more than seven percent.[11] Further, it was not unusual for companies to experience losses in excess of 30 percent in market values immediately following the news release.

Finally, Professor Walter noted that Citigroup had been unusual in the frequency of reputational incidents between 2003 and the start of the financial crisis. He argued that this recurrence begins to have a cumulative effect and people start to expect these events from a company. In other words, when businesses repeatedly behave in a manner that we find to be inappropriate, we lose our trust in them. Between the beginning of 2007 and the end of 2017, Citigroup's stock fell by 85 percent, while the S&P 500 Banking Index fell by slightly more than 8 percent. You'll recall that banks lost a significant amount of trust from the public during the financial crisis and have only recovered some of their lost reputation since then. It seems that Citigroup's investors, though, distanced themselves even further from a restoration of trust in that institution.

TRUST AND THE POTENTIAL OF RISK MANAGEMENT

Professor Walter's audience on the day of his presentation was comprised of hundreds of risk management professionals from around the world. In a survey of that group, more than 90 percent stated that shareholder costs associated with reputation-sensitive events are matters of serious concern to boards.

Likewise, these matters should be of utmost concern to risk managers, but perhaps not for the obvious reasons. Trust is also a positive attribute that can lower the cost of doing business. Too often, people with the professional title of "risk manager" focus on losses and adopt defensive attitudes towards risk, usually through control mechanisms like policies, models, oversight, and procedural checklists. Further, these titled risk managers are not typically rewarded for the success of the company. They are, however, blamed when things go wrong — for example, if risks were not successfully "managed." Risk managers are human. They will focus on and respond to what their rewards and punishments tell them is the correct behavior — control against loss rather than work towards a reward based on the broader success of the organization. If we migrate away from the idea that risk managers are a special class of employee and towards the idea that every employee is a risk manager, we can begin to change this bias in focus.

To allow the freedom to innovate, trust must be governed and maximized, subject to our tolerance for vulnerability to loss. The enablement of trust, subject to this constraint, is part of the potential of risk management to become more valuable as a broadly developed skill. We focus more on this in Parts III and IV of the book.

TRUST AND VALUE

In the end, trust adds value to our organizations because it allows for larger networks to run more successfully. Larger networks have more opportunities to receive information and to innovate through greater interaction among agents. This mutual action increases the amount of utility that our organizations can deliver, and thus raises the numerator of the value equation.

$$Value \uparrow \; = \; U_0 + \frac{U_1 \uparrow}{DR_1} + \frac{U_2 \uparrow}{DR_2} + \frac{U_3 \uparrow}{DR_3} + \cdots$$

Trust also reduces perceived risk. In general, we are more willing to be vulnerable to risk if we expect positive outcomes from our relationship with others. Hence, external agents will be willing to part with more in exchange for what we offer. This reduces the discount rate applied to our organizations and raises our value.

$$Value \uparrow \; = \; U_0 + \frac{U_1}{DR_1 \downarrow} + \frac{U_2}{DR_2 \downarrow} + \frac{U_3}{DR_3 \downarrow} + \cdots$$

Those in our network generally want us to succeed. If they are our suppliers, they look forward to long-lasting relationships. If they are our employees, they plan their professional life and, perhaps, even their retirement based upon our success. Our customers, creditors, investors, and retirees all want us to do well.

As we transition to Part III of the book, we move from the consideration of perceptions to the realm of function. What can we be doing to better meet the expectations of our network members? What does it mean to manage our risks and to govern our institutions? Is the enablement of trust a keystone objective of our businesses? What motivates people to succeed and how can we capture and distribute that feeling?

Looks do matter, but looks alone are not enough, even if you look "mahhhvellous!"

NOTES

1   See "Trust Enabling Strategies," trustenablement.com, last accessed July 14, 2018

2   Axelrod, Robert, *The Evolution of Cooperation*, Basic Books, 1984

3   Morgan, John H., *Leaves from a Field Note-Book*, Macmillan, 1916

4   In the late 1600s, the tulip market in Holland experienced a classic bubble in prices and subsequent bust. This market is taught to many in their introductory economics courses as an example of the phenomenon. See *http://en.wikipedia.org/wiki/Tulip_mania* for a Wikipedia summary of the case.

5   Kauffman, Stuart, *The Origins of Order: Self-Organization and Selection in Evolution*, Oxford University Press, 1993

6   Dunbar, Robin, "Neocortex size as a constraint on group size in primates," *Journal of Human Evolution*, Vol. 22, No. 6z, June 1992

7   Turnbull, Shann, "Mitigating the exposure of corporate board to risk and unethical conflicts," in Kolb, Robert and Schwarz, Donald, *Corporate boards: managers of risk, sources of risk*, Wiley Blackwell, 2010

8   Walter, Ingo, "Inside Job: Reputational Risk and Conflicts of Interest" in *Banking and Finance*, March 31, 2011

9   Prof. Walter cites Smith, Clifford, "Economics and Ethics: The Case of Salomon Brothers," *Journal of Applied Corporate Finance*, Vol. 5, No. 2, Summer 1992

10 Press Release, "Goldman Sachs to Pay Record $550 Million to Settle SEC Charges Related to Subprime Mortgage CDO," Securities and Exchange Commission, July 15, 2010

11 De Long, Gayle, Saunders, Anthony, and Walter, Ingo, "Pricing Reputation-Sensitive Events in Banking and Financial Services," New York University, Department of Finance Working Paper (in draft)

PART THREE

Not Everything is Dead in the Long Run

"The long run is a misleading guide to current affairs. In the long run we are all dead."

— John Maynard Keynes, British Economist

"In the long run, men hit only what they aim at. Therefore, they had better aim at something high."

— Henry David Thoreau, American Author

CHAPTER 10

Value Revisited

In Chapter 1, we discussed how to arrive at the value of any item via an exchange between two or more willing parties. In very simple terms, the value of something at a particular moment in time is what someone else is willing to give you for it, be it live ducks or money. For example, money that isn't backed by a commodity or other asset has value simply because a government will accept it in exchange for the satisfaction of tax liabilities. The exchanges in our early examples were based on relatively certain outcomes. If you traded two shoes for one live duck and five dollars, you knew exactly what you were getting. When you made a loan to Cousin Louie, you were assured that he would pay you back.

But the world is far from certain in most cases. Even in the simple exchanges above, there is an underlying uncertainty about the future value of the things that were exchanged. Relationships with businesses or interactions among political economies are also uncertain. They are highly complex and evolve over time. Further, the benefits of these relationships can vary in both magnitude and timing.

In the parlance of mathematics and finance, the outcomes of complex interactions like these are *stochastic* or, more accurately, quasi-stochastic — they are not known with certainty and may have a wide range of possible values. Don't choke on that expression too much. Know, though, that the value equation we are trying to utilize still works well even in these very complicated relationships, where the value we receive in the future, if any, is not known in advance.

A RANDOM WALK ACROSS MIDTOWN

Midtown Manhattan is always bustling with activity — people, traffic, and interesting distractions can all be found on the way to your next meeting. Thankfully for visitors to New York, Midtown is laid out on a grid pattern of streets. Actually, the grid is made up of streets and avenues, and aside from a few unusual drifters like Broadway, the avenues run parallel to each other, uptown and downtown, and the streets intersect perpendicular to the Avenues. If you're scheduled for an appointment or plan to meet someone for dinner or a play, expect them to give you directions saying, "it's on West 53rd between 5th and 6th," meaning the address is on West 53rd Street, between 5th Avenue and 6th Avenue. It's pretty hard to get lost, even if you don't have an app on your phone to show you the way!

Lots of cities around the world are laid out in grid patterns. They are easy to navigate by car or by foot and not too overwhelming for first time visitors. In addition to being easy to navigate, envisioning a walk through the grid pattern of Midtown gives us an interesting way to consider how someone evaluates the possible outcomes of engaging with our organizations.

Think of yourself as a first-time visitor to New York. Your cab driver has just dropped you off on the West Side of Midtown at the intersection of 12th Avenue and 46th Street. He says, "Take a nice walk cross-town and see what you find along the way." You decide to take his advice and begin by surveying the sites around you, including the Hudson River, the skyline, and the Sea, Air, and Space Museum of the Aircraft Carrier *Intrepid*. You like what you see and decide to walk east on 46th Street. Feeling lucky, you plan to flip a coin to decide whether to head uptown one block or downtown one block as you walk to the next avenue. You'll do this at every intersection until you get to 1st Avenue on the other side of Midtown, sometime later that day.

Figure 10.1 A Map of Midtown Manhattan
Source: iStock.com/dikobraziy

Along the way, you plan to sample one item near each intersection — food, an art gallery, street performers, or the view of the buildings. You might even decide to stop a stranger and ask how his day is going, hoping to make a new friend. At the end of your cross-town venture, you will arrive at an unknown place, but plan to have a dinner at a restaurant near the corner of 1st Avenue and whatever cross-street you wind up on. Your expectations are great!

Now, consider for a moment what you've just decided to do. You have never been to New York! You paid for a flight to get there, a cab to take you to Midtown, likely for a hotel and a cab to take you back to the airport. Further, you only have some vague ideas about what awaits you on your cross-town journey and have begun at a point on a street grid chosen for you by a cabbie you just met 45 minutes ago at the JFK terminal. You know there is some crime in New York, right? You know that even though Midtown is relatively safe, you might encounter someone who is not looking to help you — and if you really do ask a stranger how his day is going, you might not like his response. Also, who knows if you'll like the food along the way or where you wind up for dinner? There are a lot of uncertainties here!

OH, THE POSSIBILITIES

Go back for a moment to a time before you had purchased your ticket to New York. Suppose a brochure had just arrived in the mail. In it, a tour director offers to take you to New York and to arrange a certain path through Midtown and all of the activities at each street corner. From this brochure, it would be relatively easy for you to associate a value with that specific journey. The simple question to answer is what would you be willing to exchange for it, given the relative certainty of the outcome? That is its value to you.

Because there are so many different potential outcomes in the coin-toss approach to travel, it isn't possible to determine exactly what kind of value you will receive along the way. If you wanted to be a little more rigorous in your analysis, you could make some pretty good guesses about what to expect. First, since you started at West 46th and 12th, the next corner at which you stop will be either West 47th and 11th or West 45th and 11th. Because of the rules of travel you have adopted, you could not find yourself anywhere else. So, we know that whatever you see, eat, or experience at your next stop will be on one of these two corners.

Knowing this, you could search online to see what kinds of shops and restaurants are in the area. While you cannot account for the semi-random possibilities of street encounters or unexpected offerings (think the Daily

Special at a restaurant), you'd have a pretty good idea of what to expect at these two corners.

After you're done with one of these two possible experiences, you'd next walk one block to the east and toss your coin again — "heads," you go uptown one block; "tails," you go downtown one block. So, your next stop will be at West 48th and 10th, West 46th and 10th, or West 44th and 10th. Now you have three possible corners at which you might stop on your journey through New York, and two different paths that could take you to the corner of West 46th and 10th. What your experience will entail is getting a bit more uncertain — and cumbersome to evaluate in your head — as your level of satisfaction depends on what you first do on 11th Avenue and now at your present location.

As you continue your walk throughout the afternoon, the corners at which you might find yourself will form what is called a lattice pattern, which is shown in Figure 10.2. Each possible corner is represented by a dot and the lines between them connect that place to one of the two possible places from which you could have come, and one of the two possible places to which you will go from there. You cannot arrive at West 51st and 8th, because no coin-toss directed path takes you there. Likewise, you cannot arrive at West 38th and 5th because it is out of the realm of possible paths — tossing a coin and getting "tails" each time would take you only to West 39th and 5th, no further downtown.

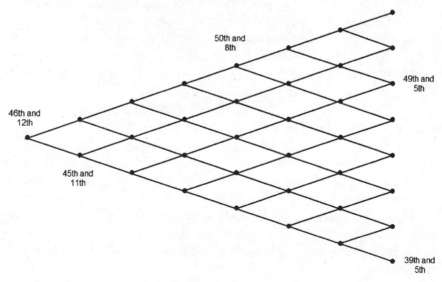

Figure 10.2 A Lattice Pattern

Figure 10.2 shows the lattice up to 5th Avenue, a pretty nice endpoint in itself. But, if you make it all the way across Midtown, you will finish somewhere between East 59th Street and East 33rd Street, on 1st Avenue. If we showed a lattice graph all the way to 1st Avenue, it would have about three times as many dots on the end as this one does, more than 100 corners on which you might find yourself during the day, and more than 16,000 paths that you could take to your endpoint. In other words, there are a lot of possible places where you might have dinner, and over 100 individual experiences you might have along the way — the satisfaction, or utility, you get from each will be dependent on the path you take to get there. With the choices at each corner and a few random encounters mixed in, the number of possible outcomes is phenomenally large.

If you were perfectly rational, as assumed in Traditional Economics, you'd know, in advance, how much you will enjoy your encounters on each corner. You'll know the exact probability of winding up on any one corner (that's the easy part) and exactly what you will do when you get there. To determine the value of the journey, you'd simply add up the value of all these possible outcomes, multiply them by their probabilities, and arrive at the average value you expect to receive from your journey across Midtown. You can then equate this to other ways to derive the same value, now or in the future, and what their cost would be to you today. The value of your cross-town walk should be no less than the cost of your trip or you will have lost value in the exchange. In the parlance of economics, you would have destroyed value (yours, personally) by making the decision to take this trip.

On the other hand, if you get more than you paid for, then the exchange of your money for this trip would have created value for you and your counterpart to this transaction. The world would have become a better place, even if just marginally.

You do have a way to estimate and represent the possible outcomes that you might realize, but it will take some work — probably more than even the most rational person can do in her head. If you use a computer to simulate your trip, you can take tens of thousands of simulated walks through Midtown, determining the value of each path taken — what you would be willing to exchange in return for that specific trip if it had been arranged in advance by the tour director.

The value of your random trip across Midtown is then derived by adding up the values of all of the thousands of computer simulations, divided by the number of simulations. This average outcome needs to be more than the cost of your trip in order for it to generate economic value for you.

In addition to knowing the average value you should expect, you might also like to know the range of possible values that you could receive and where you are most likely to be when you reach 5th Avenue. If you turn the lattice graph 90 degrees and picture yourself walking down in the same random manner, then put a ball in a slot at the end of your trip marked with the value received during each simulated walk, you'd start to get a picture that looks like that of Figure 10.3. You started on West 46th Street and there are more balls in the slots between West 45th and West 47th. So, it looks like you're most likely to get to 5th Avenue somewhere between West 45th and West 47th.

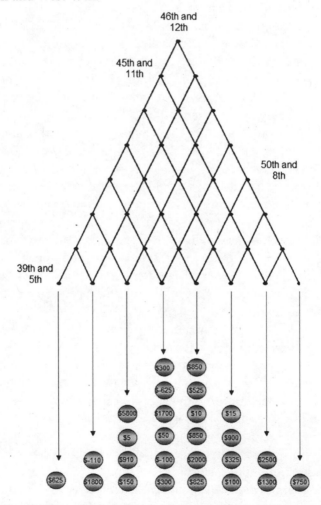

Figure 10.3 Possible Endpoints and the Value of the Path Taken to Get There

Statisticians refer to what is represented by this chart as a *probability distribution*. The one in Figure 10.3 has a shape that is tall in the middle and thin on the ends — the tails of the distribution. If we put a ball in a slot at each possible ending intersection for each of the tens of thousands of simulated trips across Midtown, the chart would stay pretty much the same shape. If we draw a line that connects all of our possible ending points on 1st Avenue, with the top ball in each stack, we'd get a graph that looks like Figure 10.4. This is called a *Bell Curve*, and it represents what is referred to as a *Normal Distribution* of outcomes.

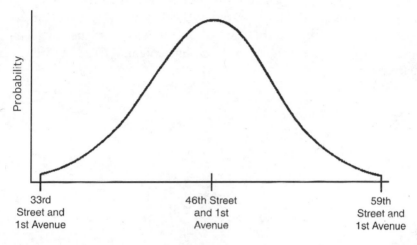

Figure 10.4 Normal Distribution of the Endpoints of Your Journey

By drawing a line from any point on the curve to the left axis, you can get a sense of how likely it is that you will end up at any one place. The farthest downtown, East 33rd and 1st, or the farthest uptown, East 59th and 1st, are not very likely destinations as there is just one path that can take you there — either 13 "tails" in a row to get to East 33rd or 13 "heads" in a row to get to East 59th. The best guess of where you will wind up is at the highest point on the graph, which is around the same street on which you began.

WHAT'S THE VALUE OF THIS JOURNEY?

Instead of arranging endpoints in buckets, let's arrange all of the values we receive from each simulated walk in order from lowest to highest, and then bucket them into small groups. From Figure 10.3, you'll see that there are different values for different trips that end up in the same place. Some of these values are even negative. Again, this is a function of the path taken to get to the last place. In some cases, you will not enjoy what you eat or see along the way, so the end result could be negative.

Figure 10.5 shows a distribution in which there are mostly good outcomes from this trip. And, the chance that you might actually derive negative value from the trip is present and shown in the left tail of the distribution of possible outcomes.

The average of all outcomes is in the middle, just below the peak of the distribution and this is your expected value of this stochastic (uncertain) process. From this graph and the simulation, you are able to measure this trip against other activities or transactions that would give you the same expected value — they are substitutes for this activity — thereby giving a sense of the value you would derive from this random walk across Midtown.

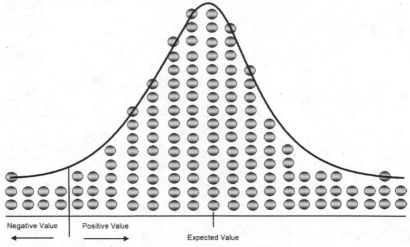

Negative Value

Positive Value

Expected Value

Figure 10.5 Positive and Negative Values in a Normal Distribution

But any town that you visit for the first time may surprise you — and this is certainly true of New York. You may find a Starbucks on so many corners that you cannot stand the thought of coffee (or the system that brought you coffee) anymore. You might wind up choosing a really bad restaurant along the way. Then, after all of your hard work and adventure, your journey might end at the doorstep of Domino's Pizza — a chain restaurant that can be found in nearly every American city. How's that for a taste of New York?

If your luck is really bad during your adventure, you might get mugged, badly injured, or even killed crossing the street! Really bad things are events that are very far to the left on the distribution of outcomes. They are much farther to the left than anything shown in Figure 10.5, and as the loss of your life is a very bad outcome, that measure of value is many multiples farther to the left than what is shown in Figure 10.5.

Fortunately, really good things can happen too. You could have such an amazing set of experiences on your trek through Midtown that the value you derive is unbelievably large. Perhaps you ran into some long-lost friends, had a fantastic lunch at Le Bernadin, met a celebrity you've long admired, found a $100 bill on the street, and saw a fabulous show at Radio City Music Hall. You then finished the day with dinner at a four-star restaurant where you subsequently, and quite by chance, met the love of your life.

You couldn't have wished for a better day than that!

Really good outcomes are farther out to the right of the distribution in Figure 10.5. And some, such as that described above, are many multiples farther to the right than what is shown on the graph.

UTILITY FUNCTIONS

To this point in the book, we've used utility and value interchangeably. That's not technically correct, except when there is no uncertainty of the outcome, or no risk. The degree of uncertainty present in any choice impacts how people perceive the value of something via a *utility function*. We discussed the role of biases in Chapter 6 and also briefly mentioned utility functions. But, now that we have developed a concept of a distribution of outcomes, the impact of Prospect Theory — which concerns utility functions, risk aversion, and loss avoidance — becomes even more important.

Not every person has the same utility function. Some people are wildly risk-averse, meaning that any kind of loss creates very high negative utility for them. Others love risk because the thrill of taking chances brings them pleasure. They may even have little regard for the losses their risk-taking might cause others. To determine the value of engaging with any one member of our network, it is helpful to understand these differences.

Broadly speaking, we can make some statements about the utility functions of those in our network collectively and how those functions affect the value of our organizations. To do so, we need to be cognizant of the biases that affect people's decisions — in other words, the things that impact their assessment of expected utility — the "somethings" in the numerator of our Value Equation that they expect to receive from us.

FAT TAILS, UTILITY, AND VALUE

In nature, extremely good and bad outcomes are much more likely to happen than the normal distribution would have us believe. This frequency in the extremes creates a graphical picture where the distribution has what are called *fat tails*. See Figure 10.6 for a comparison of a "fat-tailed" distribution to that of the normal distribution. Fat tails are common outcomes when complex systems of agents interact, as both positive and negative events are open to amplification effects.

In nature, fat tails are found everywhere from the measurements of solar flare intensity to the size of cities, stock price movements, and the magnitude of earthquakes. In fact, the Richter scale of earthquake magnitude models the fat tail of the distribution of energy released by all earthquakes using something physicists call a *power law*. Power laws are relationships that can be described when one factor changes at an exponential rate driven by a change in another factor. For example, an earthquake that measures 5.0 on the Richter scale is 10 times larger than one that measures 4.0. The power, in this power law, is 10.

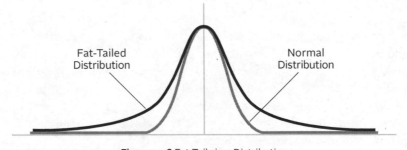

Figure 10.6 Fat Tails in a Distribution

Remember, people don't like large losses. We referred to this behavioral bias as loss avoidance. If a range of possible outcomes from a relationship or game is presented to you, and it includes your possible death, if you are like most people, you will avoid them. If you are considering an investment or charitable donation to an organization and there is a real possibility that most of your contribution will be lost or go to waste, you will demand a substantially higher emotional reward before choosing to be involved. A political economy with high risk of political upheaval will have difficulty attracting capital investments from other places.

So, take yourself back to your home and envision the Random Walk Across Midtown brochure arriving in the mail. It's highly transparent and gives you a good sense of the possible adventures that await you. Would you leave the comfort and security of your house to book the trip if it included a possible mugging? Would you be willing to part with your money if the description of your ending dinner was a chain-store pizza?

Fat-tail losses give people a reason to say "no." We, therefore, want to avoid presenting the possibility of fat-tail losses to the extent it is practical to do so.

PARALLELS TO ORGANIZATIONAL LIFE IN SYSTEMS

Exploring New York is an interaction with thousands of systems. And, this illustration is helpful to us both as a detailed way of determining the value of something that is uncertain, as well as providing us with an allegory of how others will arrive at a value of our organization.

A relationship with an employer or the decision to move to another city or country can be viewed in the same way as this cross-town adventure. You don't know exactly what to expect along the way, as there are many possible paths to be taken. Similarly, committing to be a supplier to a company, an investor in a start-up, or signing a long-term contract with another entity involves uncertain outcomes that are all path-dependent.

It is safe to assume that when you gave $10 to a charity fundraiser last week, you didn't run 10,000 computer simulations of their work to see if it was worth $10 to you. Probably, when you purchased your last stock, you only used the computer to do some very basic research on the company. And, have you ever run a computer simulation of the job that you have just been offered?

Most people don't, even if they are computer-savvy and diligent about investing. People tend to make decisions based on feelings, heuristics, input from their Strong Ties, and information gathered in the environment in which they interact. In effect, people take a shortcut for developing a probability distribution by using their networks. This process is impacted by the biases and network influences that we discussed in Part II and is especially affected when the size of potential losses is large enough to have a significant impact on the perceiver's well-being.

Still, you should be aware that some investors and businesses will commit their resources to these types of simulations, either via quantitative models or discursive analysis. And, for some financial instruments to be valued correctly, this advanced simulation work is required.

Regardless of which approach is taken, the shape of the distribution of potential outcomes matters greatly. Among the most important parts of the distribution are the tails, and most especially the left tail, where losses are depicted.

We really have a complicated picture to deal with when figuring out the value of your trip. Somehow, you have to incorporate the chance that you might not reach your final destination and all of the possible negative outcomes that you might encounter along the way. What if you get robbed within five minutes of starting your trek? You'll have no money and no credit cards to continue your trip, and therefore negative utility from the whole experience. This outcome is just like the cleaning company showing up once and then never coming back again. Or, it's like buying a WorldCom bond on the day before news that would lead to its bankruptcy was announced (I actually know someone to whom this happened).

Can we increase our chances of successfully overcoming problems that might occur?

WE'RE POSITIVELY SKEWED!

In Roger Fisher and William Ury's well-known book, *Getting to YES*, they introduce the need for avoiding "no" by noting that we are always negotiating for something — raises at work, a joint venture, a labor contract, or a number of other business or personal transactions. Negotiation is a basic means of getting what you want from others.[1] Their method of principled negotiation is focused on merits, or positive utility, that can be derived through agents joining each other's networks in some economic fashion. It seeks ways to facilitate exchanges that are perceived to be mutually beneficial.

If you are trying to attract economic capital, you have to work to avoid "no" (the left tail) and get to "yes." There needs to be a positive skew to the expectations others have of interacting with your organization and taking further steps towards achieving that positive perception is what we deal with next.

NOTES

1   Fisher, Roger, and Ury, William L., *Getting to YES*, Penguin, 1991

CHAPTER 11

The Role of Resiliency in Creating Value

As you know by now, the Value Equation increases when the utility (something good) we provide to others goes up and goes down when others perceive a greater risk that we might disappoint them. That covers two of the three factors on which we've focused so far in this book.

The third factor in the Value Equation has to do with the endurance of our ability to generate utility for those who transact with us; how we structure, or govern, our organizations will greatly affect this value.

Let's look again at the cleaning service that offered to clean your house each week for a year. You received a discount for paying up front for that whole year. Part of your risk assessment in determining the fair value of that payment was consideration of whether the cleaning company would be around for the whole year to fulfill its obligation. If it went bankrupt six months into the term of your agreement, you would have vastly overpaid for the services you received.

$$Value \downarrow = U_0 + \frac{U_1}{DR_1} + \frac{U_2}{DR_2} + \frac{U_3}{DR_3} + \overleftarrow{(\cdots)}$$

When you invest in a government bond or corporate note, you are making a loan to the government or a company. You are promised interest payments on a regular schedule and a return of your investment at the end of the agreed upon time period. But, if that company or government becomes substantially impaired or goes away before they pay you back, you will realize substantial losses.

Now, assume that someone who is an external member of your network is considering whether to be a customer of yours, or to partner with you in some contractual way. That person will think about you in the same way as you did about the cleaning company and the government or corporation that issued the debt for your investment. She wants you to be around for as long as you could possibly provide her with something of value — something that gives her utility. She doesn't want to be disappointed.

RESILIENCE

In reality, no organization operates without an occasional hiccup. The goal of our governance efforts is to successfully manage these missteps — to be resilient. This means that we have the ability to spring back; rebound; return to the original form or position after being bent, compressed, or stretched; or recover readily from illness, depression, or adversity; to be buoyant.[1] It sounds just like what we need to avoid letting people down!

In your walk across Midtown, you'd increase your resiliency by wearing a travel belt with extra cash stashed inside, or an ATM card hidden somewhere that a robber cannot see it. You'd carry a mobile phone and contact information for hospitals, friends you know, the police, and emergency services. You might even commit to memory some of the places to avoid near various intersections so that you don't make a random choice that turns out badly. A resilient organization might secure back-up lines of credit, diversify its donor base, or study what other organizations have done when faced with specific challenges so that they can be prepared to manage a similar situation.

In short, a resilient traveler, or a resilient organization, is ready to adapt and bounce back in the event of an unexpected problem.

BRITTLENESS

At the other end of the resiliency spectrum lies brittleness — a not so nice sounding word. If someone is described as "brittle," it means that person has hardness and rigidity but little tensile strength; breaking readily with a comparatively smooth fracture (like glass), easily damaged or destroyed; fragile; frail; lacking warmth, sensitivity, or compassion; aloof; self-centered.[2] Needless to say, we don't want our organization to be like that.

SINGLE POINTS OF FAILURE

In the fall of 2002, *The Atlantic* carried an article entitled *Homeland Insecurity*, which helpfully illustrates the importance of resiliency and the downfalls of brittleness.[3] The article's protagonist is Bruce Schneier, known worldwide for his work in cryptography and cyber security.

Cryptography is one element of the science of information security, allowing for data to be safely stored or transmitted across public media like the Internet in a manner that only the owner or the intended receiver is able to decipher. Schneier was so good in his work at cryptography that the FBI and the U.S. Congress wanted to ban it for fear that his technologies could be used by terrorists, criminals, and other assorted bad guys. If his work was allowed to go on, they argued, the authorities would find it nearly impossible to gather important evidence for prosecutions or to be able to interdict planned terrorist attacks. They were right, at least on the first point.

Schneier no longer believes that super-encryption is totally secure and neither do many criminals. It turns out that there is a critical flaw in the encryption process, making the technology extremely vulnerable to very large negative outcomes when one simple failure occurs. At the sending and receiving end of encrypted messages are human beings. They encrypt and decipher messages using technologies that are password-protected. Most people cannot remember complicated passwords. So, they will encrypt and decipher messages using relatively simple passwords and, once someone figures out what that password is, the encryption protection is broken and the message's secrets revealed.

This kind of vulnerability is called a *Single Point of Failure*. It describes complicated and complex systems that come undone because one thing went wrong. When they break, they break badly.

According to the *Atlantic* story, the FBI was trying to gather evidence on a suspected Mafia figure named Nicodemo Scarfo. When the FBI searched his office, they discovered that he was indeed using strong encryption on his documents and email communications. They simply installed a keyboard logger on his machine, captured the password to the public key software he used, and very shortly thereafter Scarfo was in court, pleading guilty to charges of running an illegal gambling business. For Scarfo, his security system broke badly. His system and the entire enterprise were surprisingly brittle.

In a far more serious — and by now notorious — case, a bunch of terrorists got past airline security on September 11, 2001 — one check at each airport they used. Once accomplished, they had no other serious impediments to their plans to hijack planes and crash them into buildings in New York and Washington, D.C. Airport security at that time had a single point of failure and the impact of that weakness in the system was catastrophic. This system's failure cost the lives of thousands of innocent people and continues to bring changes — such as tougher airport security, political and military conflicts, and follow-on attacks — even all these years later.

But not all failures are criminal. Companies with single products, like emerging bio-technology firms that have yet to receive full regulatory approval, have single points of failure, which, if realized, could be catastrophic for their investors. Or, businesses that have over-reliance on one customer or depend on short-term funding (which, in turn, is dependent on credit ratings issued by a few like-minded, like-acting companies), are subject to quick and dramatic ends to their existence if these keystone parties fail or walk away.

Sony, Equifax, Citigroup, and the U.S. government are just a few of many organizations which have discovered that storing large amounts of sensitive data on single networks or in single databases makes them highly desirable targets for cyber-thieves. If the security protecting them has a single point of failure, the personal or embarrassing information in those files may find its way to criminals, public websites, or other places where it could cause great harm. These may not be fatal events for those organizations, but they are bound to be costly and affect their ability to achieve corporate goals for quite some time.

As Bruce Schneier notes in the *Atlantic* article, we should expect all systems to fail at some point in time. For those seeking to better govern their organizations, the focus must therefore be on creating systems that responds well to problems — ones that break well.

THE PATH OF A PROBLEM

Every problem that emerges at a company, in technology, political economies, or other parts of our lives, has two key characteristics. First, the problem has a *potential impact*. Second, the problem needs time to develop and to reach its potential impact.

A fire on the stove in a kitchen, for example, has the potential to burn down the entire house if not stopped in time. If that house is a row house, the fire has the potential to burn down the entire block. Further, if the block of homes is large enough and the external conditions are right, the fire could spread from block to block and become quite catastrophic. The City of Chicago had a famous fire in 1871 that, legend has it, was started when "Mrs. O'Leary's cow" kicked over a lantern in a barn. The fire consumed roughly four square miles of the city before it extinguished itself at the shores of Lake Michigan. It went down in United States' history as one of that century's worst disasters.

Or, consider a calculation error in a spreadsheet that assigns an incorrectly high value to an investment product that a company has the opportunity to buy. If that spreadsheet misleads the company into believing that the market price of these securities is too low, it may begin to amass "undervalued" securities, even booking unrealized profits and reporting them in their earnings reports to investors. Over time, the company may even accumulate so much of these securities that, if forced to sell, it will discover an error of such magnitude that it leads to its demise, or, in the very least, to very large losses. Many of the losses incurred during the subprime crisis were the result of inaccurately calculated risks and overvaluation of the originated assets.

Figure 11.1 shows the "path of a problem," with the bottom axis representing time and the left axis representing the impact of the problem. If left unchecked as time progresses, over seconds or even years, the problem will cause its full potential impact. That impact may be very small or it may be large enough to break the system within which the problem is emerging. Unchecked, all problems will eventually reach their potential impact.

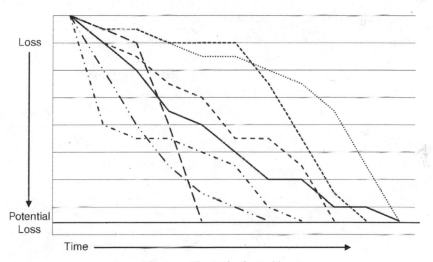

Figure 11.1 The Path of a Problem

Not unlike your walk across Midtown, any organization is also taking a walk of sorts across time, encountering potential opportunities and dangers, meeting new customers and prospective partners, and being exposed to internal and external elements that might cause it problems.

The value of that organization today is determined in the same manner as the value of your trip across Midtown — by looking at all of the possible outcomes, their value, and the probability that they will be realized. These can be represented using a probability distribution like the one we viewed in Chapter 10.

Problems result in negative values or losses for that organization and also, potentially, for those who are part of its network. The larger the potential impact of a problem, the larger its potential to reduce the value of the company to those in its network. And, as the likelihood of problems increases, so do the chances that losses could ensue.

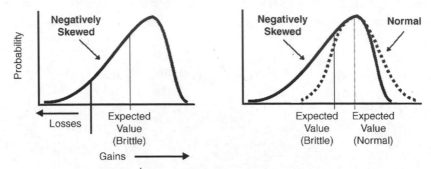

Figure 11.2 Negatively Skewed Distribution When Problems Go Uninterrupted

When looking at possible outcomes for the journey that most companies make, the probability distribution, with problems left unchecked, actually looks a bit more like that of Figure 11.2. Note that in this distribution, some very large losses — huge negative values — are possible.

In fact, with uninterrupted problems, the distribution has a rather strange shape to it, because possibilities for gain are disproportionately small compared to the possibilities for loss. This is called a negatively skewed distribution and, all else equal, an organization with this distribution as opposed to the normal distribution, will be worth less.

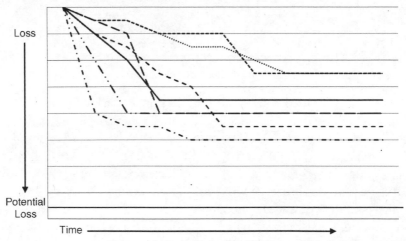

Figure 11.3 The Path of a Problem Interrupted

Now, a resilient organization will find a way to interrupt large problems before they reach their potential impact, even those that threaten the life of the system. Figure 11.3 shows the path of problems that have been intercepted by agents within a resilient system.

When growing problems can be intercepted and managed so that they never reach their potential impact, organizations are able to truncate the losses in the distribution. These cases are represented by the point at which each line in Figure 11.3 goes horizontally and never reaches its full potential loss. This is the point at which the problem was stopped. Truncating the left side, or loss side, of the distribution of possible outcomes alone will increase the value of the organization.

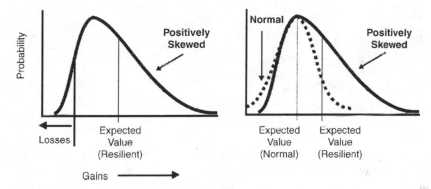

Figure 11.4 Positively Skewed Distribution in Well-Governed, Resilient Organizations

Well-governed organizations are resilient and are also structured so that positive ideas are more likely to be engendered and positive value created. In this case, the distribution is a mirror opposite of the brittle distribution, with the possibilities for gain being disproportionately large compared to the possibilities for loss. This is called a positively skewed distribution, which is shown in Figure 11.4. All else equal, an organization with this distribution, as opposed to either a normal distribution or a negatively skewed distribution, will be worth more.

THREATS TO THE SYSTEM

An organization seeking to establish practices internally that enhance resiliency would do well to develop a list of critical risks and to look for examples of where emergent problems have developed into larger issues. For example, and just a small subset of the possibilities, potential problems can develop from factors such as:

1. Changing technology or innovation by competitors

2. Loss of a high value client or supporter

3. Product recalls or liability

4. Regulatory changes or enforcement actions

5. Weather

6. Malfeasance

7. War

8. Terrorism

9. Loss of liquidity

10. Human error

11. Loss of key people

12. Supply chain disruption

13. Keystone third party failure

And we have seen results from these exact causes. For example, IBM famously missed the innovation in technology that moved computers from the mainframe to the desktop models in the 1980s. Innovators like Dell Computers took advantage of the rigidity in the IBM legacy sales infrastructure to sell directly to consumers, a change that IBM would have found very difficult to implement. Between 1988 and the end of 1993, IBM stock fell by more than 50 percent while the NASDAQ index of technology stocks more than doubled and the stock of Dell rose by over 700 percent.

Or take the case of Arthur Andersen, which began auditing Enron's accounting books in the mid-1980s. In 2001, Enron announced that it would take an after-tax charge of several hundred million dollars against earnings related to accounting errors on various partnerships, and that it would restate several years' worth of earnings. Enron's stock price fell from $90 per share to nearly zero and the company declared bankruptcy. Its President was subsequently convicted of multiple felonies and sent to jail. Conflicts of interest apparently had motivated Andersen to sign off on what some thought were questionable accounting practices at Enron. The firm was subsequently charged with obstruction of justice when it was discovered that members of its Houston office had shredded documents relevant to a SEC investigation of Enron. In August of 2002, the company shuttered its auditing practice.

Capital One Financial, one of the largest issuers of credit cards and other loans to individuals, was the subject of a regulatory review in 2002 that resulted in a supervisory action against the company. The day after Capital One issued a press release announcing the action its stock price plummeted by 40 percent. The loss in market capitalization realized over the ensuing weeks was more than $7 billion.

Even political economies are not immune from emerging issues of massive scale. Economic crises in various Latin American countries in 1982, in Mexico in 1994, in some Asian countries in 1997 and 1998, and in Russia during 1998, caused significant economic disruptions therein and losses for external members of their networks as well. Liquidity crises in these regions led to massive outflows of foreign capital, increased cost of capital, and lower standard of living for people working or residing in those countries.

And as we know, the reliance on human beings virtually assures some error, sometimes on a horrific scale. In 1984, a massive toxic gas leak at the Union Carbide plant in Bhopal, India killed thousands of people and injured hundreds of thousands of residents near the plant. Among the causes of the disaster were the failure of an employee to close a critical isolation valve which led to excessive pressurization of the tank containing the gas; the shutdown of a flare which would have neutralized escaping gas; staffing at a critical unit that was less than half of what was recommended; the elimination of a key maintenance supervisory position just weeks before the disaster; the lack of evacuation plans for the area surrounding the plant, and the government's classification of the plant as a "general industry" and not a "hazardous industry," which allowed the construction of residences close to the source of the leak.[4]

We see the potential for global warming under development. If realized to the extent that many have warned, it may cause massive famine, migration, and war.[5,6] Reactions to terrorism have a long tail in terms of time. For extended periods, people can lose freedoms and liberty. The loss of key people from an organization can greatly diminish its creative capacity, leading to an underperformance over time from its potential — a loss of prospective value.

These problems take time to emerge, but are always reaching for their full potential impact. Even this short list of sources and cases gives us a sense that both internal and external developments can create problems for organizations. If left unchecked, these problems can substantially limit an organization's ability to achieve its goals or even put an end to its existence.

LOSS AVOIDANCE REVISITED

Remember that potentially large losses factor heavily in the overall valuation of any relationship. When presented with the possibility of both large gains and large losses in a game of chance, people will usually demand positive compensation two to three times what is presented to them in terms of possible losses. Otherwise, that game will not be attractive.

For small losses, the loss avoidance effect is not present. If someone asks you to play a game where you might lose one dollar when a fair coin is tossed, in exchange for making one dollar if the coin toss went your way, you might play the game just for the fun of it. But, if the game changed in such a way that you could lose one million dollars on the toss of a coin, you likely wouldn't agree to play unless you could earn between two and three million dollars on a favorable toss.

$$Value \downarrow = U_0 + \frac{U_1}{\underset{\uparrow}{DR_1}} + \frac{U_2}{\underset{\uparrow}{DR_2}} + \frac{U_3}{\underset{\uparrow}{DR_3}} + \cdots$$

The corollary to this is that any partner or potential partner outside of your organization will assess possible negative outcomes from a relationship with your organization, looking for the possibility of large losses, and, if finding them, demanding ever-greater possibilities of large gain. Larger gains can be attained by greatly increasing the risk premium they require, making it more expensive for you to interact with them. They increase the cost to you of acquiring their economic capital and, as you recall, an increased risk premium lowers the Value Equation.

BECOMING RESILIENT

Resilient organizations can greatly reduce the possibilities of large loss for those who become part of their network. This has the effect of lowering required risk premiums and raising the value of the organization. It is less expensive for your organization to acquire economic capital when it is perceived as being, or even better, actually is, resilient.

What if Mrs. O'Leary and her neighbor agreed to keep an eye on each other's barns? What if the cockpit doors of commercial airlines had been reinforced with locks before 2001? Today, access to sensitive facilities often requires multiple forms of validation, from pass codes to secret questions, and even biometrics like retinal scans or fingerprint readers. These high-security checks must all be sequentially passed before access is granted. We refer to such systems as requiring *Multiple Points of Failure* before they break.

Interrupting problems before they reach their potential is one form of resiliency. What we are driving for in this case is a kind of attenuation or the gradual loss in intensity of any kind of negative disturbance in our systems. For instance, sunlight is attenuated by dark glasses, or sound by walls. We'd like our organization's problems to be lessened in much the same way, giving us corporate agility to respond to emerging risks.

$$Value \uparrow = U_0 + \frac{U_1}{DR_1} + \frac{U_2}{DR_2} + \frac{U_3}{DR_3} + \overrightarrow{(\cdots)}$$

Our Strong and Weak Ties will play a role in this process as will our organizational structure. We're looking for ways to make the most of our network; bringing in ideas, as well as detecting and halting emerging problems. We're striving for a high degree of return on our economic capital, while not allowing any single activity we undertake to have sufficiently large negative risks to impair or end our ability to live our values and to meet our organizational or personal objectives.

Trial by fire isn't necessarily bad. *Annealing* is a process in metallurgy wherein a material is heated to extreme levels and altered, causing changes in its strength and hardness. Organizations that face stresses like those described above are in effect going through a form of annealing and the only question is whether their reformed condition is improved or permanently damaged.

We are working to reshape our organizations — reshaping the distribution of possible outcomes — so that our organizations have a positive skew and are more valuable to others, thereby making better use of our scarce economic capital.

In the next chapter we will look at motivators, with a primary focus on the internal members of our network. What risks do we face from incentives to be productive? What drives people to attain goals? Is there a way to establish common interests to affect systems that are not presently managed well? We'll then move into Part IV of the book where we will examine the governance structures that will get us there.

Be resilient and carry on!

NOTES

1 Source: Dictionary.com, *www.dictionary.com/browse/resilient*

2 Source: Dictionary.com, *www.dictionary.com/browse/brittle*

3 Mann, Charles C., "Homeland Insecurity," *The Atlantic*, Vol. 290, No. 2, September 2002, pp. 81–102

4 Peterson, M.J., "Case Study: Bhopal Plant Disaster" IDEESE Case Study Series, 2008

5 Clark, Andrew, "Climate Change Threatens Security, UK tells UN," *The Guardian*, April 18, 2007

6 See the website of the Union of Concerned Scientists, *www.ucsusa.org*

CHAPTER 12

The Things That Motivate People

Management guru Daniel Pink relates his early journalism training to organizational behavior and design by using the "Five W's and an H" formula. Who, what, where, when, why, and how — that's what you need to write a story.[1] There is a story we're trying to write — a story about living our values and achieving our goals.

Pink says the "how" in his allegory to running a business is handled by the universities, business schools, and those who train our employees. The "who" is determined by human resources and outside recruiters. The CEO and consulting advisors determine the "what." Subsequently, the "where" and "when" are the domains of logistics, management, and the supply chain network. We would add the board, investors, regulators, customers, and others in the organization's social network to the "who, what, where, when, and how" as well.

But where is the "why" handled, he rightly asks?

We could simply move to the top of the organizational hierarchy and say that the board, through its foundational documents, determines strategy, mission, vision, and the like (in fact, we did say this in Chapter 1!). Where there is a board, it tells us the "why," as well as "where" the organization is heading. But, before a board of directors ever exists, a visionary leader with an idea assumes the role of director. Her ambition may be modest or world-changing, but just sharing her vision with someone is not enough to see it realized. Someone has to do the work and, in most cases, it's going to take more than one person to do this well.

In Chapter 3, we examined the power of self-organizing groups and in Chapter 8 we looked at how groups can amplify situations for both positive and negative results. We know that something triggers a group to form from one person's initiation. Group formation means that some kind of a threshold has been reached with the second person who joins in, and so on.

In most cases, there is a clear call for action that the group is heeding. For example, "Let's go to the pub for a beer," can prompt a group of like-minded individuals to form. "Let's end polio worldwide," can as well.

But group formation does not mean group success. That requires an ongoing motivation and the continuation of a journey whose short-term and sometimes long-term destiny is well-understood.

WHAT MOTIVATES OUR BEHAVIOR WITHIN ORGANIZATIONS?

For a moment, we'll focus on motivation within profit-making entities. We expect that money is what motivates anyone within these organizations to do their work. Profit for an individual can come in the form of salary or hourly wage — the exchange made for the economic capital that person brings to the group. Depending on the behavior desired by the governing body of the company, individual profit may also come from incentives for performance in support of corporate or individual goals and objectives. Incentives might be paid for successfully selling a product, or for a process of production that exceeds quality targets — reducing the costs of errors and related negative perceptions.

But people in these groups span a wide range of personality types and utility functions and the roles they play vary in their ability to be affected by money alone. Think for a moment about the entrepreneur who started the company. His compensation was entirely driven by the success of the firm and it is highly likely that he received no salary during the early years. If he failed, he may have lost everything he had built up to the time he began the company. He was extremely motivated to succeed, but probably didn't take the risks of going out on his own only to receive money.

It was fashionable in the 1980s and 1990s, to try to design incentive compensation systems so that everyone in the company "acted like an owner" or an entrepreneur. Stockholders are owners. So, the logic went, if employees had a right to own some company stock, they would focus their work on achieving profits to drive that stock price higher. But, rather than encourage stock ownership, many companies developed stock option plans that also broadly rewarded employees when the company's stock price increased.

To no surprise for those who understand option pricing, these plans have generally failed and have even been the source of massive abuses, as in the case of United Health Group and others.[2] Options give unlimited upside potential and, when granted, have no cost to the recipient. They have a "hockey-stick" payout profile that rewards big gains but does not penalize for large losses. In effect, they are free lottery tickets and stimulate the taking of very large and very risky bets. Being an entrepreneur is not without potential costs, therefore the misalignment of option awards begins at the moment the options are granted.

Professors William Gerald Sanders of Brigham Young University and Donald C. Hambrick of Penn State conducted research that showed CEOs who receive substantial option-based compensation take high-risk bets with firm's economic capital and don't bet very well.[3] In addition, their study found that stock option programs tend to bring about relatively large outcomes, both good and bad. In other words, stock option programs for CEOs increase the volatility of expected outcomes, making the tails of the distribution of possible outcomes even bigger — there is more risk to dealing with these companies.

Further, their research found that the heavy use of options brings about more large losses than large gains, negatively skewing results. Remember the impact of loss avoidance from those in our network when the distribution of possible outcomes includes fat tails of loss and a negative skew? Value is being destroyed by these programs when the intention was to stimulate value creation.

Monetary incentives are not to be discarded entirely. They have a role to play when crafted to fit specific desired behaviors. Still, most of us would like to think that we are motivated by other things than money. And, the good news is that most of us are. So, why is there such a strong focus on monetary incentives? Once our compensation reaches a threshold of sustenance, and maybe even a little comfort, the cost to attract additional amounts of our human economic capital probably becomes increasingly steep, unless there is something more that we can get from our work within organizations — something that money cannot buy.

DO INCENTIVES EVEN WORK?

In his 2009 book, *Drive*, Daniel Pink claims that monetary incentives fail more often than they succeed. He argues that creative and innovative work is stifled by what he refers to as extrinsic rewards, and suggests that a better focus is on what drives people from the inside, the intrinsic rewards people get from a job well done or from helping someone in need.

Pink also claims that for routine roles where processes are repetitive and where quality and speed are simultaneously beneficial, monetary rewards have been shown to work. But in other cases, they have been found to only have short-term benefits and may even have a negative long-run impact on employee performance.

Pink says that better incentive plans do not take carrot-and-stick approaches to money and performance. Rather, they look to intrinsically reward employees for creative and value-generating work. He lists three elements that lead to success via his approach:

1. *Autonomy.* This is the desire to direct our own lives. Pink believes that this is our default setting. He cites the reported success of various "Results-Only Work Environments" like that of Best Buy. He also cites research at Cornell University showing that a review of over 300 small firms found that those offering autonomy grew four times as fast as those that did not. Further, those companies had one-third of the employee turnover rate experienced by others. By autonomy, he does not mean granting complete independence. Rather, he means allowing employees to act with choice that is both autonomous and happily interdependent with others. Autonomy also does not preclude full accountability to others in the system.

2. *Mastery.* This is the urge to get better at something that matters. Pink refers to a concept called "flow," which is realized/experienced when the challenges someone faces are matched ideally to their abilities. It is a feeling we get when we are so deeply immersed in the task at hand, we lose the sense of time. Flow can lead to mastery, as long as a person has a mindset that is always seeking improvement and if goals are clear, and the efforts to achieve them, are as well.

3. *Purpose.* This is the yearning to do what we do in the service of something larger than ourselves. Purpose provides a context for autonomy and mastery. Pink describes a new "purpose motive" in goals that use profits to reach a purpose, in words that emphasize more than self-interest, and in policies that allow people to pursue purpose on their own terms.

In a well-governed organization, an environment can be created that allows employees to flourish, releasing the creativity that stimulates innovation and growth in complex systems. Employees can get more out of their organizations and their organizations can get more out of their workers. This is a key source of the "somethings" that emerge when complex systems work well and fostering it doesn't always require money.

Common ideals and goals help create more Strong Ties within an organization. There is greater trust and greater efficiency when Strong Ties abound. At the same time, there is a need for freedom, within some defined boundaries, in order to bring in new ideas and to avoid complexity collapses. Most workers want to be part of a solution to a problem or to know that their efforts have contributed to something more than they could have done on their own.

MANAGEMENT BY OBJECTIVES

Organizations where managers and workers agree to what is to be achieved and understand what is needed in the context of an organization's values is referred to as *Management by Objectives*, a term popularized by management consultant Peter Drucker in his book *The Practice of Management*.

This concept envisions collaboration in setting goals, choosing how those goals will be achieved, and how decisions will be made. In this model, actual performance needs to be measurable according to some standards and goals set by both the employee and the manager. When done success-fully, employees understand individual and corporate goals, and how their individual efforts relate to the success of the organization as a whole.

The belief is that involving employees in goal-setting and measurement will increase their sense of ownership and accomplishment when they are successful, which lowers personnel turnover and makes workers feel more empowered to make decisions.

Management by Objectives also emphasizes the role of communication, encouraging frequent interaction between managers and employees, iden-tifying problems as they emerge, and working towards course correction, if necessary.

Objectives need not be just individual and organization-wide to be successful. Rather, smaller systems can be identified within the larger orga-nization and objectives can be set for those groups as well. It is then up to successive levels of management to ensure that the goals of each sub-system are aligned with the goals of the larger system.

One advantage of Management by Objectives is that there is a certain amount of freedom given at each level of management. Pink believes that freedom, or autonomy, is essential for people to be properly motivated. Further, if freedom to create and pursue goals within a sub-system can be achieved, it will reduce the risk of communication errors when goals are merely passed through multiple layers of hierarchy, being distorted each time they are relayed.

DARLEY'S LAW

Management by Objectives can also be used inappropriately to over-quantify outcomes. In the expression "what gets measured, gets managed," Drucker attempts to affirm the wisdom of the approach. However, each of us should also take the adage as a warning, since incentives that reward the achievement of objectives are often overly designed to be based on metrics of performance.

There are also important psychological aspects to how humans within our systems will respond to incentives to perform better. In particular, work by John Darley, professor emeritus at Princeton University, finds that rigid or overly quantified incentive systems can create new risks of their own, which are unknown or unexpected to those involved in the system.

Darley's Law says, "The more any quantitative performance measure is used to determine a group or an individual's rewards and punishments, the more subject it will be to corruption pressures and the more apt it will be to distort and corrupt the action patterns and thoughts of the group or individual it is intended to monitor."[4]

Darley's Law is a good warning to organizations that employ overly objective incentive systems. Humans are quite adept at manipulating rules to personal benefit. Success in recognizing this phenomenon and in aligning incentives with behavioral objectives means that incentives must be carefully crafted so that the mix of measurable and qualitative inputs to the award, along with intrinsic rewards, match the behavior desired from the individual. We must understand how humans respond to incentives and controls before we are able to build structures to match desired behaviors with rewards.

The general intent of metric-based incentive systems is to develop measures of how individual contributions have helped the organization to reach corporate goals. By inference, the corporate goals are metrics like share price, earnings, and market share, expecting that the company will be rewarded by the market for meeting goals and punished for not doing so. Such systems are designed to pay off those who make their numbers and punish those who do not.

Incentive systems, simple or complicated, are typically based on objective measures upon which all parties agree in advance. Employers formulate a choice and employees respond to the potential outcomes perceived and the risks with which they associate them.

The appeal of such systems for the employer is in the perception that they provide more predictable budgeting, they may make employees behave more like owners, and they help retain attractive human capital.

Such systems, though, may inadvertently attract a concentration of a certain type of human capital. Employees who are averse to subjective systems under which they perceive less control are more likely to be drawn to highly objective systems. The cause of their preference may be related to a level of trust in organizations, or something deeper in the personality of the employee. Whatever the source, the more rigidity there is, the more tightly defined the personality attracted to it will be, and the greater the potential impact of concentrated misalignment — a greater chance of a single point of failure.

Prospect Theory research has yielded numerous examples of how the framing of a choice can greatly alter how that choice is perceived by humans. If the behavior that an organization is seeking to stimulate through metric-based incentives provides the employee with a choice in an incorrect manner, the organization might be creating risk of which it is not aware, or, in fact, exacerbating risk that it thought the incentive system was reducing. Further, this risk might be highly concentrated in places where its realization is likely to have high negative impact, like sales teams or business line management.

Professor Darley also suggests that highly objective systems may cause unintended and morally-surprising outcomes. Objective systems may create certain pressures on the actors within the system that may not be at all what the performance-measurers intended. This goes beyond the framing issue of Prospect Theory and into even more complex behavioral notions.

Three general sorts of occasions arise when a metric-based system is not designed well, morally:

1. A person, in hopes of advancement or in fear of falling behind, cheats on the performance measurement system by exploiting its weaknesses to make her numbers. Others who see this — and especially if this action succeeds — are then under pressure to cheat also. There is a diffusion of a corrupt innovation that corrupts the individuals within the system. This group behavior can become pervasive. Consider two employees at the same level in an organization, both seeking advancement within the organization. If one succeeds in cheating, the second may perceive his chances for promotion slipping away. That person is thus pressured to engage in the same or better cheating. The increased cheating is more likely to stimulate copycat behavior by other advancement-hungry peers.

2. A person with the best will in the world does what optimizes her performance measurements, without realizing that this is not what the system really intended. A performance measurement system is a powerful communication tool indicating that the authorities have thought these issues through and want what they reward. The individuals in the system are to some extent relieved of their responsibilities to think through the system goals, and to independently determine their contributions to those goals. In this instance, the rules of the game have been defined and the employee simply plays the game to her highest benefit.

3. A person who has the best interests of the system in mind may game the performance measurement system in various ways, to allow the continuation of the actions that best fulfill his reading of the system goals. However, this behavior takes those activities underground, and diminishes the possibilities of a dialogue about system goals or modifications in the system's measurements.

There is ample evidence of Darley's Law being realized in case studies of large financial loss like Enron, Kidder Peabody, National Australia Bank, and Barings.[5] Quality control problems were found at Ford Motor Company when it stressed metric-based approaches.[6] Even the United States Army had its bout with Darley's Law when leadership in the Viet Nam war manipulated body counts to falsely suggest success.[7] Generals in the army of the Soviet Union, when seeking to impress their visiting bosses — those who paid their bills — paved the basin of a river so that their tanks could be seen deftly cross them at high speed without delay — presumably to meet NATO forces in some massive and decisive ground battle envisioned by those in attendance.[8]

RISK-SENSITIVE FORAGING

Real life has baselines, such as a minimum caloric intake needed to live or the economic capital required to continue operations. One must not fall below these baselines in order to avoid a premature ending. These baselines can affect how a person or an organization chooses risk or processes risky options. The human response to the framing of incentives or expectations in this setting is known as *Risk-Sensitive Foraging Theory*.[9] It has its origins in the study of how animals choose where they might forage for food. But, we can apply it to human organizations as well.

One example supposes that a sales person needs to realize $2 million in sales in order to keep his job. Employment is a kind of baseline. Two sales approaches are known to this person, each with a $2 million expected value. The first approach has greater variability, meaning that sometimes sales will exceed $2 million and sometimes they will not. The other approach guarantees $2 million in sales, with no variability. Under these conditions, the typical sales person will choose the risk-free approach as only that prospect ensures his continued employment. However, if his boss, wanting to see her employee grow, shifts his sales requirements even modestly to anything above $2 million, the sales person is forced to choose the riskier approach. If he does not, he will realize the loss of his job with certainty.

With a very small change in requirements, the sales person will move from a risk-averse behavior to what is called a *risk-loving* behavior, meaning that he will seek risk, rather than avoid it. And, his risk is the company's risk. Introducing additional risk to the Value Equation, especially when it moves from a condition where no risk existed (think earthquakes where they have never happened), means that the consequences for the firm are value-destroying, even though the manager's intent was to stimulate value creation.

CASE STUDY: WELLS FARGO

Consider the case of Wells Fargo and inappropriate cross-selling. This situation illustrates the negative impact of both Darley's Law and Risk-Sensitive Foraging.

According to a report from Stanford University, Wells Fargo branch managers had been assigned quotas for cross-selling new products to customers with existing bank relationships. If those quotas were not met, the shortfall was added to the next day's sales goals, increasing their perceived baseline needs for survival. In turn, daily cross-selling targets were set for employees that put excessive pressure on them to perform or risk termination. Over a five-year period nearly two million new Wells Fargo customer accounts were created without customer knowledge or approval.[10]

The bank was criticized for failing to sufficiently monitor employees under these conditions, allowing thousands of employees to game the system and inflate their sales figures to meet their sales targets and claim higher bonuses. Following the discovery of the sales abuses, more than 5,000 employees were terminated, the company eliminated product sales goals, and re-configured incentives to emphasize customer service over cross-selling metrics. According to the bank, "[the problem] was people trying to meet minimum goals to hang on to their jobs."[11]

The bank suffered immense reputational damage. In September 2016, the company announced that it would pay nearly $200 million to settle a lawsuit. And the Wells Fargo board of directors eventually sought forfeiture of tens of millions of dollars of unvested equity awards from both its CEO and head of retail banking.

These incentive plans and minimum sales requirements were ultimately value-destroying and the reputational effects linger on long after the discovery and address of the problems.

FREE EXTERNALITIES

Of additional note, behaviors within organizations, or by organizations, can be distorted when the costs of their actions are not fully recognized or charged-for. We refer to the costs that an action imposes on others (other agents within or others outside of the organization) as *externalities*. Like ill-conceived or ill-designed incentive regimes, externalities that are not properly accounted for lead to efforts that are sub-optimal, inefficient, and misdirected.

Examples include distorting tax codes that attempt to engineer some social behavior or reward some specific supporter. In the United States, interest on mortgages is tax-deductible to a large extent. This is a very popular tax break, but it has the effect of distorting home prices and shifting wealth to those with higher incomes. The costs of those distortions are not accounted for in any measures of government spending.

Chris Matten, the former group financial controller of Swiss Bank Corporation and former Managing Director (Corporate Stewardship) of Temasek Holdings, said that risk is the single biggest expense not found on any income statement.[12] His insight is especially important for us as we consider motivation and incentives. If our incentive design, whether extrinsic or intrinsic, does not properly account for the risk it creates, then it will have a distorted impact. To take on risk, we need economic capital, which has a cost if we wish to acquire it in the marketplace. That cost should be recognized.

In the United States during the 1960s and 1970s, water and air pollution was a growing problem as many companies were able to discharge untreated chemical waste into streams, rivers, lakes, and the air without direct cost to them. At some point, those effluents overwhelmed the natural systems and produced hazards for those who had no association with the organizations, but did make use of the polluted air and water the organizations created. It may be that their actions would not have been profitable if they had to pay for the costs they imposed on others — in other words, with a true accounting, their organizations may have been value-destroying when their books and records indicated they had been creating value. China faces a similar situation with the massive pollution of its waterways. It is estimated that more than 50 percent of China's water is so polluted that it is undrinkable, and nearly a quarter of it is so toxic that it is not safe even for industrial use.[13]

If we are not charging for the costs imposed on others or for the cost of taking risk, we are not allowing for a true guide to be given to those who seek success in fulfilling their missions. The Management by Objectives approach also requires that externalities be properly accounted for; otherwise, scarce resources may be improperly allocated or actions could be taken by individuals or groups that are harmful to those outside of their group, but do not affect their measured goals. Most people who are seeking a purpose in their work do not want to be seen as negatively impacting others or taking advantage of absent pricing mechanisms.

MANAGEMENT OF THE COMMONS

Professor of Biology Garrett Hardin wrote an influential article in the 1960s called *The Tragedy of the Commons*.[14] In it, he described the potential for abuse by individuals who act in self-interested ways, depleting shared and limited resources, or *commons*, even when that resource's health is in the long-term interest of the individual. Water, air, and open grazing areas are all examples of commons that have been abused.

Yet, as we will discuss further in Chapter 15, there is ample evidence that economic governance of commons can be successful when there is engagement, a form of "ownership," by those who make use of the commons.

The values of our organizations can be viewed as a commons. The economic capital we are able to apply towards living our values — and generating value — is a commons as well. "Ownership" need not be solely stock-price-driven. Rather, successful governance and management can reward both extrinsically and intrinsically. Rewards and punishment need to be a blend of metric-based assessments, subjectivity, and organizational design. We can structure our organizations to ultimately give us greater freedom and ability to generate value.

We are now moving towards the active phase of reimagining how to govern our organizations so that they create the most value. Our goals are to manage negative risks, properly account for costs, and provide autonomy within systems that are large and interconnected enough to stimulate innovation, all while avoiding complexity catastrophes. We seek to maximize the ability of our systems to generate positively skewed distributions of potential outcomes and thus value for those who are part of our organization and its network.

NOTES

1   Pink, Daniel H., "Think Tank: Have you ever asked yourself why you're in business?," *The Telegraph*, January 29, 2011

2   "Options Backdating," Smith, Gambrell & Russell, LLP, Issue 18, Spring 2007

3   Sanders, William Gerard, and Hambrick, Donald C., "Swinging for the Fences: The Effects of CEO Stock Options on Risk-Taking and Performance," *Academy of Management Journal*, Vol. 50, No. 5, 2007

4   Darley, J.M., "Gaming, Gundecking, Body Counts, and the Loss of Three British Cruisers at the Battle of Jutland: The Complex Moral Consequences of Performance Measurement Systems in Military Settings," Unpublished Speech to Air Force Academy, April 6, 1994

5   Koenig, David R., "Aligning Compensation Systems with Risk Management Objectives," in *Risk Management: A Modern Perspective*, Dr. Michael Ong (Ed.), Elsevier Press, December 2005

6   Hughes R.L., Ginnett, R.C., and Curphy, G.J., *Leadership: Enhancing the Lessons of Experience* (5th Edition), McGraw-Hill, 2006

7   Darley, J.M., "Gaming, Gundecking, Body Counts, and the Loss of Three British Cruisers at the Battle of Jutland: The Complex Moral Consequences of Performance Measurement Systems in Military Settings," Unpublished Speech to Air Force Academy, April 6, 1994

8   Ibid.

9   See Caraco, Thomas, "On Foraging Time Allocation in a Stochastic Environment," *Ecology*, Vol. 61, No. 1, 1980; and Stephens, D.W., "The Logic of Risk-Sensitive Foraging Preferences," *Animal Behaviour*, Vol. 29, No. 2, May 1981

10 Case study information drawn from Tayan, Brian, "The Wells Fargo Cross-Selling Scandal," Stanford Closer Look Series, Stanford University Graduate School of Business, December 2, 2016

11 Ibid.

12 Speech to Asian Bankers' Summit, September 2003, Kuala Lumpur, Malaysia

13 Ewing, Kent, "China's green accidents on the rise," *Asia Times*, August 10, 2010

14 Hardin, Garrett, "The Tragedy of the Commons," *Science*, December 13, 1968

PART FOUR

The King is Dead

"*Let me tell you quite bluntly that this king business has given me personally nothing but headaches.*"
— Mohammad Reza Pahlavi, the last Shah of Iran

"*Design is not just what it looks like and feels like. Design is how it works.*"
— Steve Jobs, Chief Executive Officer of Apple Inc.

"*The real voyage of discovery consists not in seeking new landscapes, but in having new eyes.*"
— Marcel Proust, French Novelist

CHAPTER 13

The Governance of Risk

Like the game we call football, fútbol, or soccer, our organizations are a complex interaction of agents in a network working to achieve certain objectives — to score some goals. We rely on team members, coaches, fans, cleat makers, and others who can help us in this pursuit. At the same time, we constantly have to defend against both small and large attacks — problems that are emerging internally or externally, and in many cases against our competition, who are offering substitutes for what we do. Our daily operations are always in motion, transitioning and evolving, seeking to make the most of our opportunities and responding as best we can to the threats we see.

At nonprofits and other organizations not traditionally thought of as being in a score-keeping arena, the language of attack, defense, and competition might seem inappropriate. If helpful, we can substitute words like service, advocacy, efficiency, and impact. But, in the end, the goal itself remains the same: a good result from our efforts. We're looking to create and deliver value to those we seek to serve.

Let's begin this next stage of our work with a focus on the governance of risk, on both halves of the playing field.

RISK AND RISK MANAGEMENT

Risk, for most people, is uncertainty, especially in the domain of losses. But for us, risk is two-sided, with account given to both gains and losses. Consider a situation in which you find yourself walking down a hallway. You come upon a very dark room with a man standing just outside. He beckons and you cautiously approach. "I'll give you a thousand dollars if you go into this room, touch the wall on the other side, and then come back out," he offers. You have no idea what is in there and, in fact, just after this offer is made, some strange noises can be heard emanating from the room.

Your assessment of this offer will be based on many of the things we've discussed in this book, including your personal biases, utility function, and whether you have any level of trust in this person. But, who wouldn't like a thousand dollars? You might spend the money on a vacation, pay off some debt, or use it to improve the life of some deserving person who depends on the kindness of others to get by. There is value that you could derive from that thousand dollars. So, you are considering the offer.

In order to derive that value, though, you first have to ensure your survival. Those noises were not normal and the room is pitch-black. How can you prepare yourself so that you are more likely to achieve your goal?

Good news: because you are an engaging person, you also have a network of Strong and Weak Ties on which you may call. One Weak Tie can sell you a top-end flashlight for $100. With this light and for a fixed cost you can illuminate part of the room, reducing some of the downside potential. Maybe you'll be able see the source of the noises or any other potential dangers that lurk inside. However, even with this light, you cannot see everything in the room at once, so it may not be enough to entice you to take up the offer.

You recall that your neighborhood rental company has a searchlight of impressive strength. With it, you could illuminate almost the entire room, except for the area either side and above the entryway. The cost to rent this searchlight is $400. Are you ready to enter and possibly net $600 for your mission?

Finally, a good friend comes along and says, "I'll go for you if you pay me $900 upfront." Does the fact that someone else will take all the risks prompt you to take up the offer of the dark room's host? After all, if your friend makes it back, you figure you'll still be ahead $100. It's a far cry from $1,000, but at least your safety is no longer a concern.

In the end, what you're facing is a business decision, which is also a risk management decision.

In this example, the man and the dark room represent risk. They offer both upside and downside potential. The flashlight and searchlight are forms of *risk management* — things that illuminate the darkness and help you make a better (risk-adjusted) decision. Your friend-for-hire represents a concept called *risk transfer*, where, for a price, someone else will agree to assume the exposure you face. It's a form of insurance. In this case, accepting your friend's offer is the only way you can be truly resilient if the noises represent real danger. The management and oversight of the entire process from identification of the opportunity to end result is *risk governance*.

In real life, we're beckoned into rooms of varying "darkness" with great frequency. If you are offered a new job or pull up to the drive-through of a restaurant at which you've never dined, you are not quite sure what your experience will be. If you decide to launch a new product or advertising campaign, the prescience of the decision will not be known for some time. Even helping a charity may involve taking on some risks, and the diplomatic calculations made by the leaders of political economies can have an overwhelming impact on many lives. Clearly, life is not without risk and that is why we need some means of governing our exposures.

THE PROFESSION OF RISK MANAGEMENT

Evolution is one form of risk governance, albeit a slow one. If the game is to ensure the survival of the planet, or at least some kind of life on the planet, evolution will alter the make-up of species to achieve that goal. When managing our risks, however, we're after something a bit more timely, although the evolution of our organizations will be central to our method.

The intent of risk governance is to recognize that the future is uncertain so we need to plan how to adapt to circumstances that will be different in some way from today's. Tastes and preferences will change, and needs will evolve accordingly. The availability of scarce resources in the future will differ from the present, and the environment in which we operate will always be in motion, sometimes violently so.

Although we have no way of predicting these things well, we need to have a framework to do something about them. We're looking to understand, then actively and professionally manage, our risks.

Some would argue that risks have been managed by "professionals" like actuaries, doctors, or climbing guides, for hundreds of years. But, in a modern sense, professional risk managers have only come to occupy important roles in their organizations since the mid-1990s and the science of risk management has advanced greatly over that period.

The functional role of a risk manager varies widely depending on the industry and seniority of that professional. Some risk managers are responsible for health and safety issues in the workplace, as well as for the environmental impact of corporate activities. These roles are commonly found in manufacturing and natural resource exploration and extraction. Or, a risk manager may be responsible for maintaining proper insurance contracts or loan approvals for an organization.

You will also find risk managers with specializations in the following areas:

Market Risk: Changes in exchange rates, interest rates, stock prices, carbon prices, and other market-priced variables.

Credit Risk: Exposure to the failure of a counter-party to a transaction or loan.

Operational Risk: The risk of loss resulting from inadequate or failed internal processes, people, and systems.

Technology Risk: Failure of a technological agent in a system or inadequacy of technology.

Reputation Risk: The loss of the value of a brand or ability of an organization to persuade.

Legal Risk: Changes in regulation, failure to comply with existing regulations, errors in legal agreements, or litigious actions against an organization.

Security Risk: Employee safety, executive protection services, barriers to access of a company's physical infrastructure.

Cyber Risk: Barriers to access of a company's data and digital infrastructure, including data regarding its customers, employees, partners, and other members of its social network.

Political Risk: Exposures to changing political situations, either between political economies or within one.

Liquidity Risk: Loss of short-term financing to facilitate the daily transactions of the organization, or unexpected demands for funds that cannot be met in a timely fashion.

Project Risk: Delays or disruption to the scheduled implementation of key projects.

Supply Chain Risk: Exposure to other agents in our network upon which we rely to supply goods or services that are part of our organizational process or the delivery of our goods or services.

Insurance Risk: The management of risk transfer contracts with various insurance and re-insurance companies, or the failure to obtain appropriate coverage.

Environmental Risk: The potential impact of our organization's activities on its environment or changes in the environment in which we operate that affect our ability to pursue corporate values.

Business Continuity Risk: Disruption of our organization's ability to operate at its normal place or using its normal technologies due to natural or other factors.

Strategic Risk: Misalignment of corporate goals with network member needs or innovation external to the system that replaces or acts as a substitute for an organization's goods or services.

Enterprise Risk: Integration of all moving parts in the organization for maximization of value based on risk-taking capacity.

Believe it or not, this list is far from exhaustive. If you were to survey all risk management related jobs, you'd find that the number of risk management titles is in the hundreds, if not thousands, and reflects the vastness of its application. The risk management roles that have evolved most over the past few decades relate to the management of financial variables and, even more importantly, to the broad management of risks that affect an entire enterprise.

All risk management roles are important for organizations to realize their potential value. In fact, I would argue that every role within an organization is a risk management role. For our purpose here, we will look to that as an ideal and focus on the impact that risk management of the enterprise can have on enhancing our organization's value, evolving us towards that ideal construct and the essential elements for its governance.

DEFENDING THE GOAL

Defensive risk management is focused on three areas of the distribution of possible outcomes in the future: the middle (around our expected value), the left tail (where large losses occur), and the path between the two of them.

Remember, those in our network expect some level of value from us. If they receive anything less than they expect, even if it is still positive value, it will be a disappointment, or a loss of expected utility. Risk management in this part of the distribution of outcomes can be about managing forces that are often outside of the general control of the organization, but for which markets or risk-transfer options exist. Examples include the hedging of foreign currency risk. If your business reports earnings in U.S. dollars, but you sell some of your products or buy some of your supplies in other countries, your profitability can be affected by fluctuations in exchange rates, which are outside of your control. But, you can find a bank or another company willing to guarantee a fixed or semi-fixed exchange rate that allows you to plan more effectively.

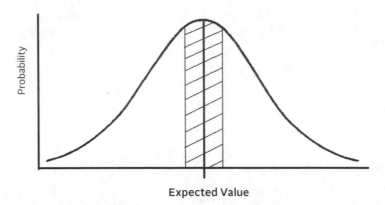

Figure 13.1 Risk Management Around the Expected Value

Risk management in the middle of the distribution is also about quality control. There is an expected rate of error in any production process, but variability of error rates makes product pricing and customer satisfaction management substantially more difficult. The organization will, when cost-effective, work towards lower error rates with increased production, while risk management will attempt to avoid drastic swings in production quality as a result. Similarly, projects are managed to specific delivery dates of various components, many of which depend on the timely and sequential completion of other tasks. Project risk management in the middle works to ensure that those delivery dates don't vary wildly.

Today's risk managers are extremely good at managing the middle of the distribution. Their work allows for boards, investors, donors, volunteers, and others to better evaluate the quality of management at organizations by identifying and controlling some sources of variability in performance that are outside of managerial control. It also gives transparency to those variables over which organizational leaders should be held accountable for results.

PROBLEMS IN THE BOX

But alas, losses will occur and some may be large. Risk governance in the left tail of the distribution (where we find these big losses) has two main objectives. The first is to understand the possible shape of the tail of the distribution and the second is to ensure that the company has enough economic capital to survive large losses at some level of probability. Let's take the second component first.

Firms that borrow money in the capital markets are assigned credit ratings, usually by companies like Standard and Poor's, Moody's Investors Service, and Fitch Ratings. These ratings are designed to indicate a probability that a company will be able to pay back its creditors. You may be familiar with ratings like "Triple A" or AAA, "Double A" or even (though we hope not), "D" for defaulted on debt.

"Triple A" is the best rating a company or country can have. Very, very few entities can achieve this because it is associated with a probability that you will not be able to pay back your debts of around 0.1 percent over five years. In other words, 999 times out of 1,000, an AAA company or country will pay you back if you lend them money for five years. "Single A" companies or countries are still pretty good. You could expect them to default about five times in 1,000 — they have a 99.5 percent probability of paying you back if you lend money for five years. A company with a "C" rating, just above default, would be more likely to default over the next five years than not.[1]

Companies will have to pay more money to creditors if their rating goes down. This is an effect of the value equation in that lenders will view the company as being more risky and thus require a greater risk premium — meaning a higher discount rate in our Value Equation. But, creditors are not alone in assigning a risk premium to companies. Everyone in the company's network will do the same consciously or subconsciously. So, the higher the perceived risk of dealing with our organization, the more expensive it will be to attract economic capital (other agents) to its network. But you know that by now!

You might think that this means all organizations would want to have AAA ratings. However, attaining such a low probability of failure can be extremely expensive, even to the point of making it difficult to do one's work. So, through managerial or board-level decision-making, most organizations will target a rating that they feel optimizes their ability to attract economic capital versus the cost of attaining that rating. As evidence of this, the Edison Electric Institute, an association of U.S. shareholder-owned electric companies, regularly produces a report that includes the credit ratings for the businesses in their industry. According to the 2016 report, the average credit rating for companies in their industry was BBB+, while only 6 percent were rated A or higher.[2] At the time of this survey, it seems that most firms in this industry were comfortable with ratings of between A- and BBB, a range that included 82% of the companies in the study.

A REGULATION SIZED GOAL?

But how many of the companies in the Edison report really know their true risk of default? To know this, you'd need to know the shape of the distribution of possible outcomes for your company's pursuit of its values and, in particular, the shape of the left tail of the distribution. This is the most difficult part of the job. What if the metaphorical goal you are defending is really twice as big as it looks to you?

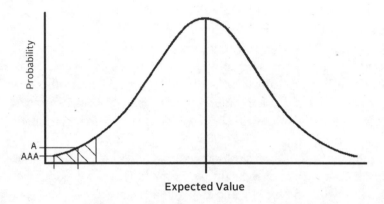

Figure 13.2 Risk Management in the Left Tail of the Distribution

The distribution of outcomes in Figure 13.2 is approximately normal in shape. If you draw a line from the left axis at the level of expected default for an A rating, you can then connect a line down to the bottom axis to tell you how much the loss would be at that level for a normal distribution. But, what if the distribution is either positively or negatively skewed? Or, what if we have fat tails? Then, the loss figures change substantially.

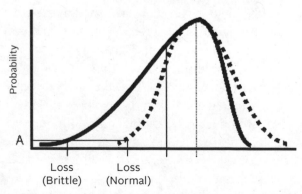

Figure 13.3 Impact of Negatively Skewed Distribution on Required Capital

See Figure 13.3 and consider our fat-tailed, negatively skewed, brittle organization. If we draw a line from the A point on the left axis, we find that the size of the loss we'd need to cover in this case is perhaps twice as large as for the normal curve. In other words, if this company wants to have an A rating, it must have twice as much financial capital on hand and that capital costs money, year after year after year. The same concept is true for an AA, a BBB, or any other credit-worthy rating.

During the financial crisis that began in 2007 many academic institutions and endowments faced cuts in their operational budgets because the outcomes realized from their investment portfolios had left tails that were not expected. There's was a problem of mismatching assets to liabilities, but the story is the same.

Suppose an organization capitalizes or budgets to a normal distribution and really is negatively skewed. In other words, it is not very well-governed but thinks that it is. In this case, it is far more likely to see an abrupt end to its existence than its executives and board members believe to be the case because it won't have enough financial capital to survive a relatively common level of loss. Or, it might have to cut operations because it was overly confident about the true possibility for negative outcomes from its investment portfolio.

In complex systems, fat tails are the norm. And predicting their size is a nearly impossible task.

Nassim Taleb's two books about probability distributions: *Fooled by Randomness* and *The Black Swan* have become quite popular. The latter is the more recent of the two and carries the subtitle *The Impact of the Highly Improbable*. The book talks about modeling the shape of the tail of distributions, as well as very rare and highly extreme events — ones that we cannot envision or understand given what we know today. In his vocabulary, these are the *Black Swan events*, so called because if you had only seen white swans in your life, you would argue that all swans are white, until you see a black one and would have to rethink your previous beliefs.

Taleb calls anyone who tries to predict the magnitude and likelihood of these tail events "fools or liars," who "can cause more damage to society than criminals," suggesting that they should "get another job." Those who believe them, he says "are suckers."[3]

The reason for his venomous sentiment likely stems from the fact that much of tail risk analysis, until recently, has had two fatal flaws. First, it has been assumed that the future would be like the past. Second, in only a small number of applications has there been account for distributions that are positively or negatively skewed and the degree of skewness they exhibit. The extent to which losses or gains might be amplified into the tail receives almost no attention outside of those who study the human reaction to physical risks.

You'd probably not "bet your life" that all swans are white, even if you have only seen white ones. But, that's exactly what many organizations do, simply by lacking a good process around understanding and managing the things in their system that might lead to a realization of the highly unlikely or the never-before-seen. Did you see the "Black Swan" in our story about risk and the dark room? Did you consider that the man might not have had one thousand dollars to give you in the first place? If you had hired your friend to go in for you, this little adventure would have cost you $900 when your focus was mostly on how you'd spend the money once you got it.

STRESS TESTS, SCENARIO ANALYSIS, AND ANTS

Good risk governance processes can help us avoid very costly or even deadly fates.

Our first step in applying risk governance to the tails of the distribution of outcomes is to accept our partial failure. We really cannot predict that which we do not know. We cannot exactly describe the tail of a distribution of future events that have not yet occurred. Sadly, we cannot even know the magnitude of the difference between something that has just a 0.5 percent chance of happening and something that will only happen once in a thousand times.

However, we can make some interesting observations about what we do and do not know that help us make better business decisions — what risk management and risk governance are really about.

Our organizations are complex systems that are full of non-linear relationships. They will experience losses that follow power laws, meaning that some factors that contribute to the loss will grow at exponential rates — they will amplify greatly. Taleb suggests that we accept this but inform organizational leaders that we do not know how all of the factors that contribute to the power law that is in effect will work, when they will interact, and to what extent. So, any attempt to assign probabilities to really bad outcomes is going to be fraught with error.

But, we can gain a non-probabilistic sense of how bad things might get by varying the factors that we believe will drive our success and failure. Our organizations can go through this exercise using three approaches.

Stress tests are a method that risk managers use to review the impact of very unlikely things on an organization's well-being. For example, one stress test would assess the impact on the need for staff at a hospital in case of a radiation leak, like the one experienced in Japan during 2011. Another would be to assess the impact on the value of an investment portfolio if interest rates increased by 3 percent in one day.

Stress tests can be based on actual historical occurrences that are then re-lived in a hypothetical exercise applied to the current construct of the organization. They may also be a set of parameters that are believed to be statistically unlikely to occur, but which would be stressful if they did happen. Or, they could be entirely invented situations — homemade Black Swans, if you will — that also subject the organization to stress.

Scenario Analysis is another technique used by risk managers to walk organizational leaders through imaginary situations to which the agents involved in the scenario have to react. These scenarios can reveal unexpected shortfalls in preparation or unintended consequences from actions taken in response to the hypothetical situation.

Suppose you run a home for disabled individuals located near an industrial factory. For risk management purposes, you might run through a scenario where there is a toxic gas leak from a rail car serving the factory to test whether the staff are adequately resourced or prepared to safely evacuate all residents in a timely fashion. You might then throw a snowstorm into the mix, a few key employee vacations, and sub-zero weather, just to make the scenario even more complicated to manage.

Both stress testing and scenario analysis are in active use at some organizations, but they are not widespread. Even less prevalent is a method based on a technique described by Dr. John Miller, Carnegie Mellon Professor of Social and Decision Sciences, as *Active Nonlinear Tests (ANTs)* of complex simulation models.[4] While his technique is applied to actual models, the concept is applicable in other ways. The idea is to systematically make large changes to the assumptions about what drives your organization's success — first making large changes to individual assumptions and then to combinations of assumptions, examining the outcome on your organization's value after each change. Eventually, and perhaps with the aid of computers, you work through a large number (or all) of the possibilities until you have a picture of what combination of changes in assumptions makes things go very, very wrong. By adopting an ANTs approach to business strategy or organizational construct, some Black Swans will emerge from the assumptions and drivers that are selected for the exercise. The organization's leadership is then more empowered to make a decision about whether to address these possible outcomes or not.

In addition to transparency and recognizing the applicability of power laws, Taleb gives us a third recommendation for mitigating the impact of errors in forecasting the shape of the tail of the distribution. Find the loss-generating situations that make the organization's leadership most uncomfortable and seek a way to transfer or re-insure them directly with investors or financial companies that take these risks for a living. Alternatively, one may issue a financial instrument that is a contingent capital claim — calling financial capital from investors or donors when things go really bad (and, notably, paying a high rate of return to them when things are fine). Consider it to be like having a couple of extra defenders who can rush the field if the problems get past your defensive line.

We have other options, too, that may be less expensive and also spare a breach of our defense.

MANAGING THE MIDFIELD

If our defensive risk management is limited to the expected value and the highly unlikely, it has failed. Very often, modern risk management programs limit themselves just so. We tend to sit back and model distributions of risk when we would be better served to get off the couch and take actions that will shape the impact of events on us in a manner more to our liking. Remember, Bruce Schneier told us that we should assume that something in a complex system will always go wrong. What matters most for our success is how we respond when things are starting to go wrong; when the path of a problem begins. We must be aware and resilient!

Defensive risk management that focuses on the path from the middle of the distribution to the tail is the kind that emphasizes and works to achieve the corporate resiliency that we discussed in Chapter 11. It seeks to ensure that all of our major systems have multiple points of failure.

One example of how this is achieved comes from Piper Jaffray, a mid-tier investment bank and broker/dealer that was owned by U.S. Bancorp from 1998 to 2003. Lisa Kenyon, then Director of Business Risk Management for the firm, created a standing committee called the Problem Response Team. It had a few regular members, including the various heads of risk management, legal, and operations groups, and floating members such as the heads of each business line. The job of the committee was to design rapid responses and make quick decisions that could efficiently interrupt an emerging problem, which, if not addressed, could lead to significant losses. The committee was not called upon often, but when it was, its actions were quite effective and saved the company millions of dollars. It was one way that Piper Jaffray became more resilient.[5]

Many organizations provide escalation hotlines and tip lines where employees can anonymously raise issues of concern to senior management. If structured appropriately, these measures can provide an early warning signal before problems reach their full potential — as long as someone is paying attention.

The midfield is critical and it takes special agility and fitness to play the position well.

SETTING UP THE OFFENSE

Even with a good midfield and defense, though, our ability to take risk is limited. The risk capital required to achieve a certain credit worthiness sets a boundary for us, as does the acceptability of risk — *risk tolerance,* or *risk appetite* — expressed by the owners of our organization or their representatives (the board of directors). For an organization to know if its activities are consistent with these constraints, we need a well-designed and disciplined managerial process that allows us to assess risk from the bottom up.

We talked about the amount of capital needed to attain a certain credit rating from a rating agency and also about how difficult, if not impossible, it is to get this calculation right. The process we described of compensating for this statistical challenge, including stress tests, scenario analysis, and ANTs allows us to paint a picture that, while not probabilistic in a pure sense, can be applied in a comparative business discussion, using subjective probabilities to measure the risks any subdivision of our organization is taking.

For example, during annual planning or monthly reviews, an in-depth discussion about each subdivision can take place with the guidance of a risk professional, designed to give business leaders a sense for the "risk" of that subdivision's activity; one that can be conveyed to the next larger subdivision of the organization. By making these quantitatively informed, but still subjective, evaluations, each subdivision can make decisions about the use of risk based on the constraints they face.

One constraint can be an actual charge for the risk they assume. Risk capital (which we write interchangeably with financial capital or risk-taking capacity) costs money to raise in the open market. It only makes sense that organizations charge the users of it internally as well. For example, if I want to buy stock in the ABC Company, I have to either borrow that money (which has a cost) or take it from some other utility generating activity (which costs me utility). The same holds true for each level of the organization. There is a scarcity of risk-taking capacity, imposed by the next higher level of the organization, for which each subdivision has to compete. It has to offer the best return to the higher level of the organization and it has to take on activities that generate sufficient utility to offset the cost of having that risk capital allocated to it, as opposed to another subdivision.

At that next level of the enterprise, the "risk" of each subdivision can be compared and contrasted for magnitude, predictability, and correlation with other activities of the larger subdivision. Like a portfolio of investments, these activities are likely to be somewhat uncorrelated. So, the risk of the larger subdivision is going to be less than the sum of the risks of all of its individual parts — it benefits from diversification. But it too will face constraints from the next higher level — the next allocator of risk-taking capacity.

This same logic applies to any new product that a subdivision wishes to launch. It must compete for the scarce and limited risk capital by showing that it provides the subdivision with a better distribution of potential outcomes, when included in the mix.

If we follow this process to its logical conclusion, the "risk" of all subdivisions will be brought up in the organization until the last highest entity is the enterprise itself and its "risk" represents an aggregation of its subdivision's risks, adjusted for diversification benefits throughout the organization. The amount of this "risk" must be less than the constraints the organization as a whole faces — risk capital and risk appetite.

The process of risk identification, facilitated risk assessment using subjective probabilities, charging for risk capital, and monitoring systems of intervention and response is our defensive risk governance process. We've laid it out in simple terms here but, in reality, it is anything but a simple task. It is very difficult to implement and manage effectively and efficiently, but it works brilliantly when done well — it adds significant value and is therefore worth pursuing by virtually any cost/benefit measure.

While this defensive work is essential for creating value, it's only a set-up for the offense. As we seek to attain our goals and serve our mission, we shouldn't be afraid to take risks, which are necessary for value creation. Rather, we should seek to create an environment that allows us to take risk confidently and more successfully — to make the best use of this scarce and expensive commodity called risk capital.

A VENTURE CAPITAL VIEW OF THE ORGANIZATION

From the ground, up, we build estimates of the risks being taken. Now, from the top down, we need to allocate our organization's risk-taking capacity in the best way possible. We'd like to open up possibilities for success, sometimes in very big, right-tailed ways!

To get there, we need to recognize and accept, or even embrace, the idea that success does not have to be achieved on each risk we take. In fact, we can do quite well by experiencing only a few big successes, as long as we manage the downside of each attempt and work to increase the chances of success for each try. This is the mindset of a venture capital fund. Such a fund allocates capital to a portfolio of smaller companies. It then nurtures each investment.

The investors in the venture capital fund — its "owners" — know that even if only a couple of those portfolio companies achieve their full potential, a good outcome will be realized. In other words, they nurture all of their companies, in hopes of realizing modest success with most of them, along with a couple of right-tail outcomes from things that go really well. They know that a few of their investments will fail, but, by limiting the size of the fund's investment in any one company, the venture investors have already limited the left tail of their distribution. Further, their involvement in oversight and governance of each investment gives them a searchlight of sorts, so that they are able to see any emerging problems and take appropriate action to intervene. Venture capitalists take care to prospectively know their risk on each investment, allowing them to allocate their risk-taking capacity carefully and to help foster an environment in which success is more likely to be achieved than failure.

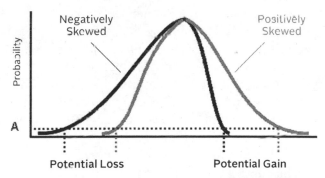

Figure 13.4 Potential Upside vs. Capital Required — Negatively Skewed and Positively Skewed Distributions

As we showed in Figure 11.4, the expected value of a positively skewed distribution of outcomes — what the venture capitalists are working to create — will be higher than either a normal or negatively skewed (brittle) distribution. Figure 13.4 shows us this again, but with a look both at the capital required to maintain a "Single A" rating and the potential upside at the same probability level. Note that the upside potential is higher but the amount of capital one needs to be as safe as an A-rated company declines dramatically. The "return on risk," or very roughly the potential gain divided by the potential loss, is greatly enhanced when a positive skew can be achieved.

Remember that all of the agents in our network, even those to whom we have weak ties or indirect connections, will use heuristics to assess our potential skew. They'll do so in either a very sophisticated way, or simply via reactive instincts. The result of their assessment, based on their expectations of the shape of our distribution of possible outcomes, will be a value they assign to us.

The investors in a venture capital portfolio believe they have found a positive skew that fits their portfolio's needs.

A PORTFOLIO VIEW OF THE ENTERPRISE

James Lam, credited with coining the job title *Chief Risk Officer* (and thereby being the first one), talks about the importance of viewing our enterprises as portfolios in his forward-looking book *Enterprise Risk Management*. James was an early leader in recognizing the value that a sound understanding of risk across the complex system of an enterprise could have on value.

A venture capital view of risk capital allocation is simply a portfolio view, albeit a little less passive one than most of us use with our own portfolios. If you have a retirement or investment portfolio, you've likely tried to benefit from diversification by including stocks, bonds, mutual funds, and perhaps even a hedge fund or private equity investment. Diversification, if done well, can limit your exposure to any single loss being excessive and, therefore, allow you to realize higher returns for less risk — what we see in Figure 13.4. If you follow this investment model, you and your investment portfolio are not that different from a venture capitalist and her portfolio.

But, it's not just businesses that adopt this mindset. If your organization is a "party for the neighbors at your house," you'll probably utilize a portfolio approach for achieving success too. If you serve only one appetizer to this diverse group of people, some of them might not like it. They'll be unhappy at your party and might even leave. So, to increase the chances of success, you diversify the choices, offering elegant hors d'oeuvres, cheeses, fancy crackers, seasoned dips, even Chex® mix, and whatever else you deem to be a crowd pleaser. Along with this food, you decide to serve cocktails, wine, water, soft drinks, and beer, rather than limiting your offering to just one of these beverages. Because of your thoughtfulness, most of your guests are going to enjoy themselves. In fact, some of them are going to have a really great time. Now, it is true that a few might be a bit disappointed. But, if you offer such a nice variety of items, it is unlikely that anyone will have a really horrible time. Because of your portfolio approach to entertaining, your party is going to be positively skewed and people will want to come back again.

Political economies are a portfolio of states, provinces, or other sub-divisions of political power. These geographical entities have further sub-divisions like counties, parishes, districts, and cities, and then wards, arrondissement, boroughs, or precincts, eventually getting down to you and your homestead or perhaps your condo association.

The United States' economy is a diversified portfolio of political sub-economies. As is shown in Figure 13.5, the distribution of growth in Gross Domestic Product, or GDP, for the U.S. is positively skewed. The United States is a lot like a big venture capital portfolio!

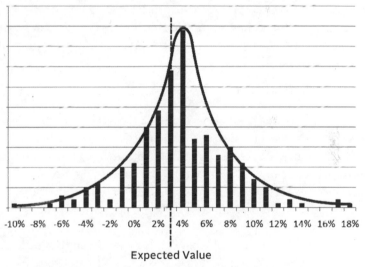

Expected Value

Figure 13.5 Quarterly Real GDP Growth (Annualized) 1947–2011
Source: National Income Product Accounts, U.S. Bureau of Economic Analysis

You can also think of the Earth as a portfolio of living entities. It is a complex adaptive system full of species that try to succeed. Some fail and some do very, very well. Like any venture capital portfolio, the Earth rebalances its portfolio from time to time to limit its exposure to large left-tail events and rewards successful innovation.

The organizational structures we find to be most successful in delivering long-tails on the right side of the distribution are the ones that are diversified and complex adaptive systems — they have many subdivisions to them that interact with agents inside and outside of the organization. If each subdivision is provided with risk capital that allows it to take risks of a small enough magnitude so that failure in one or a few of them will not give the whole portfolio a big left-tail event, the portfolio will have a truncated left tail. If the enterprise is well-governed, a few outcomes of the subdivisions' activities will be really great.

In practice, the goals of risk governance are no different from those of most managerial sciences. Good executives, to the extent possible or practical, make decisions that are intended to bring about the best returns for their organizations, relative to the risks they assume to have been assumed. Seeking to increase organizational value through maximizing returns relative to a well-informed estimate of risk, as opposed to an ad-hoc approach, is what risk governance does.

Risk governance done well gives the freedom of choice to take risks. The allocation of risk capital creates a price for taking risk. With a price, agents in systems can make free choices in a better-informed way. And, by now, we surely do not need to plot a distribution of outcomes to show you that freedom has a positive skew.

OVERALL GOVERNANCE OF OUR ORGANIZATIONS

Choices bring about change. We, as humans, have the ability to proactively and reactively design our systems to increase our chances of changing things for the better. Overall, through governance of our organizations, we are looking to stimulate a positive evolution of our systems, each time varying the attack on goal down the field, changing the mix of agents when some plans fail, and discovering and building upon some others that work extraordinarily well.

Risk governance, as part of the overall governance program, is not a black box from which answers emerge. It is a discipline, where managerial decisions are made better with enhanced information and transparency. These decisions remain managerial, subject to human error. But, they are freed to be risk-informed decisions and are thus vast improvements on any ad-hoc managerial styles that ignore the cost of risk. This is one reason why the governance of risk has moved to the forefront of attention at many organizations.

As we plan for how to best live our values, it's good to know that it's not just our goal that may be bigger than we think. Our team is much larger than we believe it to be, too. We next review a concept called *Networked and Distributive Governance* and finally consider the value that overall *economic governance* provides in bringing together all of the concepts we've developed so far.

If we're successful, we will create good and valuable things that have never yet been found to exist. These are the kind of Black Swans we're happy to discover.

NOTES

1   "Confidence Intervals for Corporate Default Rates," Moody's, April 2007

2   Edison Electric Institute, 2016 Financial Review

3   Alan Mills has an interesting article in the March 2010 issue of Risk management called "Should Actuaries Get Another Job?" from which these quotes are pulled and in which a quick review of Taleb's work regarding tail risk is given.

4   Miller, John H., "Active Nonlinear Tests (ANTs) of Complex Simulation Models," *Management Science*, Vol. 44, No. 6, June 1998

5   The author served as the Director of Market and Institutional Credit Risk Management at U.S. Bancorp Piper Jaffray and was a standing member of the Problem Response Team.

CHAPTER 14

Networked and Distributive Governance

As was outlined in the last chapter, risk-taking capacity is a scarce commodity. To the extent that it is available to an organization, it is allocated from the top-down to a portfolio of subsystems therein. Subsequently, the actual taking of risk, as measured through a disciplined approach of assessment, must be aggregated from the bottom-up to be reconciled with the organization's capacity constraints or risk appetite. The process is repeated within each subsystem of the organization. This cascading portfolio model of "allocation and assessment" is the framework we'll use as we build our full governance structure and to turn our complex organizations into complex adaptive systems.

However, before risk-taking capacity can be allocated down, our organizations need to get the capacity to take risk from somewhere within our network — from donors, voters, investors, entrepreneurs, or creditors. Our organizations also need to attract people and technologies to do the actual risk-taking — working or volunteering for the organization. Finally, other people or other systems must want what we offer for the picture to become complete and value to be created — without others willing to exchange something they have for what we offer, our products have no value.

No matter how small our objectives, we are not alone when we build a complex adaptive system. We have many relationships that will affect our success. So, an effective governance program adds an engagement of our whole network, internal and external agents alike, to the "allocate and assess" risk governance model. We're looking to create a framework of Networked and Distributive Governance, and when we do, big things can happen.

THE ROLE OF THE BOARD

Let's begin our structural design with the focus of most corporate governance initiatives, the board of directors. If an organization is large enough, it will typically elect or appoint a small group of people to be legally responsible for the overall structure and success of the organization. If the organization is too small to have a formal board, this responsibility could reside with top management. But, at this point, we'll focus on boards of directors and the legal duties they assume when given charge to govern. It is important to note that when an organization has a board, a key separation must be maintained between the roles of the governing board and management.

Numerous organizations have developed guides to board best practices including the National Association of Corporate Directors (NACD) in the U.S., the Institute of Directors (IoD) in the U.K., the Conference Board of Canada, as well as the Organization for Economic Cooperation and Development (OECD), the Directors and Chief Risk Officers group (DCRO), Commonwealth Association for Corporate Governance, the Group of Thirty, and the Basel Committee, among others. PRMIA, the DCRO, and the International Corporate Governance Network (ICGN) have independently put together helpful summaries of best practices around the specific governance of risk.[1]

Best practice guidelines often talk about the types of people needed, as well as their independence and expertise. They may even provide a helpful list of questions that the board should ask of itself and its organizational leaders. But, rather than just relying on a form with questions, we're looking for a results-driven, living system. Typically, results require accountabilities. So let's begin with a few:

1. As it relates to risk governance, the board must ensure that there is no single risk being taken by the organization that could disable the pursuit of its values. No organization of any material size that is subject to a single point of failure can be considered well-governed.

2. The board needs to be aware of the business structure and environment (the network) in which the organization operates and to understand how the risk assessment infrastructure has been designed to address the risks that may be encountered in the environment.

3. The board must ensure that the organization has proper resources and processes in place so that the allocation and facilitated evaluation, discussion, and negotiation of risk capital can be effectively and efficiently conducted.

4. The board must delegate to one of its members, or a subcommittee of the board, formal responsibility for understanding, in detail, the

risk governance infrastructure of the organization and to report on that regularly to the board as a whole.

None of these "principles" relates to any specific regulations or laws, although they are implicitly contained therein. Rather, they reflect the concept that all activities of an organization in pursuit of its objectives are fundamentally risk-taking activities. Business management is risk management. Association management is risk management. Management of our social organizations and political economies is risk management. The quality of the work that the board exhibits in living these principles sets the tone for the rest of the organization, cascading a respect for both the positive and negative sides of risk and helping us govern effectively.

PRINCIPAL–AGENT RELATIONSHIPS

Boards of directors do not, in most cases, contain the entire ownership of an organization. A typical board may represent an insignificant portion of the ownership or even none at all. A board gets its authority, though, by an allocation of authority from the organization's owners. A distribution of authority like this reflects the owners' trust in this group's ability to do the work of governance on their behalf.

With that trust comes risk. The classic term for this specific risk is the *principal–agent problem*. This problem arises when someone (the principal) hires another person (the agent) to pursue the principal's objectives, and that agent turns out to have interests that are not perfectly aligned with the principal's. In the analysis of corporate governance, this problem is generally identified with the election by owners (principals) of the small number of people who represent their interests — the board of directors (agents). It is also present in the relationship between the board (principal) and the Chief Executive Officer (CEO) or other-titled leader of the organization (agent).

In fact, at each stage of the hand-off of risk-taking capacity, the principal–agent problem is present. The problem is one of *information asymmetry*. For example, the CEO has more intimate knowledge of whether the organization is working in accordance with the board's wishes, but shares only part of this information with board members. The reduction in disclosure is due in part to time constraints as a board meets relatively infrequently and cannot possibly be told everything that the chief executive knows. However, this limited disclosure may also be due to biases and self-interest from Transmitters like the chief executive. Or, it could also be caused by malfeasance or fraud. Whatever the reason, the opportunity for abuse exists.

The board also has an information asymmetry relative to the owners of the organization. Data related to competitive advantage or strategic planning that is part of the board's regular discussions could also benefit a competitor if made public. So, it is not widely shared. Or, there may be psychological biases and self-interest in effect even to the point of forgetting who the real owners of the organization are. Failure to have full candor with owners may also be due to malfeasance or fraud.

At every place where one subsystem hands off risk-taking capacity to a member of its portfolio, the principal–agent problem is present. So, to be successful, a networked and distributive governance structure needs to also manage and control the key challenges presented by the principal–agent problem.

KEY DUTIES OF BOARD MEMBERS

One control can be found in law. As we noted in Chapter 5, those serving on for-profit and nonprofit boards of directors in the United States and Canada are likely to be aware of two duties that have been established by the courts and which set boundaries on their bad behavior.

The Duty of Care, in essence, says that a board member must pay attention to the needs and plans of an organization in a way that shows a level of care consistent with what they would do for themselves. They must attend meetings, participate in discussions, validate representations made to them, and generally represent the interest of the owners. This duty does not require that board members be good at what they do — just that they do a reasonably good job of trying. In fact, if they are prudent in their process, the courts have almost always protected directors when things do go wrong. This form of protection has become known as the *Business Judgment Rule*, meaning that as long as a director uses prudent processes in making a business decision, he or she will not be liable just because the judgment call turns out to be wrong.

In other cases, particularly in the United Kingdom and in some U.S. states, the Duty of Care may be extended to include any decisions that might reasonably be foreseen to cause harm to others. In this sense, the duty is considered to apply to anything that affects those who are part of the organization's broader system, either willingly or unwillingly.

The courts have also placed an expectation that board members act in the interests of the organization for which they serve and not in their own interests or that of a competitor. This expectation has come to be known as the Duty of Loyalty. In effect, board members are expected to avoid conflicts of interest in their decision-making, not to steal company assets, to avoid entering into an agreement with the organization that is unfairly beneficial to the director or her agents, and generally to only work for the benefit of the organization.

These two key duties are helpful in establishing minimum expectations from each subsystem's leadership because we are, in effect, distributing an owner–board relationship throughout our organization when we allocate risk-taking capacity.

We may further wish to extend expectations to include a requirement that actions taken be for a proper purpose, with "proper" being defined by law or by organizational policy. We may expect that board members remain open to new ideas and do not commit themselves to supporting future decisions before knowing the results of their most recent ones. We might require that they take into account the likely consequences of their decisions in the long-term and the impact those decisions may have on others in the network — those who are often referred to as *stakeholders*. Finally, we may expect that they uphold high standards of business conduct and ethics, as defined by law or corporate policy.

The choice as to what is required once we go beyond the requirements of the law is up to each organization and should reflect its values. But these values need to be distributed and communicated along with the risk-taking capacity.

THE CARVER METHOD

One of the most effective models for distributing accountability from the board to the Chief Executive Officer is called Policy Governance® and was developed by consultants John and Miriam Carver. Their unbreakable association with this method is the reason why the model is also referred to as the "Carver method" or "Carver model" of governance, or "Carver" for short.[2] As the commercial name implies, at the core of their model are highly descriptive policies that convey both the objectives of the organization and the limitations on how those objectives can be pursued. Its application to for-profit companies seeks to answer the question, "How can a group of peers, on behalf of shareholders, see to it that a business achieves what it should (normally in terms of shareholder value) and avoids unacceptable situations and actions?"[3] We might add that it should avoid unacceptable outcomes as well, particularly those in the left tail of the distribution.

The model is equally applicable to nonprofits and neighborhood groups, and in some ways it reflects how democratic political economies are structured already.

ENDS AND MEANS

At the heart of the Carver method is a clear distinction between *ends* — which are the prioritized objectives and intended results of the organization — and *means* — which are any decisions and actions that are not ends. "Ends" are a way to communicate why the organization exists, while "means" include activities, conduct, systems, and general operational decisions. Organizations don't exist to have a particular factory or to hire a particular person; they exist to achieve some objectives that are valuable to them. The factory and people (agents) are means to achieve these ends.

According to the Carvers, ends are most effectively controlled in an affirmative, prescriptive way, while means should be controlled in a limiting, proscriptive way. The use of ends and means in this manner allows a board of directors to be very powerful in its role, but also to grant as much authority as possible to the chief executive of the organization to achieve the ends it has established.

Under the Carver method, there are no other corporate issues besides ends and means. If an issue is not an "ends," then it is a "means," and vice versa. To control the ends in a prescriptive and positive manner, the board first expresses to the chief executive what its specific performance expectations are. These may be return on equity, share price performance, total debt, employee job satisfaction, total number of patients served, number of defects per million units produced, volunteer turnover, customer satisfaction, marketplace image, or any other quantitative or qualitative benchmarks which define success from the perspective of the owners of the risk capital that the board represents. In the Carvers' words, an organization is for whatever its owners want it to be, and these ends say what that is.

To control for means in a proscriptive way, the board's communications are limiting. In other words, they tell the chief executive what boundaries the board has around acceptable managerial decisions — risk taking capacity or risk capital, for example. This means that anything the board does not prohibit or does not define as being outside of its limits of acceptability, may be permitted, provided that it is a reasonable interpretation of what the board had intended. In this approach, the board is not interfering with the way the business is run on a day-to-day basis. It is not telling the chief executive what to do. Rather, it is telling the chief executive what *not* to do — it is constructing a ring-fence around behavior. In short, if we assume that most boards will prohibit imprudent and unethical practices, the chief executive's choices and his actions are whatever he reasonably believes will best serve the organization's goals, within these boundaries.

Control of means can best be thought of, according to C
ing the question, "What situations, activities, or decisions
would not be acceptable to the board even if they worked?"[4] In
even if the ends are being met, are there certain risks, ethical violations,
and improprieties that would be out-of-bounds for the board?

Carver notes that this ends-means distinction has several advantages:

First, it recognizes that when board members interfere with management of the organization, it is more difficult and more expensive to
achieve ends. In other words, freedom generates more value than
over-management.

Therefore, it secondly gives the chief executive as much freedom as the
board can responsibly grant.

Third, it gives room for managerial flexibility, creativity, and timeliness,
thereby creating agility and the ability to respond quickly to both
opportunities and threats.

Fourth, it rids the organization of the notion that the board knows
better than the staff how to get the job done.

Fifth, in this system, all means that are not prohibited are, in effect,
pre-approved. The board is thereby relieved of the need to review
and approve unnecessarily detailed staff plans.

Sixth, by staying out of the decisions about how things are done, except
by prohibition, the board can clearly identify the chief executive as
the sole agent responsible and accountable for the decisions made
within the organization.[5]

NESTED POLICIES

In an era of perceived frequent abuse of power by chief executives, the prospect of such freedom may seem unwise. But the Carver approach puts the
burden on the board of directors to appropriately and completely define the
ends and rules for pursuing those ends in a detailed and effective manner.
It puts the board's focus in the proper place in the domain of policy and
not in the domain of managing the organization. This is a critical re-focus
of activities for many boards.

How the board controls against abuse is a function of the detail it puts
into its policies and statements regarding ends and means, as well as the
overall governance structure it creates. For example, a statement saying the
chief executive should not put the firm at risk of default is potentially too

broad. However, a statement that says the chief executive should maintain a credit rating for the organization of BBB or better is more specific. There is no right answer for every organization in terms of how much specificity or broadness is appropriate. Carver notes that it is up to each board to take into account the interpretative range of their guidance when evaluating the chief executive's performance, and to be sure they are comfortable with what they have allowed.

Broad statements about ends and means are inevitable because a focus that is only on narrow measures risks leaving out key restrictive guidance. Further, there is a requirement stipulating that since the board is responsible to the organization's owners for everything, its policies must also cover everything.

Carver recommends a three-part principle of board decision-making to successfully balance the tension between breadth and specificity of policies.

First, the board needs to make decisions at the broadest level possible for both ends and means.

Second, the board proceeds step by step into lower levels of each ends and means statement, making increasingly specific statements about each one.

Third, the board stops this progression at the point where it is willing to accept any reasonable interpretation of those statements by its chief executive.

By taking this approach, the board manages the amount of interpretation to which its policies are open. As a result, the chief executive has either less or more freedom to use her independent judgment in pursuit of ends. Carver uses the analogy of nested boxes to illustrate this process. If the board establishes a policy, it is like a box. Everything inside that box is free to move about without the board touching it. The smaller boxes inside the larger box may be controlled directly by the board, but once the board decides its box is small enough, all of the other boxes are set by management — they fit within the larger box established by the board — and can be whatever they wish, provided they stay within the larger box.

This approach will yield large boxes in some areas of ends and means and very small boxes in others. For example, one means statement saying that bribery of government officials is always forbidden is a very small box. This approach to establishing nested boxes of policies allows the board to control the things that it must, but not all that it can.[6] It turns the board into a forward-looking and planning entity and avoids the react and rubberstamp approach that many boards take, especially if they are weak and run by their chief executive. This brings us to the third job of a board under the Carver method.

BOARD–CHIEF EXECUTIVE RELATIONSHIP

A board exists to govern, not to advise or manage the organization. It is the representative of the owners in fact and not just in words. Carver notes this forcefully and furthers the notion by saying that rather than advising, the board's job is to form the accountability link between the owners and operators of an organization. The board, according to the Carver method, cannot allow its members' natural desire to advise to obscure the central challenge it faces: how to command in such a way that management is optimally empowered and challenged at the same time? The Carvers know that the word "command" seems out of place in a model designed to beget freedom. But, they say the board not only has the authority, but also the obligation to demand, because the organization belongs to its owners and not to the chief executive or the board. They have no right not to exercise authoritative prerogatives. Command, they say, is meant in the way that the chief executive has the right to command within management. But these commands are to pursue certain ends, by not going outside of the boundaries established by the means statements.

In addition to establishing ends and means, the board has the critical role of hiring and evaluating its chief executive. The chief executive is the single person responsible to the board of directors and evaluation of her work in achieving the organization's ends is an ongoing and important process. The Carver method defines the process of clearly establishing ends and means criteria as a way to take a "define and demand" approach to the board's relationship with its chief executive. It's not that dissimilar from the "allocate and assess" concept of risk governance. The Carvers chide the "ask good questions" approach to governance as a "spotty and weak" control device.[7] They equate it to a line manager who, rather than establish objectives for his subordinates, skips that step and simply asks them good questions. Instead, the Carver approach suggests that boards systematically monitor the chief executive's performance on specific criteria. Note that these criteria need not (and should not) be solely quantitative as Darley's Law, which we discussed in Chapter 12, warns us. But, they should be systematically applied and clear.

Along with this approach is the requirement that the board speak with one voice. The individual directors should have a vigorous debate over the ends and means, but once they have been established, no one director's wishes should matter to the chief executive. Therefore, individual directors must be prohibited from evaluating the chief executive based on criteria that are not communicated to the chief executive via ends and means policies. In turn, the chief executive must have trust in the board as a whole to adhere to its guidance, as clearly expressed in these documents. Further, the board must accept any reasonable interpretation of its policies by the chief executive. Under the Carver method, this must hold for the board as a whole; it cannot be the interpretation of the most influential board member, or what the board "had in mind," but did not say explicitly. If it fails to act in this manner, the chief executive will learn that she cannot trust the board.

It should be clear at this point that the Carver model precludes the chief executive from serving as the chair of the board of directors, a practice that is widely in place across many types of organizations. This method also notes that while many boards function by allowing the chief executive to provide agendas and to train new board members, nowhere else in an organization are subordinates responsible for the conduct of their superiors, so this should not be the case at the board level either.

The Carvers go further in their critique of existing board practices by suggesting that there is no place in the board of directors for any executives of the organization because the board only has a relationship with the chief executive. It is hard to perceive that anyone reporting to the chief executive is without conflicts of interest in evaluating the chief executive's performance or setting ends and means policies as a director. Their input should be considered by the board, but they should not serve as directors.

EXTENDING THE MODEL THROUGH THE SUBSYSTEMS

Today's corporate governance discussions focus almost exclusively on the role of the board of directors and its relationship to the owners of the organization. While important, and an essential beginning point, we need to recognize that corporate governance is about how an organization as a whole works to accomplish its goals and to live its values. It goes well beyond the owner–board relationship. To achieve our success, we need a way to extend the application of owner–board governance principles to the places where the hands-on work is being done.

As noted, most current governance discussions focus on the owner–board relationship, and sometimes on the board–chief executive relationship. The Carver model is no different. However, this model also gives us a helpful framework to use towards allocating risk capital to the subsystems of our organization, the recipients of which are accountable to the "owners" of that risk capital.

Consider that, as one of its means policies, the board has handed off a limit on risk to its chief executive. It is then up to the chief executive to allocate parts of that risk capital to the respective subdivisions he identifies. It is one of his means. He is the owner of the risk from the board's perspective and has risk capital to allocate as an owner. As he does so, the recipient of the risk capital will look to the chief executive as an owner. Each recipient will likely have other subsystems that can receive a portion of this risk capital to be used as a means. At each division of risk capital a new owner–representative body is created, which is, in effect, another board that can establish ends and means for the use of that subset of the organization's risk-taking capacity. By this process, each subsystem of the organization defines smaller and smaller boxes within the larger box that was passed on to it by the board of directors in the first place.

Each of these recipients of risk taking capacity is like a venture capital company. It will allocate out its scarce resources to a number of pursuits of ends, making sure that no one failure would be big enough to deplete all of its capital, and guiding a few larger successes to continue their development, perhaps even to the point of becoming large enough to be a subdivision of the organization overall.

At each subdivision of risk capital, a Carver-style model of governance can be employed to distribute authority until it makes no more sense to subdivide the freedom to pursue ends.[8]

In many ways, the Carver model has embedded principles of the Management by Objectives philosophy. It can be summarized through ten basic principles:

1. The board governs on behalf of the owners of the organization.

2. The board must speak with one voice.

3. Board decisions should predominantly be about policy, not about execution.

4. Boards should formulate policies in nested layers, beginning with big items and narrowing as appropriate to a point where any reasonable interpretation of the policy would be acceptable.

5. The board should define and delegate rather than react and ratify.

6. The objective is to achieve ends, not to define the managerial process.

7. The board's best way to control the process, or means, is to proscribe

— prohibiting some behaviors and defining what is not acceptable, rather than what is.

8. Boards should explicitly design their own products and processes.

9. The link between the board and chief executive must be empowering and safe. The chief executive should not be subject to second-guessing, individual board member's whims, or items not explicitly covered by ends or means policies.

10. The performance of the chief executive must be monitored continually and rigorously against explicit means and ends policies.

BRINGING IN THE NETWORK

To grant the freedom to take risk confidently, we need trust, objectives (loose or specific), boundaries, subjective and quantitative assessments, and accountability. We get all these prerequisites with the Carver method.

But we also need to address the principal–agent problem and a way to maximize the positive impact that a large network of people and systems external to our organization can bring. In a Carver-type distributive governance model, it is possible to lose a critical governance element that is needed to ensure that our complex systems remain complex adaptive systems. Recall that closed systems tend toward entropy or disorganization; the Carver model can isolate groups and cause them to focus just on their subsystem. Entropy is only combated through information flowing in from outside of our relatively closed systems — the "boards" of any subsystem of the organization. To our distributive governance model, we need to add some *networked governance*. Fortunately, we have a guide for that too.

CORRUPTING POWERS OF A UNITARY BOARD

Professor Shann Turnbull, the founder of the International Institute for Self-Governance, has authored several papers and given numerous lectures about Network Governance and the need to change how our current "best practice" models of corporate governance work. Among his papers is *Mitigating the Exposure of Corporate Boards to Risk and Unethical Conflicts,* which was awarded the prize for best paper at the 2008 Loyola University Graduate School of Business Center for Integrated Risk Management and Corporate Governance symposium titled "Corporate Boards: Managers of Risk, Sources of Risk." It examines substantial conflicts of interest that are present in the model of corporate governance where an organization is governed by one board of directors, or a unitary board, and articulates a model to address them.[9]

In some countries, publicly traded companies are required to have two boards, one a management board and the other a supervisory board. Turnbull's guidance for us goes well beyond that. But, before we introduce its key elements, it is helpful to review a short list of some of the conflicts of interest of unitary boards that Turnbull highlights. These examples are representative of conflicts, which have the potential to actualize the principal–agent problem.

1. Directors have the power to obtain private benefits for themselves (and/or control groups who appoint them) by determining their own remuneration and payments to associates, directing business to interests associated with themselves, issuing shares or options at a discounted value to themselves and/or associates, selling assets of the firm to one or more directors or their associates at a discount, acquiring assets from one or more directors or their associates at inflated values, trading on favored terms with parties who provide directors with private benefits, for example.

2. They also can abuse their power by reporting on their own performance, selecting auditors and other "independent" advisers (while also determining their fees and whether they get re-hired), controlling the process by which auditors are appointed by shareholders, determining the terms of reference on which "independent" advice is provided, determining the level of profit reported to shareholders by selecting the basis for valuing or writing off trading and fixed assets, the cost of depreciation, recognition of revenues and costs in long-term contracts, defining accounting policies, and selecting those who will value assets.

3. They may not disclose full pecuniary or non-pecuniary benefits even if required to do so, but they are charged with determining how any conflicts of interest are managed, filling casual board vacancies with people who support their own positions, nominating new directors who support them at shareholder meetings, controlling the nomination and election procedures and processes, controlling the conduct of shareholder meetings, appointing pension fund managers for the firm who also provide them proxies, voting uncommitted proxies to support their own election, and other powers that often surprise the retail investor.

PEOPLE IN OUR NETWORK WHO CARE ABOUT US

Remember, we have a lot of people who want our team to do well. They'd rather not see any of these potential abuses be realized either because each abuse makes it more likely that they will realize utility from us that is below their expectations. So, let's make use of their caring interest.

Turnbull suggests we engage these stakeholders thorough various committees that are part of our formal governance structure. You probably just flinched a bit at this notion — most people would. Adding more committees to your daily routine does not seem like a way to grant freedom. In fact, it seems to be just the opposite. If you recall, we talked about how complexity collapses can occur when there are too many connections in the network — when it is too dense — and so nothing can be accomplished in a timely manner. Your reaction may be instinctive, hard-wired, and reasonable. Excessive committees are to ideas what the lion was to Thor.

However, the committees envisioned by Turnbull are not management committees. They are not designed to provide advice or to give approvals. Rather, they are designed to strengthen ties to important people and systems in our network. They are also structured to bring information in and thereby enhance the ability of our organization's work to create and deliver things that never existed before, or to do what we do already in a much more positively skewed way.

At the organization level, Turnbull envisions consultative committees of customers, suppliers, and other key stakeholders. They may meet annually or quarterly. Their objective is to discuss what the organization is doing from their perspective, what is working and what is not. They share what their future needs are likely to be and how the organization of today may or may not fit that need, giving the organization time to adapt and evolve. One study by Eric von Hippel of the Sloan School of Management at MIT found that 80 percent of ideas for product innovation came from customers, rather than from internal research and development departments.[10] Further, these kinds of stakeholder committees provide the board of directors an independent source of validation for the information that their sole executive report, the chief executive, is giving them.

Now, this may sound a little more appealing to you than a stodgy committee. But be prepared to be challenged once again. Turnbull advocates the creation of two more committees at the enterprise level — one with supervisory powers and the other with actual veto powers over actions of the board of directors where conflicts of interest exist. We're probably starting to make a few unitary board members uncomfortable with this idea. But, note that venture capital firms commonly require just this kind of oversight of a unitary board when they provide financing. This is part of their nurturing process that gives their investment portfolio a greater chance of being positively skewed.

The veto board, which Turnbull calls a *Watchdog Board*, would be given the authority to appoint the auditor of the organization, as well as other independent advisors to the board of directors. Consider that they may wish for an outside entity to evaluate the risk governance structure independently and report their findings to the board. They would hire the independent valuation firms and have the ability to veto any board actions that are subject to a clear conflict of interest.

Turnbull recognizes that this veto power is among the most discomforting aspects of his model. So he argues that representatives from various stakeholder committees form a *Supervisory Board* that could overrule the veto of the Watchdog Board if it felt the actions of the board of directors were in the best interests of the organization as a whole. Checks and balances, mixed with a separation of powers, may sound familiar and a bit more comforting than the bureaucratic lion first envisioned.

In fact, to achieve the kind of freedom we are seeking, the kind of freedom that, as Beinhocker pointed out in *The Origin of Wealth,* has allowed for over 97 percent of humanity's wealth to be created in just the last 0.01 percent of our history, we need such a structure of checks, balances, and separation of power.

A basic law of the science of corporate governance regarding complex adaptive systems is that complexity can only be regulated with matching complexity, or as it is known to others, Ashby's Law, or the "Law of Requisite Variety."[11] In a very general sense, the governance of a system must be complex and flexible or malleable enough to withstand shocks from its environment. Turnbull believes that moving towards a form of self-regulation, which is quite different from a laissez-faire "no regulation" model, is the only way to create organizations that meet the test of this law. This self-regulation is not to be confused with becoming overly complex, hierarchical, or "Interventionist." Rather it is quite the opposite, allowing a system to find a natural form of requisite complexity that grants the freedom and confidence to take risks.

CASE STUDY REVISITED: WELLS FARGO

In response to the cross-selling scandal that was discussed in Chapter 10, Wells Fargo created a Stakeholder Advisory Council charged with providing insight and feedback from a stakeholder perspective directly to the board of directors and senior management.[12]

ROLLING IT OUT THROUGH THE ORGANIZATION

As with the Carver approach, the venture capital portfolio model, and the risk governance model of Chapter 13, the Network Governance model can be cascaded throughout the subdivisions of the firm. The definition of stakeholders changes at each level, but they are likely to include representatives of subsystems within the same organization who are impacted by the subsystem's changes in focus. Or, they may be critical suppliers like IT or human resources services. We don't have to get their approval because that would invite a complexity collapse. But, we do invite their input.

When we engage these people who care about our success, they will help us intercept problems before they reach their full potential (re-shaping the left side of the distribution). They will "feed forward" information that helps our governors identify strategic opportunities. They will become stronger ties for us and, with that, bring along many of their own Strong Ties that become our Weak Ties. They can then spread the word about us and increase chances for our value-creating activities to experience positive amplification (re-shaping the right tail of the distribution). Finally, they are one of the strongest checks on the principal–agent problem that we see whenever an owner grants freedom to a user of the owner's capital.

Turnbull provides us with some examples of organizations that are following his concept of Network Governance and doing so quite successfully. Visa International was a model of Network Governance, with hundreds of boards in its governance function. In 2007, it merged with other Visa entities to form Visa, Inc. In March of 2008, Visa, Inc. listed on the New York Stock Exchange and was the largest initial public offering ever in the U.S. to that date. Since going public through the end of 2017, its stock has outperformed the broad stock market by over 20 percent, despite having issued its shares at the start of the Great Recession.

The John Lewis Partnership is a collection of over 85,500 partners who own the leading UK retail businesses — John Lewis and Waitrose. According to their website, their "founder's vision of a successful business powered by its people and its principles defines our unique company today." Further, "The Partnership aims to ensure that everyone who works for it enjoys the experience of ownership, by sharing in the profits, by having access to information and by sharing in decision making through influencing and making recommendations to the Chairman on any subject." In the 2010–11

fiscal year, all of their partners earned an 18 percent bonus based on organization-wide profits. In 2009–10, the profit share bonus was 15 percent. In
the middle of the financial crisis, partners received a bonus of 13 percent,
based on organization-wide profits. The year before that, the bonus was
20 percent and the preceding year, before that 18 percent. Between 2012
and 2016, the average distribution was 13.4 percent. Even in the incredibly
challenging environment for retail stores that was present during 2017,
partners still were awarded a bonus of five percent.[13]

The Mondragon Cooperative Corporation in Spain is another complex
adaptive system, which Turnbull cites as an example. It began in 1956 with
24 workers in one industrial cooperative and by 1979 had grown to 135
cooperatives with nearly 16,000 jobs.[14] A study of its first two decades by
Professors Henk Thomas and Chris Logan showed this cooperative's productivity, growth in sales, exposure, and employment, in both favorable and
unfavorable economic conditions, had been superior to traditional business
structures.[15] As of 2016, the organization had nearly 74,000 employees, total
sales of over 12 billion Euros, and 1.7 billion Euros of "working shareholder
capital stock."[16]

THE IMPACT OF GOVERNANCE AND
TRANSPARENCY ON TRUST AND VALUE

Another benefit of a well-developed risk governance infrastructure is that in
addition to the business intelligence that it brings, it also can provide a new
level of transparency to those whom the organization would like to draw
into its system and thereby reduce the overall cost of all its economic capital.

An investment firm seeking to raise capital from investors will have an
easier time doing so if it can confidently and accurately convey the levels of
risk it is assuming, as well as its methods for managing them. An organization seeking to attract human economic capital to relatively dangerous jobs
— physically or reputationally dangerous — will do so more effectively if it
can convince the people it seeks that the risks they are assuming do not fall
high on the Risk of the Unknown scale. An organization subject to external
regulation by a governmental authority is less likely to receive excessive
and innovation-crushing oversight if it can demonstrate a sound process for
measuring, communicating, and managing its internal risks, in addition to
those which it might impose on those external to the organization.

In short, a good risk governance infrastructure will enable an organization to be more transparent with those considering joining or evaluating
its system; that transparency will build trust. Trust, in turn, allows the

organization to become more complex and its network to grow. Larger networks have greater potential for innovation and, consequently, greater potential to create value.

THE INTEGRATION OF NETWORKED AND DISTRIBUTIVE MODELS

The Carver model, applied alone, could stand in dramatic conflict to the principles of risk governance and Network Governance that we have reviewed in this part of the book. However, it also can greatly enhance these principles when "control" — to which the Carver method alludes — is not viewed as the issuance of orders, but is one of defining by policy a structure that increases the self-control of various subdivisions. The Carver model grants freedom to determine how restrictive an organization wants to be, at any level. The tone comes from each owner-representative body.

Hanover Insurance rose from the bottom of the industry to become a top-performer when a form of distributive governance was implemented.[17] Its Chief Executive Officer at the time, Bill O'Brien, was quoted as saying, "We're not trying to eliminate control in our organizations…it's really about replacing hierarchically imposed control by increased self-control."[18] We may think of control as "orienting and adjusting," rather than "ordering." Our structure orients the organization, within which the autonomous, yet networked subsystems adjust to changes in their environment. Even the U.S. military in the 1991 Gulf War changed its emphasis from "just follow orders" to one that allowed units to semi-autonomously interpret "directional intent." This was, in effect, a Carver "nested box." They also were expected to learn from other units, which is a feature of Network Governance.[19]

Networked and Distributive Governance is intended to be in alignment with biological governance systems that have proven to be highly resilient. Diversity of behavior is a source of resiliency and the variety of agents, products and ideas that arise from a networked and distributive governance model are like an eco-system, making the entire system more resilient. This form of governance does not seek to override order that forms naturally, but provides an environment where the freedom to create and innovate is stimulated. Nature uses *Mass* (enough members to cover the territory), *Engagement* (networking deeply in local external environments), *Randomness* (allowing for variety in the pattern of search for new ideas or rewards like food), and *Roles* for team members to successfully create networks like ant and bee colonies.[20] *The Economist* magazine highlighted this concept in a 2001 article on Artificial Intelligence, noting, "A single ant is not God's brightest creature. But as colonies, ants engage in food cultivation, temperature regulation, mass communication (using scent trails), and bloody, organized warfare. Ant colonies run themselves with an efficiency that outstrips human society. But no single über-ant manages the show."[21]

The board of directors, or overall governing body, by whatever name it goes, gives power to the chief executive of an organization, who may be viewed as an über-ant, and in many cases believes he is. However, a transformation, or re-governing of our organizations, replaces this mind-set with one similar to an architect who is creating a highly adaptable and malleable portfolio of risk-takers. The Mondragon group utilizes a type of venture capital firm to seed new initiatives, each time imprinting the general DNA of the organization onto the new venture.[22] When one of these new entities experiences right-tail growth, it is forced to divide, ensuring that it does not get so big as to create single-point-of-failure risk to a larger subsystem.[23] This also frees the creative elements of the subdivided group to pursue new uses of the risk-taking capacity that was generated by their previous success.

MIT professor Peter Senge uses the term *chaordic*, a combination of chaos and order to describe systems like Visa International, where order is produced from chaos. That means the systems must bring in information from the outside — from their network — to be well-governed. At Visa International, there were five principles used for its governance design:[24]

1. It must be equitably owned by all participants

2. Power and function must be distributed to the maximum degree

3. Governance must be distributive

4. It must be infinitely malleable, yet extremely durable

5. It must embrace diversity and change

Equitable ownership may seem like a buzzword for some kind of political agenda. It is not, and it need not be. Rather, it leads us to a final stage of our governance structure, the identification, creation, and management of commons among participants. It is those commons, which must be perceived to be equitably "owned," and for us to realize the full potential of the vision that got us started in the first place.

SUMMARY

In summary, our networked and distributive model of corporate governance is an addition to our "allocate and assess" risk governance model with the following features:

1. Each "owner" of risk-taking capacity empowers a small group to take risks.

2. Each empowered group, when allocating the owner's risk capital, defines ends and means that are subsets of any ends and means policies under which they live.

3. Ends are prescriptive and means are proscriptive. The former allow for evaluation, which must be ongoing, while the latter grants freedom by defining the bounds within which ends may be pursued.

4. Customers, suppliers, and other stakeholders of each subsystem are invited into the governance process via stakeholder committees.

5. A Watchdog Board ensures that the distributors of risk capital are not abusing their power by actualizing the principal–agent problem. It can veto any ends and means decisions where conflicts arise.

6. A representative committee of the stakeholders, a Supervisory Board, is established with the power to over-ride any veto that it believes was not in the best interest of the entire network of the subsystem.

Networked and distributive governance of our organization's risk creates freedom to confidently take risk in pursuit of our ends, or values. Freedom gives the opportunity to create value from the pursuit of those values.

And that's why we do what we do!

NOTES

1   PRMIA Principles of Good Governance (original and revised), DCRO Guiding Principles, and ICGN Corporate Risk Oversight Guidelines

2   For full details of the model, see *carvergovernance.com*

3   Carver, John, "A Theory of Corporate Governance: Finding a New Balance for Boards and Their CEOs," *Corporate Board Member*, April 2001

4   Ibid.

5   Carver's Policy Governance Model in Nonprofit Organizations, *Canadian journal Gouvernance – revue international*, Vol. 2, No. 1, Winter 2001

6   *Op. cit.* Carver, April 2001

7   Ibid.

8   For a detailed look at the Carver Policy Governance Model, see *Corporate Boards that Create Value* (Jossey-Bass, 2002) and *Boards that Make a Difference* (Wiley,

2006), among other texts authored by the Carvers.

9 Turbull, Shann, "Mitigating the exposure of corporate board to risk and unethical conflicts," in Kolb, Robert, and Schwarz, Donald, *Corporate Boards: Managers of Risk, Sources of Risk*, Wiley Blackwell, 2010

10 Von Hippel, Eric, "Lead Users: A Source of Novel Product Concepts," *Management Science*, Vol. 32, No. 7, July 1986

11 Tunbull, Shann, "A New Way to Govern," Organizations and Institutions Network 14th Annual Meeting on Socio-Economics, University of Minnesota, June 2002

12 See "Inside the Stagecoach: Wells Fargo launches Stakeholder Advisory Council," *Wells Fargo Stories*, December 21, 2017. See also Kilroy, Meaghan, "Wells Fargo forms stakeholder advisory council," *Pensions & Investments*, December 21, 2017.

13 John Lewis Partnership Annual Reports

14 Thomas, Henk, and Logan, Chris, *Mondragon: An Economic Analysis*, George Allen & Unwin; HarperCollins, 1982

15 Ibid.

16 Mondragon Corporation Annual Report 2016

17 Ibid.

18 Williamson, Craig, "Biological Governance," Chapter 10, *Sinisterpapers*, 2009

19 Ibid.

20 Thompson, Ken, "The Law of Requisite Variety and Team Agility," *Bioteams Features*, October 22, 2007

21 "Artificial Intelligence, 2001: a disappointment?" *The Economist*, December 20, 2001

22 Turnbull, Shann, *op. cit.*, 2002

23 Ibid.

24 Ibid.

CHAPTER 15

Economic Governance

Throughout this book we have referred to "organizations" without always distinguishing among political, social, profit-seeking, or not-for-profit entities. These associations of agents are otherwise called companies, firms, charities, countries, etc., referring to their specific type of incorporation or reason for assembly. Some organizations come together spontaneously, with an expected temporary existence, while others are formed with a vision of permanence or, at least, endurance.

Why do organizations even exist in the first place? Do they have common characteristics that allow for a universal approach to governance, or can one type of organization learn from the successes or failures of other types? The first question has been a focus of studies in the field of economics since early in the 20th century and several notable efforts have been made to describe the reasons that prompt "firms" to form. We're interested to know this as well. Newer research helps us in knowing what to do with an organization, regardless of its purpose, once it has been created. From this new knowledge we can further refine our governance framework, so that our organizations can generate the most value from the initiative that caused them to form in the first place.

MARKETS AND/OR HIERARCHIES

The classic debate of why companies exist has a similar dichotomy to that of the dominant division in Traditional Economics between Interventionists and the Invisible Hand crowds we mentioned in Chapter 1. The Invisible Hand perspective is one that competition for scarce resources like economic capital best takes place in an open market exchange where individuals are free to contract with each other but do not necessarily have to join an organization. The Interventionist approach believes that hierarchy is necessary to protect larger systems. Hierarchy and control can prevent negative externalities when participants see no ongoing relationships with other agents and, therefore, focus only on extracting the most from the environment in which their system operates.

Professor Ronald Coase, who was awarded the Nobel Prize in economics in 1991, noted in his classic paper "*The Nature of the Firm*" that the choice between using market transactions or hierarchies in an organization had been viewed as a discreet choice to that point in the economic literature (circa 1937), and believed that such a view of exclusivity was not to be taken as a given.[1] More recently, the work of Professor Oliver Williamson of the Haas School of Business at U.C. Berkeley, suggests the "markets *or* hierarchies" choice was a false dichotomy. The real choice, he states, is how much of a mix of markets *and* hierarchies is best.[2] In his work, the impact of partial information on the enforceability of contracts played a key role. He was informed and guided by the likes of Herbert Simon and others during his graduate studies and incorporated concepts like Bounded Rationality into his work, for which he too was awarded the Nobel Prize, in 2009.[3]

Williamson postulates that the nature of the relationship between two agents, particularly when one agent is providing an asset that is specially designed for use by the other agent, will determine whether work is done within an organization or by contract outside of that structure — by outsourcing to the market. His work suggests that transactions are more efficient inside of an organizational structure when they are complex and highly tailored to the needs of one or both parties to the transaction. The reason in this case is that contracting to an outside party could be very expensive in terms of writing complete and enforceable contracts that cover all eventualities. Further, once such a contract has been written, "the market" for that exchange becomes very narrow because of the specificity of the asset. A narrow market has few participants, and, hence, there are many opportunities for either party to use its leverage over the other to extract excess gains. If both parties in such a specific transaction are part of the same organization, this kind of a "rent extraction" problem goes away because the organization's management can resolve conflicts.

Consider the relationship between a coal mining company and an electricity producer that generates power with coal.[4] These are unrelated processes, except at the point where a transaction between the generator and miner occurs. Since coal is costly to produce and transport, if there is a mine close to the power plant that provides a satisfactory product, both the coal miner and power generator can find a beneficial relationship through contractual relationship. On the downside, such a relationship has the potential to create a high codependency between the entities. It becomes increasingly expensive to end the relationship, especially if there are no close competitors nearby. Williamson's theory says that the further away a mine and power generator are from other mines and power generators, the more likely it is that the two will eventually become jointly owned to alleviate the conflicts that may arise from codependency.[5]

Williamson also notes that when firms make the choice between raising capital via investors or creditors, the appropriate nature of the financing is in part dependent upon the same criteria as whether a transaction is best done internally or in the marketplace. Since creditors have no control over assets unless things go wrong, assets that are more generic are more easily disposed of by those creditors and may be more suited to debt financing. More specific assets, like the coal mine or electricity generator, are less suited for financing by creditors because the liquidation value outside of the existing, codependent relationship is greatly reduced if the controlling firm has financial problems that give the creditors ownership of both assets.

But bringing all transactions inside of a firm — the Interventionist model — is not a perfect solution either. Williamson notes that when complex relationships are brought into the organization, the executives may act in their own self-interest when profits or gains from these transactions are distributed. Their individual actions may not be in the best interest of the organization as a whole.

Because of these issues, there is no unitary solution — either market or hierarchy. Rather, the answer to optimal organizational size lies in finding the right mix of markets *and* hierarchies. Firms that do not realize the appropriate mix tend to be less profitable and are also less likely to survive.[6] Empirical research has shown very strong validation of Williamson's construct, which is, in part, why his work has been so influential. We should, therefore, expect the governance framework of our complex adaptive systems to also feature markets and hierarchies, with appropriate checks and balances in place to manage the issues of internal management and conflicts of interest, as well as appropriate signals to tell us when the organization is out of balance.

While Williamson's work is specific to "firms" or companies, there are many other types of organizations that need to appropriately design governance of their activities — of their systems — and which face the "markets and hierarchies" conundrum. It's helpful to look across organizational types for any positive common traits that are likely to help us achieve a higher value for our organizations. Doing so yields some surprising relationships and insights.

CITIES, ORGANISMS, AND ORGANIZATIONS

Geoffrey West is a distinguished professor of physics and former president at the Santa Fe Institute.[7] You may recall from Chapter 4 that the Santa Fe Institute is known for its leading work on Complexity Science. In July of 2011, West presented *The Surprising Mathematics of Cities* to the TED Global conference in Edinburgh, Scotland, outlining his research of various organizations — systems.[8] He and his research colleagues looked for commonalities among various types of systems including companies, living organisms, and cities. They studied the relationship between size, growth, and mortality in thousands of systems. It turns out that no matter their size, evolutionary history, or geographic location, cities, living organisms, and companies grow in a surprisingly predictable ways. The relationships between characteristics like size and energy consumption among all systems tend to follow very neat and narrowly defined power laws and do so universally.

You may recall the mention of power laws in our discussion of large tail risk events and other natural phenomena. Power law relationships are surprisingly common. What West and his colleagues have found is that natural organisms tend to become more efficient in terms of their energy consumption as they grow. In fact, the power relationship in this regard is on the order of 75 percent, meaning that for every 100 percent increase in size of an organism, only 75 percent more energy is needed to sustain it. The relationship is universal across all living species.

Large living things also tend to have similar growth patterns. They increase in size quickly when young, then their growth rate flattens to zero and they eventually collapse and die.

Cities also experience energy efficiency that follows a power law like that which applies to living organisms. They do so universally, regardless of their size and regardless of their geographic location. Unlike living organisms, though, cities experience other growth patterns that follow power laws with exponents of greater than one. For every 100 percent increase in the number of people in a city, there is approximately a 115 percent rise in creative output like patents, in income, jobs, but, unfortunately, also in crime rates, as well as rates of AIDS and other viral infections.

Cities, West points out, don't collapse and die like mammals do. Rather, they have shown extreme resiliency even to the point of surviving nuclear attack. Cities are extremely difficult to kill, he states.

Where do companies fall on this power law spectrum? Are they more like an animal or more like a city? In their study of over 23,000 companies, West and his colleagues have found that companies are, unfortunately, more like single living organisms. They grow rapidly in their early years, level off in terms of growth and innovation, and ultimately collapse and die. A similar phenomenon occurs within organizations as it does to rats, birds, and individual humans — and it is not good.

So, what are the differences that may cause this? Cities and other organizations we seek to govern are made up of agents in networks, each one facing the same constraints and the same benefits of networks. West wonders if companies and living organisms might be able to have the same properties as cities do, and vice versa. "Is London like a big whale?" he asks. "Is Microsoft like an ant hill?"

The divergence between the disparate powers of growth may be a result of the relatively mobile and self-organizing social network of people in cities, which contrasts with most organisms and most companies. Living organisms are made up of lots of subsystems that do not change much or cannot be changed without a lot of effort. Most of us keep the same heart and same brain throughout our lives, for example. Within companies, once bureaucracy and administration take over, they begin to realize the bounded growth of living organisms too. They don't change their systems much and, as a result, will eventually collapse and die. We can speculate that this is in part due to the effect noted in the markets and hierarchies model of organizations: when firms bring market relationships in-house to realize efficiencies (exponents of less than one in terms of energy use), they simultaneously expose these relationships to administrative biases, principal–agent problems, and problems of communication.

We would like to get the exponent of the growth in value power relationship to be greater than one, so that our organizations can live on. But while exponential growth at a factor greater than one may at first seem ideal, any system with such a growth rate will eventually become so large, complex, and dense that it too will collapse — unless it reshapes itself and innovates, over and over again and at a faster and faster pace, each time. This requirement may sound a bit hopeless for us in our quest to govern organizations. How can we innovate faster and faster, over and over again? Is this not impossible? Are our organizations not doomed to a tragic course of death or complexity collapse?

The portfolio approach to risk governance, via a Networked and Distributive Governance structure, will actually allow us to achieve this. The challenge is to let go of the "boundaries" concept between organization and market.

Think of the owner who allocates risk-taking capacity to her organization as having allocated such to a small "city." The redeployment of capital by the "city" is done in a cascading fashion, effectively creating "smaller cities" each time it is subdivided. Each subdivision is thus able to grow internally at the fast pace of early life. But when its success pushes it to a sufficient size, where its growth rate may start to level off if it does nothing new, it uses the additional risk-taking capacity that its success has brought to spawn more new "small cities." These, in turn, may grow rapidly and create even more "small cities." It is this pace of division and multiplication of success that can yield an exponent of growth that is greater than one and also allows us to avoid complexity collapses — our "cities" are subdivided to avoid becoming too dense.

One successful portfolio spawns three; with success, each spawns three more, for nine. These processes may eventually spawn 27. Our one "city," all the while growing in total (it is now 27 small cities), distributes control to the smaller cities, preventing them from ever reaching the stage of collapse. It allows each one to operate within a very large policy box and to establish its own nested boxes as well for each time they subdivide. If one is locked into the mindset that the "big city" must control everything, as might come about if one only considers "markets *or* hierarchies" as the choice, then companies will remain like individual living (for now) organisms.

MANAGEMENT OF THE COMMONS

Professor Elinor Ostrom of Indiana University was a co-recipient of the Nobel Prize in economics the same year as Oliver Williamson. Not unlike Williamson, Ostrom critically examined the dichotomy of choice — "market" or "government" — in terms of approaches taken to manage Common Pool Resources or commons. Again, commons are resources to which more than one individual has access, but where each person's consumption reduces availability of the resource to others — examples include fish stocks, pastures, potable water, the air, and oceans.[9] Her research concluded that the best approaches to governance do not always fit well into one or the other of these strict approaches, and better ways to manage commons were driven by the interaction of interested agents — those who care about the system.[10]

She was influenced by the work of her husband, Professor Vincent Ostrom, who, along with Professor Charles Tiebout and Professor Robert Warren, interestingly studied the governance of services in cities. They developed a concept of polycentric systems of governance for services in cities like police and water, that in line with the results more recently modeled by West, showed economies of scale in some areas of production and the ability to avoid diseconomies of scale in others.[11,12]

Elinor Ostrom's research found that three mechanisms increased the productivity of these polycentric governance models:

1. Small and medium sized cities were more effective than large cities in monitoring performance of agents — this is familiar to us in regards to the most effective group size researched by Dunbar and noted by Gladwell, as well as our concerns over complexity collapses when networks become too large and too dense.

2. Agents who were dissatisfied could move to other subsystems. In organizations, this means that human capital is free to change jobs or to no longer engage an organization. Risk capital could be re-allocated to other uses.

3. Local communities can contract with larger producers and change contracts if not satisfied, while neighborhoods in a larger city cannot. This gives these subsystems the ability to outsource some work, making use of the market as well as the organization.

It turns out that trust, as we discussed in Chapter 9, plays a key role as well.

Recall from Chapter 12 Garrett Hardin's work, *The Tragedy of the Commons*. It assumed that unless there was government intervention, depletion of commons would happen. That's because people who think others will use up the resource before they do, selfishly speed up their consumption first. In effect, he sees users of common resources as being trapped in a type of Prisoner's Dilemma out of which they cannot escape. Ostrom's research found that when agents are constrained in this game in the way in which the classic Prisoner's Dilemma is played — they are not allowed to communicate or to plan future decisions in the game — this negative outcome is, indeed, sure to be realized.

However, Ostrom's research also found that when cooperation among agents is allowed, when they have repeated face-to-face communication, and particularly when the agents have the ability to change how the game is played, they can easily break groups out of this trap of commons abuse. In fact, when these conditions prevail, self-governance structures are extremely successful in increasing returns, not depleting the resource.[13] They are substantially more efficient than those overseen by some centralized governor that is distant and remote to the users of the resource.

In successful self-governing systems, users create *boundary rules* about who can use the common resource, *choice rules* about how to use the commons, and active forms of *monitoring and sanctioning* rule breakers.[14] Some of the governance design principles Ostrom identified include:

1. Boundaries: Clear and locally understood boundaries between legitimate users and nonusers are present and clear boundaries that separate a specific common pool resource from a larger social-ecological system are present.

2. Congruence with Local Conditions: Appropriation and provision rules are congruent with local social and environmental conditions, while appropriation rules are congruent with provision rules; the distribution of costs is proportional to the distribution of benefits.

3. Collective-Choice Arrangements: Most individuals affected by a resource regime are authorized to participate in making and modifying its rules. It is a democratic process.

4. Monitoring: Individuals who are accountable to the users, or are the users themselves, monitor the appropriation and provision levels of the users, while individuals who are accountable to the users, or are the users themselves, monitor the condition of the resource.

5. Graduated Sanctions: Sanctions for rule violations start very low but become stronger if a user repeatedly violates a rule.

6. Conflict-Resolution Mechanisms: Rapid, low-cost, local arenas exist for resolving conflicts among users or with officials.

7. Minimal Recognition of Rights: The rights of local users to make their own rules are recognized by the government or higher level of the organization.

8. Nested Enterprises: When a common-pool resource is closely connected to a larger social-ecological system, governance activities are organized in multiple nested layers.

This last condition will be recognizable as a Carver-type distributive form of governance. Ostrom's research found that in over two-thirds of studies of the management of commons, the most effective governance structures for managing the resource were characterized by most of these design principles, while those that failed were not.[15] These design principles appear to be the ones that increase the likelihood of long-term survival of an organization managing a common resource and the commons itself.

Ostrom's work calls into question the blind faith in markets to manage commons. It appears to be very important that the monitoring and sanctioning element of design be active and carried out by group members themselves, or someone over whom they have control. In experiments, Ostrom found that with communication and the principles above, including sanctioning, the management of commons could achieve a nearly optimal outcome in repeated games of resource allocation, when expectations in a "tragedy model" would otherwise be the depletion of the resource.

She notes some of the failings in the assumptions of Traditional Economics which we discussed in Chapter 4, saying, "The assumption that individuals have complete information about all actions available to them, the likely strategies that others will adopt, and the probabilities of specific consequences that will result from their own choices, must be rejected in any but the very simplest of repeated settings."[16] To get to an ideal outcome, people and groups will use heuristics and iterative learning to develop reasonably good decision-making tools.

Markets also are generally dispassionate and impersonal. Ostrom finds that individuals who regularly work in teams are more likely to adopt norms and to trust each other more than individuals working alone — or perhaps we should say feeling alone if the orders of governance come from too distant a place. While Williamson looked at the boundaries of the firm being based on efficient contracting and the ability to resolve conflict within a single organization, the benefit of working together within a firm seems also to be tied to trust and the ability to self-regulate using the design principles Ostrom has identified.

More evidence from her work indicated that the required cooperation becomes more difficult as the size of the group of users increases or as the time horizon of users' engagement shortens. The Nobel Scientific Committee summary of Ostrom's work also seems to indicate support for the distributed, portfolio approach to construction of a larger organization:

> "Large-scale cooperation can be amassed gradually from below. Appropriation, provision, monitoring, enforcement, conflict resolution, and governance activities can all be organized in multiple layers of nested enterprises. Once a group has a well-functioning set of rules, it is in a position to collaborate with other groups, eventually fostering cooperation between a large number of people. Formation of a large group at the outset, without forming smaller groups first, is more difficult."[17]

Our Networked and Distributive Governance model is a form of polycentric governance, in that the distributive aspect creates multiple centers of independent authority, all of which are under a larger umbrella. It also takes into account the input of stakeholders — others with whom we interact in our system. Ostrom's work finds that the successful management of commons requires frequent communication among users of the commons. In our case, the larger "umbrella" is what we have been referring to as the organization — the top-of-the-house portfolio.

CASE STUDY: BLOCKCHAIN GOVERNANCE

As of mid-2018, the markets or hierarchies debate is rapidly being played out in the evolving governance structures of blockchains — distributed ledger technologies. Initial emphasis in this field was on fully decentralized structures, avoiding or even rejecting the centralized or hierarchical models that dominate traditional corporate structures. Not surprisingly, some of these fully distributed networks became too dense to remain efficient. The movement towards a blend of both markets and hierarchies, or decentralization with requisite hierarchies mixed in based on levels of trust and overall complexity, is underway. Greater emphasis on identifying and managing the commons in blockchain also is being witnessed as governance practices in this area rapidly evolve.

RISK CAPITAL AS COMMONS

In our networked and distributive risk governance model, the commons, or common pool resource, around which our governance is framed is risk capital. This risk-taking authority and capacity is provided to subsystems in the network that can allocate it to productive uses, but each allocation means that less is available for others within the group. For the commons of risk capital to be most effectively governed, the application of Ostrom's principles is required.

1. *Boundaries* in this case are the specific subdivisions to which risk capital is allocated.

2. *Congruence with Local Conditions* is the box within which ends and means have been defined, but allowing for any reasonable interpretation of them within the box.

3. *Collective-Choice Arrangements* is the freedom to define smaller boxes within the larger box.

4. *Monitoring* is conducted by all agents, but also through stakeholder committees and watchdog boards.

5. *Graduated Sanctions* are penalties for the misuse of risk capital that

would be applied by the market to the organization as a whole, but which each subdivision applies to its portfolio investments.

6. *Conflict-Resolution Mechanisms* include escalation lines, problem response teams, and stakeholder committees' representatives who have the right to overturn vetoes form the Watchdog Committee.

7. *Minimal Recognition of Rights* is the definition of the box in which any reasonable interpretation of ends or means is allowed by the subsystem.

8. *Nested Enterprises* are the portfolios that result from our networked and distributive risk governance framework overall.

CONCLUSION: BRINGING IT TOGETHER

Under the right conditions, self-organized groups of people can do amazing things. We can create products and services that never existed before. We can invent new and better ways of performing both simple and complex tasks, including running political economies and improving our communities. In short, given the right setting, we can create things that are of substantial value to others in our network, while also creating value for ourselves.

Reimagining governance is about creating that right setting.

To increase the value of what we do today, the Value Equation demonstrates that we need to:

1. Increase the utility that others in our network expect to receive when they interact with us.

2. Increase the number of times that others in our network can expect to receive utility from us.

3. Lower the perceived risk that we will disappoint them.

Our organizations are systems, interacting with other agents and systems — our network — in a very large environment. Bigger, more open networks have the capacity to bring in more ideas and information, begetting a greater potential to create value. They also have a greater ability to realize positive amplification effects and tipping points of growth. That is why we should aspire to make our networks as big as possible.

However, we have to recognize that there are natural limits to the size of any network. Density often becomes too great when networks grow large. Hence, systems must be able to divide, spawning new sub-systems that have the potential to experience the innovation found in self-organized groups that have not yet reached their capacity.

Trust among agents in these networks is essential for growth, as it enables systems to become larger than they could otherwise. Trust also allows for more effective risk-taking by yielding greater freedom to operate and innovate within boundaries. It lowers the cost of gaining the capacity to take risk and the perception that others have of the negative risk involved in doing business with us.

Risk is not to be feared. It offers both upside and downside potential. Owners, investors, donors, voters, and other parties allocate risk-taking capacity to some governing body of an organization. In our ideal setting, this risk-taking capacity, or risk capital, is allocated by that governing body from the top down with a venture capital portfolio mindset — one that nurtures investments to large gains (in a few cases), while limiting the downside of any one failure, and building an organization with great resiliency and a relatively low level of perceived risk.

Resiliency and appropriately perceived risk are realized via organizational design, managing the middle of the distribution of possible outcomes, intercepting problems before they reach their potential, and guiding a bottoms-up risk assessment that ensures a consistency of risk-taking with the top-down risk capital portfolio allocation.

With the recognition that risk-taking capacity, or risk capital, is a commons, the governance framework design principles which Ostrom has devised, combined with the Carver's work and some of the concepts advocated by Turnbull and others, allow us to develop a universal framework for polycentric economic governance of our pursuit of value and values. The ideal setting for our organization is achieved through a combination of ends and means policies that beget freedom within boundaries, checks, balances, and information flow from those in our network.

By following the design principles that allow for the effective management of commons, in a networked and distributive environment of governance, we can govern our organizations to realize power-law growth to an exponent greater than one, along with positively skewed distributions of outcomes for those in our network — those who care about us and about whom we care deeply.

Our organizations can deliver more utility, live longer, and be perceived as trustworthy and reliable deliverers of value — allowing us to create value by more completely fulfilling the values which we most dearly pursue.

And the reason that all organizations exist is to do just this.

NOTES

1 Coase, Ronald H., "The Nature of the Firm," *Economica*, Vol. 4, No. 16, 1937

2 See Williamson, Oliver, *The Economics of Governance*, January 2005 and *The Theory of the Firm as Governance Structure: From Choice to Contract*, January 2002, as helpful overviews.

3 For a summary of Williamson's work, see the Scientific Background on the Sveriges Riksbank Prize in Economic Sciences in Memory of Alfred Nobel 2009, Economic Governance, complied by the Economic Sciences Prize Committee of the Royal Swedish Academy of Sciences

4 Joskow, Paul, "Vertical Integration and Long-term Contracts: The Case of Coal-burning Electric Generating Plants," *The Journal of Law, Economics and Organization*, Vol. 1, No. 1, March 1985

5 Economic Sciences Prize Committee of the Royal Swedish Academy of Sciences, *op. cit.*

6 Ibid.

7 For more on Prof. West's work, see his website at the Santa Fe Institute

8 West, Geoffrey, "The surprising math of cities and corporations," TEDGlobal 2011

9 Ibid.

10 For a summary of Ostrom's work, see the Scientific Background on the Sveriges Riksbank Prize in Economic Sciences in Memory of Alfred Nobel 2009, Economic Governance, complied by the Economic Sciences Prize Committee of the Royal Swedish Academy of Sciences

11 Ostrom, Elinor, "Beyond Markets and States: Polycentric Governance of Complex Economic Systems," Nobel Prize Lecture, December 8, 2009

12 Ostrom, Vincent; Tiebout, Charles; and Warren, Robert, "The Organization of Government in Metropolitan Areas: A Theoretical Inquiry," *American Political Science Review*, Vol. 55, No. 4, 1961

13 Ibid.

14 Bloomquist, William, Schlager, Edella, Tang, Shui Yan, and Ostrom, Elinor, "Regularities from the Field and Possible Explanations," in *Rules, Games, and Common-Pool Resources*, edited by Elinor Ostrom, Roy Gardner, and James Walker, University of Michigan Press, 1994

15 Ostrom, Elinor, "Beyond Markets and States," *op. cit.*

16 Ibid.

17 Scientific Background on the Sveriges Riksbank Prize in Economic Sciences in Memory of Alfred Nobel, 2009, *op. cit.*

GLOSSARY

Adaptive Walk | A process by which a simulated agent takes a random step on the fitness landscape searching for higher ground. If a step in one direction results in an improvement in fitness, the agent will take another step in the same direction until a step in any direction results in lower levels of fitness.

Affective Paradigm | How risk events are processed in a quick and reactive manner, generally designed for survival or response to a threat. The Affective Paradigm relies on images and experiences and their link to emotions, both good and bad.

Agents | Animate and inanimate components of a system which interact with each other.

Amplification Stations | A type of Transmitter that has a particularly high level of influence over other agents (akin to Mavens or Strong Ties), an expert in a field, news media or public agency.

Anchoring | A behavioral bias whereby expectations of an unknown value are based on the known value of something else, regardless of whether it is related to the unknown value.

Annealing | The process of heating metal to an extremely high temperature and reshaping it, changing its strength and hardness.

ANTs | Active Non-Linear Tests of complex simulation models.

Behavioral Economics | The study of behavioral biases in economic exchanges.

Behavioral Finance | The study of behavioral biases in financial valuations.

Bell Curve | A probability curve representing frequencies of values realized in a Normal Distribution.

Bounded Rationality | The notion that people make decisions based on the limited amount of information they have and the limited amount of time in which they can make that decision. These decisions may not be completely "rational" in the sense of Traditional Economics, but are as rational as they can be given the bounds of the aforementioned constraints.

Boundary Rules | Rules that define the places where an agent cannot go in a simulation game or the actions an agent cannot take within a controlled system. Also found in successful management of commons or Common Pool Resources as a definition of which agents can use the commons.

Business Judgment Rule | As defined in law, this guidance suggests that as long as a person with fiduciary responsibilities, for example, a board member, uses prudent processes in making business decisions, that person will not be personally liable for losses if the decisions turn out to have been incorrect ones.

Catastrophic Failure | Failure within a system of a magnitude that severely reduces or eliminates the value of that system or its capacity to create value.

Chaordic | A hybrid of the terms chaotic and order, suggestive of a complex system within which some chaos is allowed to develop in a subsystem which is subject to the controls of a larger system or a system of greater standing within a hierarchy.

Chaos | A system that is lacking in order or predictability, sensitive to initial conditions and full of non-linear relationships.

Chief Risk Officer | The person given responsibility for the development and execution of an enterprise-wide assessment of risk within an organization and the education of agents regarding the use of risk capital.

Choice Rules | Rules regarding the use by approved agents of the resources of a commons or Common Pool Resource.

Closed System | A system which has no transactions with other systems or agents outside of its system.

Cooperation | Two or more agents communicating in game theory to enable a better outcome for both.

Commons | Also Common Pool Resource, or CPR, is a resource whereby consumption by one agent reduces the availability of that resource to other agents who share access to it.

Communication | One of three methods for processing information in systems whereby agents exchange information within the system or with agents in another system.

Complex | As in Complex System or Complex Adaptive System, this describes a system which has a total value different than the sum of its parts. It is contrasted with a complicated system which is simply the sum of its many parts and can be disassembled and re-assembled to arrive at the same system with which one started.

Complexity Catastrophe | A result of overly dense networks which causes the exchange of information in a complex system to fail and a catastrophic failure to be realized.

Complexity Economics | The study of systems and value creation, most commonly associated with the Santa Fe Institute.

Controlled System | A system which has a method to automatically bring variables within the system that move outside of a normal range back to acceptable levels.

Culture | Learned patterns of communication, positive, and negative feedbacks, within a system.

Darley's Law | Coined by Professor John Darley of Princeton University, it warns that the more any quantitative performance measure is used to determine a group or an individual's rewards and punishments, the more subject it will be to corruption pressures and the more apt it will be to distort and corrupt the action patterns and thoughts of the group or individual it is intended to monitor.

Defecting | The act of agreeing to testify against the other suspect in the Prisoner's Dilemma game.

Dense Network | A complex network with a high number of average connections between agents in the system.

Discounting | A mental or mathematical process by which something of value that we will receive in the future is translated into a present value today.

Dread Risk | Aspects of a risk that make us anxious as we contemplate its potential realization.

Duty of Care | A legal duty under some statutes that a member of a governing body with fiduciary responsibilities will use care in the execution of his duties

Duty of Loyalty | A legal duty under some statutes that a member of a governance body with fiduciary responsibilities will take actions and make decisions that are in the interest of that organization and not in her self-interest or the interest of another entity.

Economic Capital | A scarce resource that has value as an input to a system.

Editing | The first step in a two-step process of risk-based decision making in which agents order possible outcomes according to some experience-based technique that has been learned. Roughly identical outcomes are used as a reference point, better outcomes are viewed as gains and worse outcomes as losses. Associated with Prospect Theory.

Embeddedness | The degree to which an agent is enmeshed in a social network. An agent with many relationships is said to have a high level of embeddedness.

Ends (Policy) | The goals of an organization, or sub-system of an organization, as expressed by policy of the governing body of that organization or sub-system. Used with the Carver Method of corporate governance.

Engagement | A term from natural systems that describes how agents network deeply with local, external systems and environments.

Enterprise Risk Management | A process of evaluating and addressing the risks of an entire organization or system in a holistic manner.

Environment | The space in which a system operates and interacts with other systems.

Equilibrium | The state in which competing influences in a system or subsystem are in balance.

Evaluation | The second step in a two-step process of risk-based decision making in which agents review possible outcomes to decide which ones provide them with the most utility. Associated with Prospect Theory.

Evolutionary Psychology | The study of evolution of the mind, believing minds to be modular, evolving over time to serve certain functions and to solve problems.

Evolution of Cooperation | The process by which cooperation has evolved as a valuable human activity.

Expected Utility | The amount of utility an agent expects to receive from a game, exchange or consumption decision.

Exponential Discounting | A process of discounting that changes in a consistent manner for each unit of time added between now and when the item of value is to be received.

Externalities | Costs or actions imposed by one agent on other agents without their consent and without compensation or cost to the first agent.

Error Terms | The amount by which a forecast or model estimate varies from the actual value of something.

Fairness | A behavioral phenomenon whereby an agent may make a decision that results in a loss to itself because it believes the situation is unfair, generally, according to that agent's values.

Fat Tails | A term used to describe probability distributions in which large gains or losses are more likely to occur than in a Normal Distribution.

Fitness Landscape | A virtual terrain made up of "rods," each of a height that represents the fitness of a DNA sequence associated with that specific rod. See Chapter 3 for a discussion of The Game of Evolution and the fitness landscape therein.

Framing Theory | A theory developed by Daniel Kahnemann and Amos Tversky that describes how the framing of choices can dramatically change decisions.

Function | The role that an agent plays in the operation of a system.

Game Theory | Primarily used in economics, it is an attempt to analyze human behavior in games of choice where the value of the outcome to an agent is dependent upon the choice of another agent, in addition to the choice made by the first agent.

Herding | A form of mass behavior, generally associated with seeking protection or evading a perceived risk.

Heuristics | Experience and knowledge that help us to make decisions when risk is present and there is only partial information or limited time available.

Hyperbolic Discounting | A time-inconsistent manner of discounting the value of something to be received in the future. In this type of discounting, valuations fall rapidly for very small periods of delay initially, but less so for value expected to be received far into the future.

Information Asymmetry | When one agent has more information than another agent about the value of something.

Information Sources | A person, group, or organization that sends out a message full of Signals to Transmitters and Receivers.

Information Value | The value derived by one system from information provided to it by another system or agent in a system.

Intervention | A form of control in systems where some agent takes action to correct elements within the system seen to be outside of the system's comfort zone.

Key Person | Used in reference to a critical person in an organization whose loss could affect that organization's ability to perform as expected. As in "Key Person Insurance," an insurance policy that pays a benefit to the insured party when a "Key Person" departs an organization, dies or is incapacitated.

Keystone | A critical component to a structure or system. Without its presence that system or structure could easily collapse under stress.

Kinship | The degree to which people share a genetic code.

Liquidity | A measure of how easily something can be sold or exchanged for another item without a change in its current value. Also, the availability, on very short notice, of financial capital to an organization.

Loss Avoidance | A strong preference by people to avoid the prospect of large losses from a choice or game, even in the face of equally large opportunities for gain.

Macroeconomics | The study of large social/financial/economic systems.

Management by Objectives A management theory developed by Peter Drucker whereby managers and employees agree, ex-ante, on goals, objectives and how decisions will be made, with performance measured ex-post based on these agreements.

Mass | A description of how natural systems work that refers to having enough agents to cover a wide territory.

Means (Policy) | In the Carver governance model, these are policies that describe the rules for pursuing Ends. These are restrictive, designed so that anything that is not prohibited is pre-approved, provided that it is a reasonable interpretation of the meaning of the policy.

Monitoring | The process whereby agents keep track of the use of a common or common pool resource in an attempt to manage it successfully.

Multiple Points of Failure | A concept associated with resiliency suggesting that a system will only experience a catastrophic failure if multiple parts of that system fail simultaneously or in rapid sequence. Contrast with Single Points of Failue.

Negative Feedback | An action taken by a system or agents in a system to restore a variable in that system which has moved out of line with a range that is acceptable to that system.

Networked and Distributive Governance | A form of corporate governance which combines models for distributing accountability for the effective use of risk capital and freedom to make decisions within defined parameters along with oversight from key external parties that have a vested interest in the success of the organization. See Chapter 14.

Networked Governance | Governance processes that incorporate stakeholders or other interested parties outside of the organization or subsystem of the organization.

Non-linear | A function that changes in value at anything other than a linear rate. For example, $y = x^2$ is a non-linear equation as each unit change in x results in a change in value of y that is the square of x.

Normal Distribution | The statistical distribution that arises from a large number of small, individual effects, often referred to as the Bell Curve.

Open System | A system that receives information from other systems or agents from outside of its system.

Partial Failure | A loss in value from some action or event that is not a catastrophic failure.

Path-dependent | The concept that the value of something today is dependent upon its value in one or multiple periods before today. An example is the balance of a savings account when interest is paid. Interest earned in one year is dependent on how much interest was earned in every prior year.

Portals | Quick routes to a higher place on the fitness landscape when a small change in a DNA sequence results in a highly positive change in the fitness of a living organism. See Chapter 3, The Game of Evolution.

Positive Feedback | An action taken by a system or agents in a system that drives a variable in that system to a larger value.

Potential Impact | The loss in the value of a system that would be realized by a problem in the system if it is left unchecked and there is no effort by agents in the system to control it.

Power Law | Describes a relationship between two variables whereby one changes at a rate which is an exponent of the change in the other. For example, $y = x^2$ is a non-linear equation as each unit change in x results in a change in value of y that is the square of x, or the power of 2.

Power of Relationships | In Network Theory, a way to represent the influence that one agent can have on another.

Present Value | The value of something today that will not be received until a future date.

Principal–Agent Problem | Whenever one agent (the principal) entrusts another agent to act on their behalf there is a negative risk that the second agent will act in its own interest and not that of the principal.

Prisoner's Dilemma | Associated with Game Theory, it is a particular choice example wherein two suspects are offered different outcomes in terms of sentencing if they will testify against the other suspect, but they are not allowed to communicate and do not know if the other suspect will agree to testify against them.

Probability Distribution | A statistical or graphical representation of values arrived at through a repeated process.

Prospect Theory | The study of choice in risky situations whereby agents follow a process to determine the prospect of getting something of value, or utility, from that choice.

Punctuated Equilibria | Periods of relative stability in systems that precede or follow periods of relative chaos.

Randomness | In natural systems this describes the variety of patterns of search for new ideas or rewards, like food.

Receivers | The ultimate recipients of a message from an Information Source.

Reciprocal Altruism | An expectation that a good act towards another agent in a system will be rewarded with a good act from that agent at some point in the future.

Reciprocity | The act of reciprocal behavior, both good and bad.

Risk | An attempt to quantify uncertainty. Risk can be both positive (the possibility of gains) and negative (the possibility of losses), quantified ex-ante.

Risk Appetite | The stated tolerance of a organization for the realization of negative risks. This may take the form of a corporate policy containing limits on risks which are taken or may be reflected by the amount of Risk Capital allocated to any part of a system or subsystem.

Risk-averse | Someone is said to be risk-averse if they are reluctant to play a game or make a choice of uncertain value rather than another game or choice with a more certain, but possibly lower, expected value.

Risk Capital | An allocation of risk-taking authority based on a measure that expresses the amount of loss expected at some probability associated with the activities of an organization or sub-system of that organization.

Risk Dimensions | See Dread Risk and Risk of the Unknown.

Risk Governance | The organizational framework within which the risk management function operates and wherein risk is assessed, priced, monitored, and charged-for.

Risk-loving | An agent with a preference for risk, often considered to be the opposite of being risk-averse.

Risk Management | The process of acting upon information regarding the risk that an organization or system faces. Via risk management an organization or system accepts a risk, transfers it or alters the way in which the realization of a risk will impact the organization or system.

Risk of the Unknown | The extent to which a risk is judged to be unobservable, unknown, new, or delayed in producing harmful impacts.

Risk-sensitive Foraging Theory | A concept that examines how animals look for food and the change in their behavior/risk-taking that takes place when requirements for survival change.

Risk Tolerance | See Risk Appetite.

Risk Transfer | The process of transferring the cost of a negative risk to a third party through contract. Examples include insurance, derivative contracts or other hedging operations.

Rules | One of three methods for processing information in systems, rules determine how the system makes decisions based on information.

Sanctioning | The process whereby agents punish other agents who have access to a Commons or Common Pool Resource who have violated the rules established for its successful management.

SARF | See Social Amplification of Risk Framework.

Scenario Analysis | A form of stress testing whereby a specific sequence of events, a scenario, is used to evaluate its impact on the value of the organization or system.

Sensitivity to Initial Conditions | The concept that the impact of an event is dependent upon the conditions the system faces when the event occurs. For example, saturated ground cannot absorb heavy rainfall. Therefore, flash flooding may occur more rapidly if such is the initial condition of the ground.

Signals | Information contained in a message sent by an Information Source.

Single Point of Failure | When a system reveals its brittleness and experiences a catastrophic failure because of the failure of one element in the system.

Small Changes in Probability | When the likelihood of an event changes slightly. This is especially important when the change in likelihood is from zero to any positive value or from one (certainty) to any value less than one.

Social Amplification of Risk Framework (SARF) | A framework for explaining mass reactions to realized risk events that occur in some cases, but not in others, when conditions appear to be the same. Associated with the work of Roger and Jeanne Kasperson and Paul Slovic. See Chapter 8.

Stakeholder | Someone who has an interest in the success of an organization or system, but is not an owner of that organization or system.

Stochastic | Random, as in a process or game whose outcome is entirely driven by chance.

Stress Test | A risk management and risk governance technique whereby market or other variables that impact the value of something are changed by highly improbable amounts to assess their impact on the value of the organization or system.

Strong Ties | Agents within a system or outside of a system to which an agent maintains an existing relationship with relatively high power of influence.

Supervisory Board | In a Networked Governance structure, this group is comprised of stakeholders who can override any veto of a Watchdog Board. In a two-tiered board governance system, it is a body made up entirely of directors who are not executives of the organization.

Thresholds of Collective Behavior | The point of participation by a subset of group members at which an entire group will exhibit mass behaviors. Associated with the work of Professor Mark Granovetter, trying to distinguish why mass actions are realized in some cases and not in others, when conditions appear to be the same.

Transact(ion) | One of three methods for processing information in systems whereby agents exchange goods, services or money (things of value) with agents in that same or another system.

Transmitters | Agents in a system that pass along a message from an Information Source to other Transmitters or Receivers.

Trust | The willingness to accept and/or increase one's vulnerability to the actions of another agent or system.

Utility | Something that makes us "feel good" provides us with utility, which is a measure of the value that something has to a particular agent.

Utility Function | A mathematical function that describes how utility is derived by an agent in a system. It is particularly relevant when risk is present in a choice.

Value | The amount of one thing that an agent is willing to exchange for something owned by another agent.

Values | Associated with principles and beliefs, values guide our perception of the value of something. They are what help us to evaluate utility.

Watchdog Board | A group of stakeholders with important authorities in the governance of an organization, including the appointment of auditors and independent advisors to the board, as well as the authority to veto board decisions where a conflict of interest is present.

Weak Ties | Agents within a system or outside of a system to which an agent maintains an existing relationship with relatively low power of influence.

ABOUT THE AUTHOR

David R. Koenig's work over the past four decades has been focused on helping organizations to be more successful in achieving their goals. He's served on multiple for-profit and nonprofit boards and has advised board members and executives around the world. His executive leadership roles have included the creation and development of corporate risk management programs at three different companies, the management of complex portfolios in excess of tens of billions of dollars in size, the risk oversight of a complete suite of public mutual funds for one of the largest banks in the U.S., and the development of the first firmwide risk management program in the mortgage banking business. Many of David's initiatives have begun with ideas about things that didn't yet exist at his employer or client, and working to make them a reality.

Because of his innovative concepts and initiatives, David has been invited to present his ideas at more than 100 events on five continents, and his travels have taken him to nearly 40 countries. In 2010, one of his visionary governance concepts was honored with an inaugural M-prize for management innovation in the category of Reinventing Leadership. In 2008, he was honored as the recipient of the PRMIA Higher Standard Award — the top recognition bestowed on any member of the Professional Risk Managers International Association.

David is a widely published author, lends his time to numerous industry initiatives to advance best practices, is a founder of two global professional associations, and is an active volunteer in his community. He is a proud member of Rotary International and has earned multiple Paul Harris fellowships.

David earned his M.A. in economics from Northwestern University, and B.A. degrees in mathematics and economics from Miami University in Oxford, Ohio. He practices his work from an office in the beautiful college town of Northfield, Minnesota.